V&R Academic

Axel Wieandt

Unfinished Business

Putting European Banking (and Europe) Back on Track

With 41 figures

V&R unipress

MIX
Papier aus verantwortungsvollen Quellen
FSC® C083411

Bibliographic information published by the Deutsche Nationalbibliothek

The Deutsche Nationalbibliothek lists this publication in the Deutsche Nationalbibliografie; detailed bibliographic data are available online: http://dnb.d-nb.de.

ISBN 978-3-8471-0715-6

You can find alternative editions of this book and additional material on our website: www.v-r.de

Printed in Germany.
Cover image: "Forex Trading Blue Concept", © Tomasz Zajda (Fotolia: #112494750).
Printed and bound by CPI buchbuecher.de GmbH, Zum Alten Berg 24, 96158 Birkach, Germany.

Printed on aging-resistant paper.

Contents

Part IV – Crisis becoming existential

Part V – Finishing the business, in a principled way

Acknowledgments

First and foremost, I would like to acknowledge the patience, comments and questions of the full-time MBA students who attended my leadership seminars "European Banking and the Financial Crisis" at the J L Kellogg Graduate School of Management (KGSM), Northwestern University, in Evanston, Illinois, in the spring of 2016. I would like to thank KGSM for the invitation to teach these seminars, and for my appointment as Adjunct Professor in the Finance Department. I benefited greatly from numerous stimulating conversations with my colleagues in the Finance department, most importantly Donald P Jacobs, former Dean, and Kathleen Haggerty, former Senior Associate Dean of Faculty and Research at KGSM.

I am grateful to Hans-Helmut Kotz, fellow of the Center for Financial Studies in Frankfurt, Germany, and fellow of Harvard University, Cambridge, Massachusetts, for his input on the outline of the book. My former colleague Frank Altrock, now professor at the FH Trier, and my brother Carl, a former principal with McKinsey & Company, have read earlier versions of the book and provided helpful comments.

I would also like to acknowledge the interesting discussions I had with the Masters in Finance Students at WHU – Otto Beisheim School of Management in Vallendar, Germany, where I have also been teaching a course on "European Banking and the Financial Crisis". I am similarly grateful to Sascha Hahn, Tom Lesche, and Sebastian Mönninghoff, "my" Ph.D. students, for many insightful discussions on the topic over the last few years.

Most importantly, I would like to thank Valerie Maysey for her outstanding editorial support, Jan Ohlendorf from WHU for his research and editing assistance, Gerald Olgemöller for helping with the production of the figures, and Oliver Kätsch from V&R Academic for his continued encouragement and support of this project.

Of course, I remain fully responsible for any remaining errors and omissions in the final text. And I am fully aware that this book itself is very much "unfinished business".

Without the continued support of my family this book would not have been possible.

Königstein i Ts, April 2017 *Axel Wieandt*

Prologue

"I believe that banking institutions are more dangerous to our liberties than standing armies. If the American people ever allow private banks to control the issue of their currency, first by inflation, then by deflation, the banks and corporations that will grow up around [the banks] will deprive the people of all property until their children wake-up homeless on the continent their fathers conquered. The issuing power should be taken from the banks and restored to the people, to whom it properly belongs."

attributed to Thomas Jefferson, 3rd president of the USA

"Thus, our national circulating medium is now at the mercy of loan transactions of banks; and our thousands of checking banks are, in effect, so many irresponsible private mints. What makes the trouble is the fact that the bank lends not money but merely a promise to furnish money on demand – money it does not possess." [1]

Irving Fisher, American economist, (1935)

This spring, I am again teaching a class on "European Banking and the Financial Crisis" in the Master of Finance Program of WHU – Otto Beisheim School of Management, my alma mater. Most of the students in my class were not even born when I graduated from WHU in 1990. They are part of the post-crisis generation. A generation that has not yet experienced a banking crisis. Not that I wish that they experience one. On the contrary.

The reason why I have been teaching a class on banking in the Great Financial Crisis is because I want the next generation to understand what has happened, how it has happened, why it has happened, and what can be done to prevent it from happening again. But they must also understand that it could happen again. A financial crisis is like an organizational failure, only on a larger scale. That is exactly what a financial crisis is! Nobody wants it to happen. Nevertheless, it may still happen. My students need to understand that it is easy to explain the Great Financial Crisis with the benefit of hindsight. And they need to acknowledge that it could happen again.

I have written the book for all of them, the next generation that will, hopefully,

1 See Fisher (1935), Chapter 1: Introduction.

contribute to finishing the business, to help putting European banking and Europe back on track.

As I am preparing for class, I find an old article from the Financial Times, dated 29th September, 2008. Lehman Brothers was collapsing and the tsunami of the Great Financial Crisis was reaching the very core of Europe; it was hitting Germany:

"Hypo Real Estate bailed out by German peers

Germany's financial sector was in turmoil on Monday after Hypo Real Estate, one of its biggest lenders, had to be rescued by other banks and the government to solve a €50bn ($72bn, £40bn) liquidity crisis.

Shares in HRE plunged more than 70 per cent, and other banking stocks nosedived after the intervention, the most serious sign of strain in Germany's financial sector since the collapse of Lehman Brothers aggravated the global credit crisis this month.

HRE, one of Europe's biggest commercial property and public sector lenders, was handed a €35bn liquidity lifeline by other German private sector banks, the Bundesbank and the European Central Bank. The lender is also selling €15bn of assets to cover its liquidity shortfall.

The rescue is likely to lead to a sale of assets from HRE's €400bn balance sheet. Peer Steinbrück, Germany's finance minister, said HRE's remaining businesses would be placed in a special purpose vehicle for an orderly wind-down. But people close to HRE rejected the suggestion.

The government and a consortium of German banks will underwrite €35bn of credit guarantees for HRE, with the banks standing for a 60 per cent share of an initial €14bn guarantee. The government will provide the remainder of the first-loss piece and a further €21bn guarantee, meaning the state's exposure could rise to more than €26bn.

The urgent bail-out was agreed in the early hours of yesterday with Mr Steinbrück and Angela Merkel, German chancellor, in telephone contact with bankers and officials meeting in Frankfurt. A finance ministry official said: "We are walking on the edge – this is really serious. We don't know what will happen tomorrow."

HRE is one of Germany's most prominent financial companies and one of the 30 companies in the Dax index, which fell 4.2 per cent. The rescue was organised after HRE's inability to refinance short-term borrowing within Depfa, its Dublin-based subsidiary that lends to the public sector. HRE admitted it faced "extremely challenging conditions on the international money markets".

Bafin, Germany's financial regulator, and the Bundesbank said the package of short and mid-term financing would ensure the viability of the company.

Only a few months ago, JC Flowers, the private equity investor, led funds investing €1.1bn in HRE, buying almost 24.9 per cent of the bank for €22.50 a share.

Shares in HRE had fallen 74 per cent to €3.52 by the close in Frankfurt.

> *Stocks of banks with substantial property exposure were also savaged, with Commerzbank and Deutsche Postbank falling 23 per cent.*
>
> *A failure of HRE could also have had repercussions for Germany's important market in ultra-safe covered bonds, or Pfandbriefe. HRE is an important issuer of such bonds."*[2]

The article brings back memories from those dark days. I was head of Corporate Development at Deutsche Bank at the time, and had spent most of my career with the German lender. Our Corporate Development team was responsible for strategic transactions. We had been working on the Postbank deal for some time. After the announcement of the acquisition of a 29.75 percent stake in Postbank on 12th September, 2008, I had hoped for a quieter autumn. The Great Financial Crisis and the HRE situation, however, did not leave a lot of breathing space. Before I knew it, I would be in Munich. With HRE. As CEO. In the eye of the storm, where we were fighting the tsunami, stabilizing, restructuring and ultimately nationalizing the group.

Since then, almost 9 years have elapsed. And the banks in Germany are still raising capital and restructuring. The situation has improved: significantly improved, no doubt, but is has taken a long time to make progress. And more effort, significant effort, is needed to put European banking back on track.

The state of affairs in European banking reflects the situation of Europe, the political disunion and looming Brexit, the ECB's extraordinary monetary policy with ultralow interest rates and Quantitative Easing (QE) and the structural crisis in Europe. It also reflects the geopolitical situation. In fact, the banks are like a mirror, in which we can see reflections of both the past, and the expectations for the future. Let us a take a closer look and face up to the realities. Putting the situation in context and beginning to ask questions is a first step.

An important step.

This book is my attempt at making a first step.

---

2 See Financial Times (2009).

Chapter 1:
Unfinished business – an introduction

"There are deep fault lines in the global economy, fault lines that have developed because in an integrated economy and in an integrated world, what is best for an individual actor is not always best for the system. Responsibility for some of the more serious fault lines lies not in economics but in politics. Unfortunately, we did not know where all these fault lines ran until the crisis exposed them."[3]

Raghuram G Rajan, economist and 23rd Governor of the Bank of India, (2010)

"As he (Sir George Blunden) put it, since a country's banking system was central to the management of its economy, its supervision would inevitably be a jealously guarded national prerogative."[4]

David McKittrik, Ulster-born journalist, Obituary of Sir George Blunden in The Independent, (2012)

In 2017, a decade after the outbreak of the Great Financial Crisis in the US subprime mortgage market, Europe's banks (and Europe) are still off track. Profitability and returns on equity are depressed, balance sheets continue to shrink and in some countries, such as in Italy, banks continue to be an acute threat to financial and political stability. Despite recent progress, and extraordinary monetary policy measures, the Continent of Europe continues to be held hostage by three interrelated crises: a chronic economic growth crisis; a peripheral sovereign debt crisis; and a lingering banking crisis, which, together, are all feeding into a political crisis:[5]

(1) *Economic growth crisis:* as measured by Gross Domestic Product (GDP), the European Union (EU) only regained its 2007 output level in the first quarter of 2016. This economic performance is in sharp contrast to the US, which had already regained 2007 GDP levels by 2011. At the time of writing, the US is over 10 percentage points ahead in terms of GDP growth since the crisis.

3 See Rajan (2010), p 4–5.
4 See David McKittrik's (2012) obituary of Sir George Blunden, former Deputy Governor of the Bank of England, and first Chairman of the Basel Committee on Banking Supervision (BCBS).
5 Compare Shambaugh (2012) for an in-depth analysis of the Euro's three interlocking crises.

Moreover, the US is also ahead in terms of employment: the unemployment rate there has fallen below 5 percent, with labor market participation on the rise. The unemployment rate in the EU, however, is still well above 10 percent: in some countries in the periphery it is still above 20 percent, and yet still higher at the younger end of the employment scale in countries like Greece, Portugal and Spain. This weak growth performance negatively impacts sovereign and bank solvencies, via lower tax revenues and rising borrower defaults respectively.[6]

(2) *Sovereign debt crisis:* sovereign debt levels are still elevated after almost a decade of economic stand-still, and have reached a level of 90 percent of GDP in the Eurozone. While this is still below the level of the US, where public debt has topped 100 percent in the wake of the Great Financial Crisis, the lower Eurozone average masks much higher sovereign debt levels in the southern periphery of the continent. Public debt in countries like Greece, Italy and Portugal is only sustainable in the current environment of ultra-low, negative interest rates. And austerity measures, imposed to improve the fiscal position of the indebted sovereigns, have further reduced growth.

(3) *Banking crisis:* the profitability of European banks is still anemic. At the end of the 3rd quarter of 2015, Eurozone banks reported a 5.7 percent annualized return on equity (RoE), up from 3.4 percent in 2010, but still below their cost of capital.[7] As a consequence, valuations of Eurozone bank stocks are still depressed: in many instances, well below tangible book value. The weakness of the banks in Europe is simultaneously both cause and symptom of the European economic and political crisis. And the weakness of the banks still weighs heavily on the sovereigns, particularly those on the periphery, where slow growth is preventing a recovery of public finances and non-performing loans (NPLs) continue to burden banks' balance sheets.

(4) *Political crisis:* the European project has taken a significant step backwards with the 2016 Brexit vote across the Channel. In addition, in the wake of the election of Donald Trump as president of the USA, populism is on the rise on the continent. EU exit forces are gaining momentum in a number of EU regions and member states, emphasizing the urgency of overcoming the economic and financial crisis in Europe.

Two fundamental questions follow from this diagnosis: in what ways, and to what extent, does the recovery of the European economy depend on the health of

---

6 Compare ECB (2015a), in particular slide 4 for an analysis of the post 2007 output gap in Euroland.

7 Compare DB Research (2013) for a detailed comparison of US and European bank performance.

the banking sector? And why then, almost ten years after the Great Financial Crisis, have we not yet finished the business of putting the banks back on track? Let us look at both of these questions and, subsequently, outline in what ways this book attempts to contribute to the public discussion on banking and banking policies in Europe. Ultimately, and this is the core proposition of this book, we need to repair European banking if we want to get Europe economically, financially and politically back on track.

Why does banking matter? The importance of banks in the European economy

Europe, unlike the US, is not one state, but a union of 28 independent countries. Of these, 19 countries belong to the Eurozone. However, the EU and US economies are comparable in size. The US economy comprises 321 million inhabitants and, as of 2015, has a GDP of USD 18 trillion. The EU economy has a GDP of USD 16.3 trillion and, as of 2015, 510 million inhabitants. The Eurozone (EU-19) economy alone has a 2015 GDP of USD 11.6 trillion with 339 million inhabitants.[8]

Banks perform an important role in the economy. Essentially, they provide for, and channel, financing into longer term investments.[9] This role can, to a certain degree, also be performed by financial markets. But, this role is primarily performed by banks in Europe, unlike in the US. Banks are at the heart of the economic and financial system of Europe. Households in the Eurozone own significantly fewer financial assets than in the UK or in the US, and they hold a much larger portion of their assets in bank deposits and insurance and pension funds. US households, on the other hand, have significantly more exposure to financial markets and have relatively few assets with banks.[10] In many European countries, the economy is characterized by small and medium sized enterprises (SMEs). Unlike larger corporates, they do not have ready access to financial markets and must rely solely on the banks for external financing.

There is not one single banking system but many different banking systems in Europe. Total banking assets in the Eurozone were 270 percent of GDP in 2015[11], in some individual member states even higher, with some individual bank

8 Compare World Bank (2015).

9 The traditional model of banking as Intermediation of Loanable Funds (ILF) has been recently superseded by a description of the role of banks as Financing through Money Creation (FMC). See Jakab and Krumhof (2015) for a detailed analysis of intermediation and financing models of banking.

10 Compare Allen et al. (2012).

11 See ECB (2016).

balance sheets of more than 50 percent of national GDP. For example, Deutsche Bank's balance sheet of USD 1.75 trillion in 2015[12] was equal to 52 percent of German GDP. This contrasts with the US, where total bank assets amount to just 87 percent of GDP[13], and the largest banks are much smaller relative to overall GDP (eg, J.P. Morgan's balance sheet of USD 2.4 trillion[14] in 2015 equaled 13 percent of US GDP). In total, as of 2015, there are over 7,100 credit institutions (of which 4,700 are in the Eurozone) and close to 1,000 foreign branches in the EU (thereof 700 in the Eurozone).[15] The EU credit institutions still have over 200,000 physical branches, many of which are expected to close over the next few years. The banking market is still fragmented in many countries and characterized by overcapacities.

In 2011, bank credit to the private sector reached 136 percent of GDP in the EU (27)[16], compared with 55 percent of GDP for the US.[17] Corporate bond and stock market capitalizations amounted to only 15 percent and 43 percent respectively in the EU (27), as opposed to 35 percent and 104 percent respectively for the US.[18] The EU (27) averages, however, mask great differences among the EU member states. Bijlsma and Zwart (2013) recently analyzed the financial systems of the EU member states along 23 different dimensions, including the size of the banking system, household deposits, credit to non-financial firms, market capitalization of listed firms, and bank profitability, to name just a few.[19] Their analysis has enabled them to classify the EU countries into four categories:

(1) *The market-based countries:* the Netherlands, UK, Belgium, France, Finland and Sweden; these countries are closer to the US than other EU member states.
(2) *The bank-based countries:* Austria, Denmark, Germany, Greece, Italy, Portugal, and Spain; these countries resemble Japan more closely, as far as their financial system is concerned.
(3) *The Eastern European countries:* Bulgaria, Czech Republic, Estonia, Hungary, Lithuania, Poland, Romania, Slovakia, and Slovenia; these countries accessed the EU relatively recently and are still in at an earlier stage of their

12 Compare Deutsche Bank (2015), Balance Sheet Data. Balance Sheet size converted with 1.08 USD/EUR.
13 See FDIC (2015).
14 Compare J.P. Morgan Chase & Co. (2015).
15 See ECB (2016).
16 Croatia only became a member of the EU in 2013.
17 Compare Bijlsma and Zwart (2013), Appendix B, Table B.1, p 41: Bank credit to the private sector as a fraction of GDP, drawing on IMF financial statistics and World Bank data.
18 Compare Bijlsma and Zwart (2013), Appendix B, Table B.3, p43: Corporate Bonds as a percentage of GDP, drawing on BIS data: and Appendix B, Table B.6, p 46: Stock market capitalization as fraction of GDP, drawing on World Bank data.
19 Compare Bijlsma and Zwart (2013).

economic and financial development. Therefore, they have, in overall terms, smaller financial systems.[20] They are also typically more reliant on bank financing, as financial market development tends to follow economic development.

(4) *The outlier countries:* Ireland, Cyprus, Malta and Luxembourg; they have large banking sectors that function as important financial hubs in the EU and extend a sizeable amount of cross-border credit.

European banks today are more international than their US counterparts. In addition, the introduction of the Euro facilitated cross-border banking within the Eurozone. In fact, since the negotiations of the Maastricht treaty in the late 1980s and early 1990s, the European banking system has changed along several dimensions:[21]

(1) *Rising leverage:* the lending activity of Eurozone banks increased significantly. A sizeable portion of this lending was short-term cross-border interbank lending, ultimately fueling the expansion of bank lending, and bolstering the development of a real-estate bubble in several countries of the European periphery. Another aspect of this rising leverage was the build-up of commercial real estate exposures.[22] The implementation of the Basel framework in Europe created special incentives for the build-up of sovereign and collateralized real-estate exposures. In particular, the expansion in sovereign debt was, practically, neither constrained by any regulatory equity buffer nor by any large exposure limits.

(2) *Globalization:* the European banks, particularly the respective national champions, significantly expanded their global activities and began to push into investment banking and capital markets businesses. They raised large amounts of short-term funding in the US money markets, and became significant lenders and buyers of securitizations in the US market, impacting domestic credit conditions and contributing to the rise of the (subprime mortgage) housing bubble.[23]

(3) *Increasing complexity:* banking has become more complex, and has evolved beyond the simple channeling of savings and the provision of financing to firms, households and governments. Interbank funding, both unsecured and secured (via the Repurchase Agreement or Repo markets) had been growing significantly in the run-up to the Great Financial Crisis. Intermediation chains have lengthened as a consequence of the rise of securitization tech-

20 Croatia only accessed the EU in 2013 and is therefore not part of the Bijlsma and Zwart study.
21 See Brunnermeier et al. (2016), chapter 9, pp 157–159.
22 See Antoniades (2015).
23 See Shin (2011) regarding the global banking glut impacting US credit conditions.

nology and off-balance sheet vehicles[24] and the number of transactions has increased. All in all, the European banking system has evolved from a set of largely self-contained national banking systems to a globally integrated and interconnected web of funding and financing arrangements.

(4) *Explicit and implicit government guarantees:* after 2001, the German state-sponsored "Landesbanken" aggressively increased their state-guaranteed bond issuance and invested these cheap funds into US subprime mortgage securities. Subprime mortgages are characterized by poor credit histories and high interest rates. The Landesbanken were taking advantage of a transition agreement that the German government had negotiated with the EU Commission. This transition agreement allowed them to issue state-guaranteed bonds until July, 2005 with a maximum maturity up to the end of 2015. Bonds issued after July 2005 were no longer eligible for state guarantees, in line with European competition law.[25] Not only the Landesbanken, but also the largest banking groups in the Eurozone benefited from implicit government guarantees: they were obviously considered "too-big-to-fail". Rating agencies and financial markets would assume that these banks would be bailed out by their respective sovereigns, significantly lowering the cost of funding and driving the build-up of leverage in these institutions.[26]

These developments made the European banking system more vulnerable to the fall-out from the US subprime mortgage crisis, and fueled the build-up of a real-estate bubble in certain countries in the periphery. In other words, they created hidden vulnerabilities too, that only became apparent when the crisis was hitting – and by then it was far too late.

What did go wrong in the Great Financial Crisis? – Getting Europe's Banks (and Europe) back on track

The Great Financial Crisis of 2007–2009 emanated from the US subprime mortgage market and spread to Europe via securitizations bought and sold by banks and other institutions. As a consequence, the interbank markets were hit by turbulence, as the delinquencies of US subprime mortgages began to increase. The interbank markets ultimately came to a complete stop in the after-

24 See Adrian and Shin (2010) for an analysis of the changing nature of financial intermediation leading up to the Great Financial Crisis.
25 Compare BMF (2002).
26 See for example Schich and Kim (2012) for evidence on the value of implicit government guarantees.

math of the Lehman failure in the fall of 2008. Central Banks on both sides of the Atlantic were forced to come to the rescue, as lenders and market-makers of last resort. The Federal Reserve Bank (Fed) and the European Central Bank (ECB) put in place a swap facility to ensure access to US dollar (USD) funding for European banks, which had been relying extensively on roll-over funding in the US money markets. At the institutional level, the first response was increased coordination among supervisory agencies.

Whereas the US opted for swift recapitalization of its banking system the European response was characterized by protracted forbearance. Unlike in the US, where the top banks were virtually forced to take government recapitalization money, the European banks had to apply for state aid on an individual basis, and to both their national governments and the EU Commission. The latter had to sanction this financial support and negotiate compensatory measures with the national governments. Between 2007 and 2009, the US spent 74 percent of its GDP on bailing out the financial services industry, including the banks. The UK 86 percent of its GDP, whereas the Eurozone spent only 18 percent of its GDP.[27] Policy coordination and sequencing in the US was better, with stress-testing conducted to determine whether the banks could repay government money soon or later. With the solvency of the banking system restored, QE could then reach the economy faster via the bank lending channel. In addition, QE in the US was supported by fiscal stimulus. In the Eurozone, however, the banking system was never properly recapitalized and, consequently, monetary stimulus could not work as well as in the US. In fact, the need to keep interest rates "lower for longer" to reflate the European economy comes at a significant cost, as sub-zero interest rates erode both deposit gathering and lending franchise values. Stress testing of banks' regulatory capital without a fiscal back-stop in place added to the uncertainty, rather than rebuilding stability, as the 2009 stress testing did in the US.

With the outbreak of the so-called "Euro" Crisis (a sovereign debt crisis on the EU periphery) the crisis became existential in Europe. It started in Greece and quickly affected Italy, Ireland, Portugal, Spain and Cyprus, all of which, with the exception of Italy, had to be bailed out by the EU, its member states and the International Monetary Fund (IMF). Greece, in actual fact, received three bailout packages, the second one with Private Sector Involvement (PSI), which "bailed in" banks and other institutional investors still holding Greek sovereign bonds at that stage. Several important fault-lines had existed under the surface since the launch of the Euro, notably (1) weak public finances due to a lack of

27 Compare Figure 1.2 in Huertas (2014), p 12, based on the December, 2009 Financial Stability Report of the Bank of England (2009a), Figure 1: Public sector interventions during the financial crisis, p 6.

budgetary discipline, (2) divergence in financial cycles (boom in the periphery and sluggish growth in the core)[28], (3) diverging competitiveness evidenced by growing current account balances in the periphery, and increasing surpluses in countries like Germany and the Netherlands, and (4) the negative feedback loop of sovereign funding problems associated with the banking sector, as the latter had large holdings of sovereign debt on its balance sheet. Losses in the banking system in Ireland, Greece and Cyprus were so high that they ultimately forced the governments in those countries to ask their European partners for help.

The slow recovery of the European economy relative to the US after the Great Financial Crisis raises the question to what extent this is caused by the difference in financial systems. Recent work by Allard and Blavy (2011) of the IMF, finds supporting evidence for a faster recovery of market-based economies as opposed to bank-based economies.[29] In fact, the comparative advantage of market-based economies in recovery is amplified when comparing strongly market-based economies with those which are strongly bank-based. To a certain degree, however, the superiority of market-based economies in recovery is due to higher employment and product market flexibility. Intuitively, market values for tradeable securities adjust faster than loan loss provisions (LLPs) can be booked. Market prices can fall off the chart on a screen in milliseconds, as market participants react to news on unexpected losses with sell-orders, whereas banks, at least to date, are only required by international accounting standards to book provisions for loan losses they have actually incurred.[30] Loan losses cannot be hidden in the market, but they can be on a bank's balance sheets for a long time.

The circumstances of the European banks today are characterized by multiple challenges and uncertainties, notably (1) the ongoing wave of regulatory changes and increased requirements for solvency capital, (2) low interest rates/flat yield curves pushing the deposit and lending franchise values into negative territory, (3) broken reputations and skyrocketing costs of misconduct, (4) elevated levels of non-performing loans (NPLs) and non-core legacy assets, as well as (5) growing investment requirements to make a successful transition into the digital world. These challenges are reflected in the valuation discount to book, making recapitalizations difficult.

Getting the banks back on track is key. What has been done so far and what needs to be done to finish the business? Let us look at an outline for this book.

28 Compare de Haan et al. (2015).

29 Compare Allard and Blavy (2011), WP/11/213.

30 This will change with the introduction of IFRS 9 which will require banks to recognize impairment losses over the full life time more quickly.

Finishing the business – an outline for this book

This book is aimed at the well-informed and interested public as well as bankers, regulators, supervisors, politicians and academics. As we obviously have not yet managed to get the banks bank on track in Europe, we need to take the debate to the next level and come up with specific suggestions. This will involve taking an historical perspective and looking at the evolution of the banking system, both from a macro-economic as well as a micro, bank-management standpoint. The book refers to the most recent academic research on the issues at hand, putting the findings into perspective through the eyes of an "insider". The general tone of the discussion is investigative – trying to identify the underlying root causes and uncover hidden fault lines. Getting the European banks and Europe back on track is as much about asking the right questions as it is about providing guidance and making actionable suggestions.

The book is divided into a total of fourteen chapters, including this introduction, and falls into five parts:

Part I – Where we started from: the starting point for this book in *Chapter 2: Europe's banking landscape* is a brief description of the evolution of the European banking landscape prior to the Great Financial Crisis. The chapter traces the evolution and integration of European banking since the Second Banking Directive of 1989, through to the launch of the common Eurozone currency a decade later. *Chapter 3: Banking – from the bottom up* – complements this description with a fundamental analysis of the economics of banking and banks. Specifically, this chapter attempts to answer the questions of why we need banks, how banks earn money, and how they create value for their shareholders. *Chapter 4: Banks' specialness – and the need for regulation and supervision* builds on this analysis by examining the specialness of banks resulting from their transformation of readily-available, liquid deposits into long-term, illiquid loans to the economy. This transformation creates an inherent vulnerability to panic and runs on banks, because the withdrawal of deposits is subject to a serial service constraint and the liquidation of loans is costly. Bank runs are socially wasteful: the resulting need for regulation, supervision and safety nets is the topic of chapter 4. This chapter tries to answer the questions of why we need to regulate and supervise banks (instead of just relying on market discipline), how we can prevent socially wasteful bank runs and contagion across the financial system, and how much regulation and what safety nets are really needed.

Part II – European banking and finance in less troublesome times: on the basis of the foundations laid in Part I, chapters 5 and 6 set out to trace European policy-making with regards to integration of financial markets and banking services. *Chapter 5: Re-engineering of European Banking* analyzes the most important steps towards financial and monetary integration, in particular, the

First (1977) and Second European Banking Directives (1989), the Financial Services Action Plan (FSAP) (1999), and the implementation of the international Basel regulatory framework in the European Union. Financial and banking integration further accelerated with the launch of the common currency in 1999. Banking in the monetary union is therefore the topic of *Chapter 6: One market, one money – (too) many banking systems.* However, while monetary policy was unified and wholesale money markets were beginning to integrate, banking politics and supervision remained a national prerogative. This created a critical fault line that few appreciated in less troublesome times and which only became apparent in the burgeoning financial crisis.

Part III – Crisis hitting and multiplying: Chapters 7 and 8 analyze the Great Financial Crisis and its impact on European banking. *Chapter 7: From "turbulences" to the Great Financial Crisis* traces the origins of the Great Financial Crisis back to the US subprime crisis. It raises the important question of why this Crisis was able to seriously affect European banks, and identifies the interbank market as the key transmission channel of turbulences across the Atlantic. *Chapter 8: Mopping up – containing the crisis* compares the crisis response in the US with the crisis response in Europe. The case studies of the Lehman failure and the AIG bail-out on the US side and the HRE bail-out in Germany on the European side provide the background for this comparison. The crisis response in Europe was characterized by a lack of both speed and policy coordination.

Part IV – Crisis becoming existential: just as the crisis is coming under control in the US in 2010, it is suddenly becoming existential in Europe. *Chapter 9: Early lessons drawn: shackled by principles?* analyzes the early lessons drawn in Europe, particularly the de Larosière report[31] of 2009, which led to increased coordination, but not to the much-needed integration of banking, capital markets and insurance supervision in Europe – at least, not yet. It also takes a closer look at the nexus between sovereigns and banks. This nexus turned into a spiral of doom not only in Greece, Ireland, Portugal, Spain but also in Cyprus. The resulting "Euro" crisis is the topic of *Chapter 10: Then come Greece and Ireland: "unnecessary, undesirable, and unlikely".* The main focus of this chapter is on the Greek and Irish sovereign debt crises.

Part V – Finishing the business, in a principled way: chapters 11, 12, 13, and 14 are devoted to finishing the business of putting the banks back on track in a principled way. Europe clearly needs to improve the institutional crisis management framework and move beyond a time-consuming and incomplete national policy coordination. *Chapter 11: Centralization of financial policies – If Greece (or Ireland) were Texas,* is devoted to the need for centralization of banking policies in a monetary union. It compares the Texas banking crisis in the

31 Compare European Commission (2009a).

US with the recent Greek and Irish banking crises and draws important lessons for the European banking system by looking at the evolution of the US banking system. *Chapter 12: Blueprints, optimal policies to choose from* takes us back to the drawing board and analyzes the shortcomings of the current Basel framework, which is at the heart of international banking regulation. It draws important lessons from the bank and sovereign (creditor) bail-outs between 2008 and 2014, and looks at the issues of state aid, competition policy and bank resolution schemes. In particular, it sheds light on the issue of moral hazard and the link between liability and accountability. It critically discusses the need for further structural reforms, especially the question of separation of investment banking from retail banking. *Chapter 13: Banking union –realm of the possible*, finally, is devoted to an in-depth assessment of the current state of play in the implementation of Banking Union. Last, but not least, the discussion is elevated to the level of the overall architecture of the European Union in *Chapter 14: The larger context – how much political union European Monetary Union (EMU) needs.* This chapter concludes the book by trying get at the fundamental question of how much more political union is ultimately necessary in a monetary union, in order to achieve sustainable growth and financial stability in Europe.

In summary

The banking system in Europe is large relative to the size of the economy and characterized by universal banking, and a significant number of systemically relevant, globally active national champions. Banks perform a vital role for the economy. Their leverage and deposit funding makes them inherently vulnerable to bank runs. Hence there is a need for safety nets in the form of supervision, a lender of last resort facility, and deposit insurance. In the run-up to the Great Financial Crisis, European policy makers were pushing towards more financial and monetary integration, culminating in the creation of the single Eurozone currency at the turn of the millennium. Monetary integration and a naive and inconsistent implementation of Basel II capital rules allowed for an increase in sovereign debt and a significant build-up of bank leverage, and made the European banking system vulnerable to the US subprime crisis. Since then, Europe has been held hostage by three overlapping crises, a banking crisis, a sovereign debt crisis, and an economic growth crisis. Resolving these crises means putting the banks back on track: this requires a centralization of banking policies and a careful recalibration of rules and regulations. Europe needs to (re-) establish a clear link between liability and accountability to contain the moral hazard created by multiple safety nets and reinforced by bank rescue measures in the aftermath of the crisis.

Part I – Where we started from

Chapter 2: Europe's banking landscape

"... banks were and are consciously employed by the group in control of the government to assist them in their competition with other states."[32]

Charles W Calomiris and Stephen H Haber, professors at Columbia and Stanford Universities respectively, (2014)

"As concerns banking, it is a clear conclusion that the introduction of a single currency will not only make the creation of a single market irreversible, but that it will, ..., alter fundamentally the nature of several businesses. ...., there is little doubt that it will reinforce the competitiveness of European banks operating in the capital markets of third countries such as those of the United States, ..."[33]

Jean Dermine, Professor of Banking and Finance at INSEAD, (1996)

Let us start with a look at Europe's banking system before the outbreak of the Great Financial Crisis – with the benefit of hindsight, of course, and with a view to uncovering hidden vulnerabilities. What was the situation of the European banking system before the outbreak of the Great Financial Crisis? How has European financial integration progressed since the Second European Banking Directive (89/646/EEC) in 1989? And, finally, how did the introduction of the common currency a decade later accelerate the integration of Europe's financial markets and banking landscape?

Pre-crisis landscape – national variety, universal banking and national champions

The pre-crisis banking landscape in Europe was characterized by different banking systems, each dominated by several, large, internationally active, national champions. The differences in national banking systems reflected deep-

32 Calomiris and Haber (2014), p 59.
33 Dermine (1996), p 56.

rooted differences in economic structures and financing traditions, in particular:

(1) *differences in firm structures* eg, the French economy was dominated by large corporations; this contrasts with the importance of SMEs which characterizes the German and Italian economies), and
(2) *corresponding financing habits* eg, larger corporations have easy access to the bond markets (in normal times); smaller SMEs are highly dependent on the availability of bank financing to fill the external financing needs,
(3) *various degrees of government* involvement eg, the German state-owned "Landesbanken" and locally-owned Savings Banks with a dual objective of operating commercially, but also implementing the developmental objective of state and local governments; the UK banking system with virtually no direct government involvement, and last, but not least,
(4) *different degrees of liberalization and deregulation* eg, the French banking sector was deregulated early on; the Italian banking market was deregulated later, with limited access for foreign banks.

Moreover, among other factors, differences in:

(1) *economic growth rates and demand for banking services*, especially lending services eg, higher demand for bank lending in the developing Eastern European countries and the periphery than in the core countries,
(2) *market structures* eg, high concentration in the Nordic, Benelux and UK domestic banking markets; fragmentation and "over-banking" in Italy,
(3) *exposure to fee-generating wholesale and investment banking activities* eg relatively high investment banking exposure for the leading UK, French, German and Swiss banks, and
(4) *the level of government involvement in domestic banking* eg, high in Germany and Spain; virtually no government involvement in domestic banking in the UK.

led to varied profitability and RoE levels in the different national banking sectors. RoE levels over the period 2000–2006 were rather low in the German and Italian banking sectors, at 3.7 and 10.0 percent respectively, whereas the banking sectors in the Nordic countries, the UK and the Benelux exhibited RoEs above 15 percent throughout the same period.[34] Similarly, growth in bank assets accelerated significantly at that time. In France, Germany, Italy, Spain and the UK combined, the increase in nominal banking assets between 1995 and 2006 was in excess of 400 percent.[35]

34 See Goddard et al. (2010), Table 32.8, p 828.
35 See Goddard et al. (2010), p 826 and Table 23.7, p 827.

London and Luxembourg had emerged as the predominant financial centers, given their favorable infrastructure and tax rulings. London was the major hub for both international and wholesale / investment banking into Europe, and Luxembourg had become the hub of choice for the European mutual fund industry. Both hubs benefited from the "passporting" rules in the Single Market that allow market participants to distribute financial services and products throughout the EU with a single banking or fund management license.

Even at the time of writing, the banking markets of most European member states are still dominated by domestic banks. Cross-border penetration of European banking, as measured by assets of banks from other EU countries relative to total banking assets, had steadily increased since the creation of the common currency: in 1999, it stood at 13 percent, and in 2007, just before the outbreak of the Great Financial Crisis, it peaked at 21 percent (see Figure 1). The share of assets of banks from third countries, ie countries outside of the EU, remained steady between 1997 and 2013 at a level of less than 10 percent. Cross-border banking penetration is highest in Eastern Europe, and in Belgium, Finland, and Luxembourg.

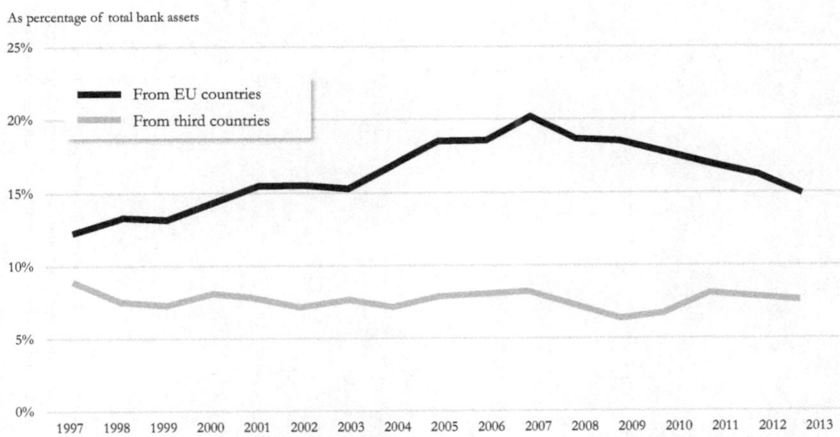

Note: Share of assets from other EU countries and third countries measured as a percentage of total banking assets. The share is calculated for the EU-28.

(Figure 1: Cross-border penetration in European banking 1997–2013 (as a percentage of total bank assets), from: de Haan et al. (2015), Table 10.1, p 337)

In 2013, the top 30 largest banks alone (selected by Tier 1 capital published in "The Banker") accounted for over EUR 24 trillion in assets, representing more than half of the total banking assets of EUR 42 billion of the European banking system (see Figure 2).

Banking groups in 2013		(1) Capital strength a) Euro billion	(2) Total assets Euro billion	(3) Business in home country as percent of (2)	(4) Business in rest of EU as percent of (2)	(5) Business in rest of world as percent of (2)
Global banks b)						
1. HSBC	UK	115	1,937	37	11	52
2. Barclays	UK	67	1,568	36	26	38
3. Deutsche Bank	Germany	51	1,612	28	30	42
4. Credit Suisse	Switzerland	37	710	23	22	55
5. UBS	Switzerland	35	821	33	25	42
6. Standard Chartered	UK	31	489	16	5	79
European banks c)						
1. BNP Paribas	France	72	1,800	34	44	22
2. Santander	Spain	61	1,116	29	41	30
3. UniCredit	Italy	43	846	40	59	1
4. ING	Netherlands	38	788	38	48	14
5. Nordea	Sweden	24	631	24	75	1
6. Danske Bank	Denmark	22	432	48	51	1
Semi-international banks d)						
1. Royal Bank of Scotland	UK	60	1,228	61	16	23
2. BBVA	Spain	40	583	51	9	40
3. Commerzbank	Germany	26	550	51	33	16
4. DNB Group	Norway	16	285	74	18	8
5. KBC	Belgium	14	241	53	45	3
6. SEB Bank	Sweden	12	280	63	34	3

Notes

a) Top 30 banks are selected on the basis of capital strength (Tier 1 capital as published in *The Banker*)

b) Global banks: less than 50% of assets in the home country and the majority of their international assets in the rest of the world

c) European banks: less than 50% of assets in the home country and the majority of their international assets in the rest of Europe

d) Semi-international banks: between 50% and 75% of assets in the home country

Banking groups in 2013		(1) Capital strength [a] Euro billion	(2) Total assets Euro billion	(3) Business in home country as percent of (2)	(4) Business in rest of EU as percent of (2)	(5) Business in rest of world as percent of (2)
Domestic banks [b]						
1. Crédit Agricole	France	63	1,707	81	11	8
2. Groupe BPCE	France	47	1,124	77	11	12
3. Lloyds Banking	UK	46	1,012	82	12	6
4. Société Générale	France	41	1,235	76	13	11
5. Rabobank	Netherlands	35	674	76	6	18
6. Intesa Sanpaolo	Italy	34	626	86	12	2
7. Crédit Mutuel	France	30	659	84	11	5
8. La Caixa Group	Spain	18	351	91	7	2
9. ABN AMRO	Netherlands	17	372	80	13	7
10. Landesbank Baden-Württemberg	Germany	15	274	75	18	7
11. DZ Bank	Germany	14	387	75	19	6
12. Bayerische Landesbank	Germany	14	256	75	18	/
Top 30 European banks		**1,135**	**24,592**	**53**	**24**	**23**

Note

a) Top 30 banks are selected on the basis of capital strength (Tier 1 capital as published in *The Banker*)

b) Domestic banks: 75% or more of assets in the home country

(Figure 2: Biggest 30 banks in Europe in 2013, from: de Haan et al. (2015), Table 10.2, pp 341–342),

The 30 largest European banks can be categorized into four groups:

(1) *Global banks:* HSBC (UK), Barclays (UK), Deutsche Bank (Germany), Credit Suisse (Switzerland), UBS (Switzerland), and Standard Chartered (UK) are global banks. They have less than 50 percent of their assets in their home country and the majority of their international assets in the rest of the world, outside of the EU. They are also large in size relative to their home country's GDP, making them "too-big-to-fail" both individually and in aggregate at the EU level. The two Swiss banks are, of course, not domiciled in the EU, but are globally active banks with important interconnections to the European banking system.

(2) *European banks* with less than 50 percent of their assets in the home country and the majority of their international assets in the rest of Europe include BNP Paribas (France), Santander (Spain), UniCredit (Italy), ING (Netherlands), Nordea (Sweden), and Danske Bank (Denmark).

(3) *Semi-international banks* with 50 to 75 percent of their assets in the home country include Royal Bank of Scotland (UK), BBVA (Spain), Commerzbank (Germany), DNB Group (Norway), KBC (Belgium), and SEB Bank (Sweden).

(4) The biggest *domestic banks* with more than 75 percent of their assets in their respective home countries include Crédit Agricole (France), Groupe BPCE (France), Lloyds Banking Group (UK), Société Générale (France), Rabobank (Netherlands), Intesa Sanpaolo (Italy), Crédit Mutuel (France), La Caixa Group (Spain), ABN AMRO (Netherlands), Landesbank Baden-Württemberg (Germany), DZ Bank (Germany), and Bayerische Landesbank (Germany).

On the eve of the Great Financial Crisis, the top European banks were more global than their US and Asia-Pacific counterparts (see Figure 3). This is not only due to larger cross-border activity within an integrated European banking market, but also due to substantial business activities in the rest of the world, particularly in the US and Asia-Pacific. In 2008, the top 30 European Banks had, in aggregate, close to 50 percent of business outside their home country, thereof 28 percentage points in the rest of the world outside Europe; the top 15 banks for the Americas were more domestically oriented, with just 27 percent of their business abroad. The top 15 Asia-Pacific banks were even more domestically orientated, with just 18 percent of their activities outside their respective home countries.

In line with a similar trend in the US, the total number of banks in the EU decreased from over 12,200 to slightly more than 7,700, ie a reduction of almost 40 percent.[36] This reduction was mainly due to consolidation and has led to

36 Compare de Haan et al. (2015), Table 10.4, p 347.

	2000			2004			2008			2011		
Continent	h	r	w	h	r	w	h	r	w	h	r	w
Europe	55	20	25	54	22	24	51	21	28	53	23	24
Americas	77	8	15	78	9	13	73	9	18	70	11	19
Asia-Pacific	80	6	14	86	4	10	82	7	11	87	5	8

Notes

Share of business in home country (h), rest of the region (r) and rest of the world (w) of the top banks by continent.
The top 30 banks for Europe; the top 15 banks for Americas and Asia-Pacific. The shares add up to 100%.

(Figure 3: Development of international banking by continent 2000–2011, from: de Haan et al, (2015), Table 10.2, p 343)

increased market concentration in some of national banking markets. Whereas market concentration is low in Austria, Germany, Ireland, Italy, Luxembourg, Poland and the UK, it is high in Estonia, Finland, Greece, Lithuania, Malta, and the Netherlands.[37]

Another important distinguishing feature of the banking market is the degree of competition; competition in the banking sectors of the Czech Republic, Ireland, the Netherlands, Spain, and the UK, is stronger than in France, Germany, Malta, and Romania, all of which have an intermediate level of competition, while banking competition in Austria, Cyprus, Finland, Hungary, Italy, Poland, and Portugal is low.[38] The respective geographical market for various banking services differs. While the market for banking services to households and SMEs is still national and the market concentration can be expected to have an impact on competition, the market for wholesale banking services to larger corporates is certainly European, and the investment banking market is even more global.

Before the outbreak of the Great Financial Crisis, the RoE for listed Eurozone banks was, in some cases, well over 20 percent, considerably above Cost of Equity (CoE). This positive gap between RoE and CoE translated into stock market valuations significantly above their book value for most banks.[39] However, unlike in the US, the driver for these high RoE levels was not the return on assets (RoA) but rather balance sheet leverage. This is best illustrated by comparing the development of J.P. Morgan and Deutsche Bank before 2008.

At the turn of the millennium, globalization of business was accelerating. For corporate banks this meant that they had to provide a full range of commercial and investment banking services to clients, and they had to do so in all of the places their customers were doing business. As Deutsche Bank increased its global banking reach in international markets, several competitors followed suit.

37 See de Haan et al. (2015), Table 10.4, p 347.
38 Compare Bikker et al. (2006).
39 Compare Constancio (2016), Figure 3.

As a result, rivalry intensified within the international investment banking market. To finance the asset growth on their balance sheets, banks had three primary options:
(1) use profits earned in previous periods,
(2) issue new equity capital thereby diluting existing shareholders, or
(3) borrow debt capital thereby increasing leverage.

Until 2007, Deutsche Bank achieved remarkable growth in per-share earnings, which grew from EUR 0.63 in 2002, to EUR 13.05 in 2007, ie an 83 percent annual growth rate. But this earnings growth did not only come purely from an increase in RoA, but mostly from an increase in leverage: RoA increased from 0.05 to 0.36 percent in 2007, but leverage, expressed as total assets to Tier 1 capital, increased from 33.3 to 71.3 in the same timeframe. This pushed RoE from 1.75 percent in 2002 to 24.97 percent in 2007: a 13-fold increase in five years. In comparison, J.P. Morgan achieved a higher RoA (increasing from 0.21 to 1.13 percent) but a lower RoE level (increasing from 4.3 to 17.6 percent) over the same period. In the case of J.P. Morgan, however, these RoE levels were achieved with far less leverage (just 17.6 times total assets to Tier 1 capital in 2007, down from 20.2 times total assets to Tier 1 capital in 2002).

In the case of Deutsche Bank and other large European banks, the increased leverage was partly due to regulatory arbitrage and the adoption of the Internal Ratings-Based Approach (IRBA) to the risk-weighting of assets. It was also due, however, to significant amounts of secured and unsecured funding provided by non-bank financial institutions. In fact, as Schmidt et al. found in their empirical analysis of the alleged transformation of the financial systems in the three major European economies, France, Germany, and the UK, "the intermediation chains are lengthening.... Non-bank financial intermediaries are taking over a more important role as mobilizers of capital from the nonfinancial sectors".[40]

Ever since the passing of the First Banking Directive (77/780/EEC) in 1977, which required full harmonization of the relevant bank supervision standards such as solvency, liquidity, and financial controls, EU legislation has been directed consistently toward the reduction of barriers to cross-border banking activity. Let us look at the evolution of European banking and the impact of monetary integration on Europe's banking landscape to fully understand what level of financial integration had been achieved in Europe pre-crisis.

40 See Schmidt et al. (1999), p 36.

From fragmentation to integration – evolution of banking policies in the EU since the Second Banking Directive of 1989

The EU has its origins in the European Coal and Steel Community (ECSC), formed by six European countries, Belgium, Germany, France, Italy, Luxembourg and the Netherlands, in 1951. With the Treaty of Rome (1957) entering into force in 1958, the European Economic Community (EEC) came into being.[41] In 1973, Denmark, Ireland, and the UK joined what was then called the European Communities, followed by Greece (1981), Spain and Portugal (1986), and Austria, Finland, and Sweden in 1996. After the end of the Cold War and the collapse of the Soviet Union, various Eastern European countries became candidate members of what was then the European Union. In 2004, Cyprus and the Czech Republic, Estonia, Hungary, Latvia, Lithuania, Malta, Poland, Slovakia, and Slovenia joined the EU, followed by Bulgaria and Romania in 2007 and Croatia in July, 2013[42] At the time of writing, following a referendum in 2016, the UK is about to trigger their exit from the EU under Article 50 of the Maastricht Treaty.

The Treaty of Rome, which sees its 60th anniversary this year, proposed the creation of "a unified economic area with a common market" as a key task of the European Community, including a single market for financial services. It paved the way for the creation of a common market where goods, services, labor, and capital could move freely and steered Europe down the path to a single financial market. But it was not until the late 1970s that concrete steps were taken in this direction.

The First EU Banking Directive of 1997 was an important first step towards the synchronization of prudential supervision of banks. It required the full harmonization of relevant banking standards, such as solvency, liquidity, and internal controls. Unfortunately, national approaches to even basic prudential standards, including capital requirements, continued to diverge.

In the second half of the 1980s, the completion of the internal market moved higher up on the agenda of EU policy makers, resulting in the 1985 White Paper

41 In addition to the European Atomic Energy Community (Euratom), which was also agreed in the Treaty of Rome.

42 In line with Article 49 of the Treaty of Maastricht, that any state that respects the "principles of liberty, democracy, respect for human rights and fundamental freedoms, and the rule of law", other neighboring countries may apply to join the EU: (i) Turkey applied for membership in 1987; (ii) Albania, Bosnia and Hercegovina, Kosovo, Macedonia, Montenegro, and Serbia are recognized as official candidates; Montenegro and Serbia have set a goal to finish accession talks by 2019; (iii) Moldowa, Ukraine and Georgia signed Association Agreements with the EU in 2014; (iv) Switzerland (withdrawn 2016), Norway (withdrawn 1992) and Iceland (withdrawn 2015) have applied for membership but withdrawn their applications in the meantime.

on the Completion of the Internal Market[43], which provided for the free circulation of goods, services, and capital within the EU. The Cecchini (1988) Report[44] calculated the costs of nationally fragmented markets and estimated the benefits of the internal market to be approximately 4–7 percent of GDP. The White Paper led to the adoption of the so-called Single European Act (SEA) in 1986, which aimed at completing the internal market by 1992.

As regards banking, the European Commission called for: (1) a single European banking license, and (2) home-country control of banking groups (as opposed to host-country supervision):

(1) *Single European banking license:* the Second Banking Directive determined that a credit institution that is authorized in any member state is allowed to establish branches or supply cross-border financial services in the other member states. The single banking "passport" has, therefore, contributed significantly to the stimulation of cross-border banking. The banking model adopted by the EU gives national supervisors responsibility for financial conglomerates, the ownership structure of banks, and their relationship with the industry.

(2) *Home-country control in the supervision of branches:* importantly, the Second Banking Directive also introduced the principle of home-country control in the supervision of branches, albeit with some exceptions. Home-country authorities were to be responsible for the supervision of solvency that extended to the bank itself, its foreign and national subsidiaries and its foreign branches. EU member states retained the right to supervise an EU bank's activities in their country only to the extent that this supervision was necessary to protect "public interest". Thus, the way in which a bank markets its services and deals with customers (ie its "conduct of business") could be regulated by the host state. The host state could also intervene in matters of liquidity, monetary policy and advertising. Moreover, in emergency situations the host-country supervisor could – subject to ex post control by the Commission – take any precautionary measures deemed necessary to protect investors and customers.[45]

The main limitation of the Second Banking Directive is that the single license does not extend to subsidiaries in host member states. This is unfortunate, as the expansion of cross-border banking more often takes place via subsidiaries, especially when the cross-border activities involve major banking operations. As

43 Commission of the European Communities (1985).
44 See Cecchini (1988).
45 Compare Walkner and Raes (2005).

Dermine (2005), explains, based on his case studies of ING and Nordea[46], two European banks that expanded via significant cross-border M&A, that the motivation for a bank to keep a subsidiary structure is driven by eight arguments, of which four are temporary in nature, to help with the integration of an acquisition. A subsidiary structure serves to: (i) maintain the original brand, (ii) reassure management, and (iii) reassure shareholders that original functions will be retained in the entity in the home country, thereby also (iv) increasing the likelihood of (national) shareholder approval. Transforming a subsidiary into a branch subsequent to a merger (v) could create a tax liability, and (vi) trigger additional contributions to the home deposit-insurance fund. Even if tax laws and deposit insurance schemes were harmonized and (already) fully integrated, there are two more fundamental arguments in favor of maintaining a subsidiary structure: keeping the legal entity (vii) allows for a separate listing, and (viii) a later sale of the business.

The European legal framework is based on the international banking standards of the Basel Committee on Banking Supervision (BCBS). An important element in banking regulation are the so-called Capital Adequacy Requirements, ie regulations concerning the minimum amount of (equity) capital that banks must hold in order to withstand adverse economic shocks. The Solvency and Own Funds Directive (89/647/EEC and 89/299/EEC), which laid down the solvency rules for banks, was based on the 1988 Basel Capital Accord (also referred to as Basel I).

Instead of fully harmonizing rules, the principle of minimum harmonization is used to define a common minimum standard. Member states must observe this minimum standard when they implement a Directive into national law, but can move beyond this minimum ("gold plating"):

(1) the Second Banking Directive called for harmonized capital adequacy standards and large exposure rules, as well as supervisory control of banks' permanent participation in the non-financial sector;
(2) the minimum harmonization principle was also applied to deposit insurance. The Directive on Deposit Guarantee Schemes (94/19/EEC), which was accepted by the Council in 1994, provided for a mandatory coverage per depositor of a minimum of EUR 20,000. Deposits at a branch were covered by the deposit insurance of the home country. In implementing this Directive, member states adopted an explicit deposit insurance scheme with compulsory participation. Practical arrangements with respect to coverage limits, funding, and co-insurance, however, differed substantially across EU member states.

46 See Dermine (2005), p 20.

A major supporting piece of legislation for financial market integration was the 1988 Directive on Liberalization of Capital Flows (88/361/EEC). It contained a safeguard clause allowing members to take any necessary measures in the case of an acute balance of payments problems. A certain degree of uncertainty persisted, therefore, with regards to the complete and permanent freedom of capital flows.

The 1992 Treaty of Maastricht confirmed the Single Market program. The Treaty is explicit on the principle of decentralization and allocation of regulatory and supervisory powers to the national central banks (Articles 105 (2) and (5)). It would only be in very special circumstances, and with unanimous agreement of the European Council, that the ECB would be allowed to regulate or supervise financial institutions (Article 105 (6)).

The European Council of Cardiff in 1998, underlined the importance of financial market integration as a political priority. In May 1999, this resulted in the launch of the Financial Services Action Plan (FSAP) by the European Commission. The FSAP had four objectives: (1) creation of a single EU wholesale market, (2) creation of open and secure retail markets, (3) state-of-the-art prudential rules and supervision, and (4) improvement of the wider conditions for an optimal single financial market:

(1) *Single EU wholesale market:* the Markets in Financial Instrument Directive (MiFID, 2004/39/EC) was, to a large extent, the cornerstone of the FSAP. The directive provided securities firms with an updated EU passport, allowing them to offer a broader range of financial instruments and services across Member States on a home-country control basis.

(2) *Open and secure retail markets:* the Commission acknowledged that certain barriers prevented consumers and financial services providers from reaping the single-market benefits of increased choice and competitive terms. For example, the Distance Marketing Directive (2002/65/EC) aimed to protect retail customers dealing with a financial services firm in another member state. Specifically, it ensures that retail customers receive a certain minimum of specified information about financial services or products before entering into a contract, and that they also have the right to cancel some type of contracts even after entering into them.

(3) *State-of-the-art prudential rules:* the Capital Requirements Directive (CRD) laid down new capital adequacy rules for banks and is based on the 2004 Basel II Capital Accord. It stipulates the minimum amount of own funds which must be held by the bank. The aim is to ensure that the banks can weather difficult periods and absorb unexpected losses, thereby protecting depositors and clients, and fostering the stability of financial systems. This directive has been revised a number of times, resulting recently in CRD IV.

(4) *Improved wider conditions for an optimal single financial market:* the FSAP also addressed disparities in tax treatment and attempted to create an efficient and transparent legal system for corporate governance. An example was the Savings Directive (2003/48/EC) that established automatic exchange of information as the way of combating cross-border tax evasion on savings-related interest income.

In 2004, the European Commission concluded that the FSAP had been delivered on time, with 40 out of the 42 measures being adopted before the 2005 deadline.

The Lamfalussy approach, which was put forward in 2001 was pivotal in the drafting of new regulations and the harmonization of supervision of banking, the securities markets and insurance[47] as it allowed for the distinction between legislative principles and technical rules. The Commission was, and still is, supported by the European Banking Committee (EBC) which advises the Commission on policy issues related to banking activities and assists the Commission in implementing measures for EU legislation. The Committee of European Banking Supervisors (CEBS) was an independent advisory group responsible for the uniform application of directives and institutionalized the exchange of information among supervisors. It was dissolved in 2011 and its role assumed by the European Banking Authority, the EBA, which sets technical standards for banking regulation.

After this brief review of financial integration policies let us now turn to Economic and Monetary Union (EMU) and its impact on the European banking landscape.

European Banking and Monetary Union

Whilst financial integration had been progressing gradually and in smaller steps, European monetary integration was characterized by two major steps: the introduction of the European monetary system (EMS) in 1979, and the introduction of the common currency in 1999.

(1) *Step 1 – the EMS:* the EMS was introduced in 1979, with the aim of creating a 'zone of monetary stability' in Europe. The core principle was the so-called Exchange Rate Mechanism (ERM), within which the currencies of participating countries were supposed to fluctuate within a band of plus and minus 2.25 percent. In the early 1990s, the EMS was put under strain by the differing

47 The Lamfalussy approach was set out by the Commission of Wise Men on the Regulation of European Securities Markets (2001). That committee was chaired by Alexandre Lamfalussy, former President of the European Monetary Institute, a precursor to the ECB.

economic policies and conditions of its members, and the band of fluctuations was subsequently widened to plus and minus 15 percent.

(2) *Step 2 – ECB and Euro:* in 1989, the Committee for the Study of Economic and Monetary Union recommended, in the "Delors Report"[48], a three-phase transition spread over 10 years. The conclusions of the Committee were incorporated into the 1992 Maastricht Treaty on European union. In 1999, the ECB took over responsibility for monetary decision-making and a common currency, the Euro, was introduced in 11 EU member states in the same year. Retail markets continued to operate in legacy national currencies until January 2002, when Euro notes and coins were finally introduced. Legacy currencies were completely withdrawn by May 2002. At the time of writing, 19 member states are part of the Eurozone. An important feature of the single currency system is the payment and clearing system, which remains organized at the national central bank level, while real-time settlements between financial institutions flow through the ECBs "Trans-European Automated Real-Time Gross Settlement Express Transfer System" (TARGET).

With the establishment of the ECB and the introduction of the Euro, monetary policy was fully integrated, but fiscal policy remained fragmented and subject only to certain loosely enforced rules under the Stability and Growth Pact of 1997. Financial integration, while accelerating in wholesale markets – money markets, and bond and equity markets – as expected[49], remained incomplete. This was particularly the case in retail financial services. The ECB's annual "Financial Integration in Europe" report of April 2008 concluded that "in the euro area, while interbank market and capital market related activities show clear signs of increasing integration, retail banking markets continue to be fragmented"[50] According to Dermine, (2002), the "law of one price" which represents the theoretical benchmark for integrated markets, is unlikely to hold in retail banking markets for various reasons:[51]

(1) *Trust and confidence in local banks:* customers want to ensure that their money is in safe hands. Local knowledge of the bank, the banking system, local language, proximity, etc. may lead to a certain preference for a domestic bank.

(2) *Bundling of financial services:* retail customers generally buy a bundle of services; the "law of one price" may hold for the bundle of products and services but not for the individual banking product.

48 Committee for the Study of Economic and Monetary Union (1989).
49 See Dermine (1996).
50 ECB (2008), p 17.
51 See Dermine (2002).

(3) *Asymmetric information in lending:* local knowledge can help to overcome asymmetric information. Local banks may, therefore, be in a better position than foreign banks to lend to retail customers and SMEs.
(4) *Differences in legislation:* differences in tax and consumer-protection rules can create barriers to entry for foreign banks.

M&A in the banking sector accelerated significantly in the wake of monetary union (see Figure 4). European banks in most countries prepared themselves for the Single Market by merging with other domestic banks. The rate of cross-border mergers increased after the beginning of the EMU. Consolidation was driven by the objectives of realizing economies of scale and scope, reducing labor and other variable costs, cutting operational inefficiencies, and spreading risk through product or geographic diversification.

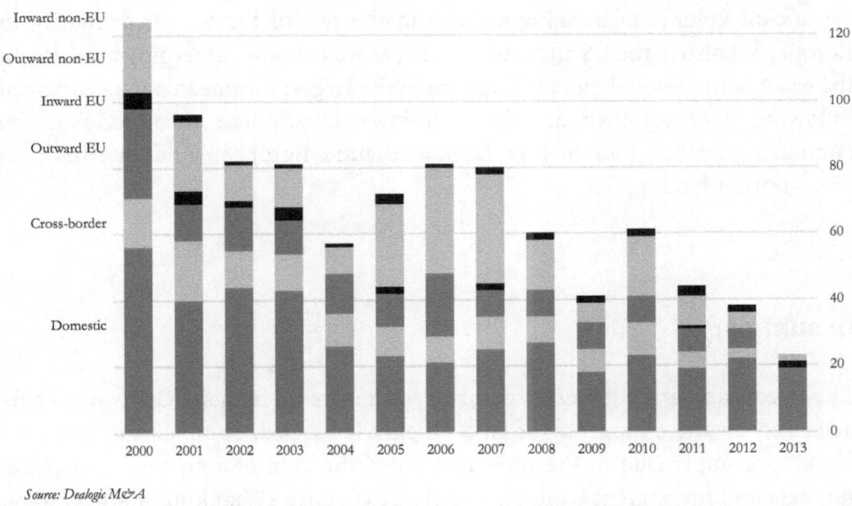

(Figure 4: Banking M&As in Europe 2000–2013 (value of competed deals, Euro billion), from: de Haan et al. (2015), Figure 10.11, p 344)

Early cross-border mergers in the 1990s created regional banks, such as Fortis in the Benelux and Nordea in the Nordic countries. Conversely, they were aimed at adding a US investment banking franchise to build out the bank's market position in global investment banking, as demonstrated by Deutsche Bank's acquisition of Bankers Trust in 1999. More recent transactions at the beginning of the millennium, however, were more widely spread across Europe. Examples are the takeover of Abbey National (UK) by Banco Santander (Spain) in 2004, and the takeover of Bank-Austria Creditanstalt (Austria) by HypoVereinsbank

(Germany), in 2005. The peak in transaction values in 2007 reflected the merger of the Italian banks Sanpaolo IMI and Banca Intesa and the acquisition of ABN AMRO (Netherlands) by a consortium of Royal Bank of Scotland (UK), Fortis (Belgium), and Banco Santander (Spain). This deal was the largest transaction in banking history, but it has since then become symbolic of overstretched M&A activity in the banking industry immediately prior to the outbreak of the Great Financial Crisis: already seen as having paid too high a price, both Fortis and RBS were among the first large European banks to be adversely affected by the crisis.[52]

Since that time, overall M&A completed deal volumes have declined steadily from over EUR 120 billion in 2000 to just over EUR 20 billion in 2013. Domestic deal volumes declined throughout this period whereas non-domestic deals continued to increase until 2007.

Significant cross-border M&A activity at the beginning of the millennium resulted in the creation of large, complex multinational banking groups with a significant volume of banking activity in the rest of the world: primarily in Europe, but also in the US and Asia-Pacific, as well as other emerging markets. In the wake of the general globalization trend the largest European banks had been following their customers and financial flows globally. The introduction of the common currency had further facilitated intra-European and international cross-border lending.

In summary

The European banking landscape prior to the Great Financial Crisis was characterized by the emergence of large, highly leveraged, complex international banking groups. Due to the introduction of the common currency, financial markets and investment banking and (large corporate) banking markets were, more or less, integrated, whereas retail banking markets remained fragmented. Harmonization of rules and regulations was incomplete. Supervision was somewhat coordinated but neither integrated nor centralized. All in all, integration and consolidation in EU banking remained very much unfinished business.

Let us now look at the fundamental economics of banking, banking regulation and supervision in the following two chapters before we revisit European banking and financial policies in less troublesome times.

---

52 Santander was able to sell the Italian bank Antonveneta, that it had received a spart of the carve-up of ABN AMRO, for a sizeable profit to the Italian Banca Monte dei Paschi di Siena.

Chapter 3: Banking – from the bottom up

"Adventure is the life of business, but caution is the life of banking." [53]

Walter Bagehot, British journalist, businessman and essayist, (1962)

"A banker is a fellow who lends his umbrella when the sun is shining and wants it back the minute it begins to rain."

attributed to Mark Twain, US writer, humorist and critic

If we really want to understand what is happening in European banking, what needs to change and why, we must take a close look at the banks themselves. We need to understand the role that banks play in the economy, how they are compensated for their services, and how much profit they need to generate for their shareholders, so that they both benefit and to continue to invest.

Why do we need banks? The role of banks in the economy

Banks are an important part of the financial system. At the macro level the financial system allocates scarce resources to their most productive use in the business sector. Merton and Bodie (1995), distinguish six basic or core functions performed by the financial system:

(1) *"To provide ways of clearing and settling payments to facilitate trade.*
(2) *To provide a mechanism for the pooling of resources and for the subdividing of shares in various enterprises.*
(3) *To provide ways to transfer economic resources through time, across borders, and among industries.*
(4) *To provide ways of managing risk.*
(5) *To provide price information to help coordinate decentralized decision-making in various sectors of the economy.*

53 See Bagehot (1962), p 5.

(6) *To provide ways of dealing with the incentive problems created when one party in a transaction has information that the other party does not or when one party acts as an agent for another.*"[54]

The financial system relies on different institutions to perform these core functions. In principle, two different ways exist to achieve the appropriate allocation of resources: via financial markets or via financial intermediaries (see Figure 5). The allocation of resources via financial markets is often referred to as direct finance (such as the foreign exchange and fixed income or equity markets), whilst the allocation of funds via financial intermediaries is referred to as indirect finance (via banks or non-bank financial intermediaries, such as insurance companies or fund managers). In terms of indirect finance, the intermediation chain can be long and complex. For example, fund managers, insurance companies, or other non-bank financial intermediaries gather financial resources from the non-financial sector and either deposit them directly with a bank or invest in the bank's bonds.

For the financial system to work properly, the government must first provide a stable legal and regulatory framework which will protect property rights and be able to enforce (financial) contracts. The system also needs both government regulation and supervision to ensure adequate and equitable information disclosure to all market participants. Sustainable economic development and financial stability go hand-in-hand: therefore, the government must ensure the stability and soundness of individual financial intermediaries as well as the financial system as a whole. However, regulation and supervision must still allow a degree of competition among financial institutions to encourage these institutions to perform their core functions efficiently. Financial services regulation and supervision should also ensure that sufficient headroom exists for financial innovation, which in turn can lead to greater efficiencies in performing these basic financial functions.

For a variety of reasons, mostly historical and political, financial systems differ in the relative importance of banks versus financial markets. Bank-oriented economies are arguably better at dealing with non-diversifiable risk than financial markets. The typical household asset in a bank-oriented economy, such as Germany, is the deposit account, as opposed to the securities account holding stocks and bonds in a financial market-oriented economy such as the US. Arguably, intertemporal risk-sharing is also more effective in a bank-oriented economy, whereas the financing of new technologies works better in economies

54 See Merton and Bodie (1995), p 2.

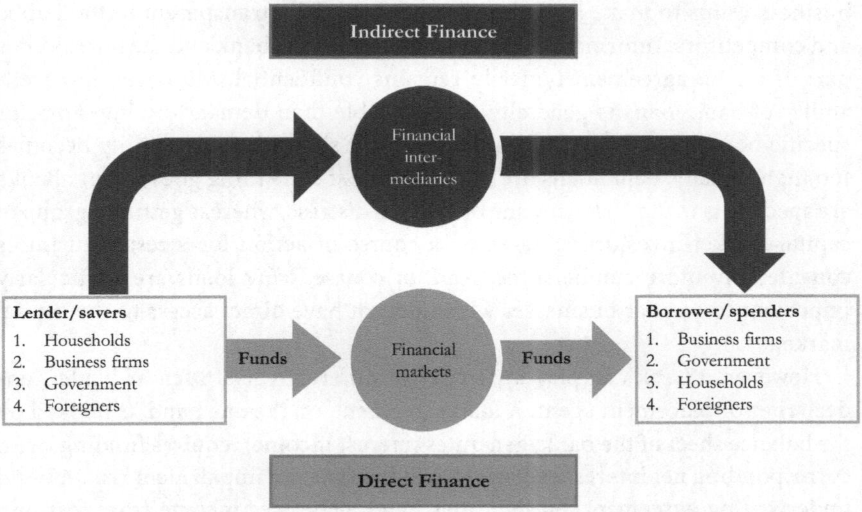

(Figure 5: Direct versus indirect finance, based on de Haan et al. (2015), Figure 1.1, p 5)

based on financial markets.[55] In other words, banks and financial markets are complementary institutional frameworks.[56]

On one level, banks and financial markets compete with one another by each executing bundles of individual core functions. On another level, they complement each other: for example, when a core function moves to the financial markets but the product offering is not viable without a bank offering the complementary function. The process of migrating financial functions from banking to the financial markets is often referred to as dis-intermediation, and the reverse process as re-intermediation. Securitizations in the capital markets can be a substitute for bank loans. But issuers typically need the assistance of a bank in terms of originating, warehousing, structuring, pricing the underlying financial assets and providing the cash flows necessary to access the capital markets. Issuers also need banks to access the payment, clearing, and settlement systems.

From the perspective of a borrower, who has the choice between taking out a loan from a bank or issuing a bond, what are the decision-making criteria? Firstly, size is a key parameter: loan size is more flexible and typically smaller than the minimum size for a bond issuance. There are fixed costs – mostly legal – for a bond issuance, and costly ongoing reporting requirements to both the markets and to the regulators. This is an important consideration since not every

55 Venture Capital financing in the US works well because the stock market allows for lucrative exits from these investments.

56 See de Haan et al. (2015), pp 33–35, for a concise summary of these issues.

business wants to make its financial statements fully transparent to the public and competitors. Information exchanged between the bank and the borrower as part of a loan agreement typically remains confidential. Moreover, the availability of bank loans is generally more reliable than demand by investors for specific bond issuances; primary markets can shut down if volatility becomes too high. Finally, bank loans are more flexible if something goes wrong. Banks are specialists in the restructuring of loans in distress, whereas getting a group of capital market investors to agree on a course of action for a restructuring is considerably more cumbersome. And, of course, bank loans are particularly important to smaller businesses which do not have direct access to the capital markets.

However, a bank can play a number of different roles, such as lender, underwriter or placement agent. A loan agreement, on the one hand, is booked on the balance sheet of the bank, generates interest income, requires funding (with corresponding net interest expenses), and is subject to impairment risk. A bond underwriting agreement, on the other hand, generates income from fees and does not require immediate funding. Bond underwriting only requires contingent funding if the bond cannot be placed with investors. Where this is the case, the underwriting risk for the bank crystallizes and the banks' balance sheet becomes subject to market risk (as opposed to credit risk arising from a loan exposure). As a business grows, it will seek to diversify its funding sources. Bank loans signal credit worthiness to the capital markets and are typically a prerequisite for a bond issuance.

The financial system, consisting of financial markets and financial intermediaries, plays an important role in fueling economic growth. Economic research frequently uses the relative size of financial assets as a percentage of GDP as a proxy for financial sector development. As Rajan and Zingales, (1996), remark: "Financial development has a substantial supportive influence on the rate of economic growth and this works, at least partly, by reducing the cost of external finance to financially dependent firms."[57] But if financial sector development reaches a certain threshold, it can have a negative effect on economic growth: the debt overhang restricts the ability of the business and public sectors to invest, and the financial sector attracts human capital away from the business sector.[58] Moreover, higher debt levels also mean higher risk of financial instability.

57 See Rajan and Zingales (1996), p 584.

58 Reinhart and Rogoff (2010) show empirically that high debt levels are associated with notably lower growth rates.

Following the functional perspective introduced above, there are broadly speaking five different types of banking services[59]:

(1) *underwriting and placement* (eg, share or bond offerings),
(2) *portfolio management* (eg, the on-balance sheet management of the loan book or off-balance sheet management of mutual funds),
(3) *payment services* (eg, cash management services),
(4) *monitoring and information-related services* (eg, monitoring of borrowers),
(5) *risk management or risk-sharing services* (eg, liquidity insurance through revolving working-capital lines or sight deposit accounts).

From a legal and regulatory perspective, the EU Banking Co-ordination Directive 89/646/EEC provides a list of banking activities (see Figure 6).

- Deposit taking and other forms of borrowing
- Lending
- Financial leasing
- Money transmission services
- Issuing and administering means of payments (e.g., credit cards, traveler's checks, and bankers' drafts)
- Guarantees and commitments
- Trading for the bank's own account or the accounts of customers in
  - Money-market instruments
  - Foreign exchange
  - Financial futures and options
  - Foreign exchange- and interest-rate instruments
  - Securities
- Participation in share issues and the provision of services related to such issues
- Money brokering
- Portfolio management and advice
- Safekeeping of securities
- Credit reference services
- Safe custody services

(Figure 6: Banking activities according to the EU Directive, Dermine (2015), p 35)

In the modern economy, most money takes the form of bank deposits.[60] Deposits and currency together are referred to as "broad money," as opposed to "base

59 Compare for example Dermine (2015), chapter 4.
60 Compare McLeay et al. (2014) who build on Tobin (1963).

money" which consists of currency and central bank reserves. Deposits are created by other banks when they make loans: whenever a bank makes a loan it is creating a matching deposit in the borrower's bank account with the same or another bank, and providing liquidity to the customer. Borrowers, however, can rapidly neutralize the effect of newly created liquidity if they decide to repay existing debt instead of buying goods and services, and making investments. And banks, despite the fact that they can provide this additional liquidity (albeit within the limits of the regulatory and supervisory framework), have a continued responsibility to generate profits and create value for their shareholders.

How do banks make profits? Banks' balance sheets and income statements

How are banks compensated for their services? And how do they generate profits? To answer this question, understanding a bank as an "institution whose current operations consist of granting loans and receiving deposits from the public" is helpful.[61] Banks are quite opaque institutions. They receive deposits in various forms from the public and other institutions, and use these funds to provide liquidity, again in various forms, to those needing funds for projects and investments. An important outcome of this taking-in and giving-out of funds is a mismatch between financing and funding cash flows in terms of size (aggregating many small deposits to a larger loan), maturity (funding a longer-term loan with sight deposits), and denomination (collecting Euro deposits and providing a USD-based loan). In a sense, banks act like brokers: households want their deposits to be safe and available on demand, whereas businesses are looking to the bank to fund longer-term investments with uncertain outcomes. Households are not equipped to monitor a bank: they expect their money to be safe and not subject to volatility caused by external factors such as market information. In contrast, banks are specialists in the analysis and monitoring of long-term investment projects, and in dealing with highly information-sensitive forms of funding. This is one of the reasons why banking activities are regulated: to protect the retail customer, who is relatively unsophisticated as regards financial services products, and to ensure that banks meet their obligations.

The banks' balance sheets reflect their core lending and deposit activities. Banks grant loans to both retail and corporate customers, as well as other banks and non-bank financial institutions. They also hold cash and reserves with central banks and "safe" government bonds to enable them to remain liquid

61 Freixas and Rochet (2008), p 1.

when faced with high, unplanned levels of cash withdrawals from their depositors, should this happen. Their balance sheets contain relatively small positions as regards fixed assets. Banks fund their assets by collecting deposits from the public, specifically from retail and corporate customers, as well as from other banks. Deposits can be on demand or term, that is, with a specific maturity. Deposits are supported by equity and subordinated bonds issued to institutional investors, meaning that such investors are the first in line when it comes to absorbing losses.

Core lending and deposit activities also drive the banks' Profit and Loss (P&L) statements (see Figure 7). The difference between the interest income generated by loans and bonds on the asset side of a bank's balance sheet and the deposits and bonds on the liability side produces the net interest income in the P&L. Other core revenue components are fee and commission incomes generated from other services. The sum of the net interest income and the fee and commission incomes is referred to as gross revenue on the P&L. To arrive at earnings before taxes (EBT), the bank must provide for loan losses and account for their operating and other expenses, such as regulatory supervision, professional fees, etc.

Assets	**Liabilities and Shareholders' Equity**
Reserves with central banks	
Retail loans	Retail deposits ▪ Demand deposits ▪ Savings deposits ▪ Term deposits
Corporate loans	Corporate deposits ▪ Demand deposits ▪ Term deposits
Interbank loans	Interbank deposits
Government bonds	Subordinated debt
Fixed assets	Equity

	Interest income
./.	Interest expense
=	*Net interest income*
+	Fee/trading income
=	*Gross revenue*
./.	Loan provisions
./.	Operating (noninterest) expense
=	*Earnings before taxes*
./.	Taxes
=	Earnings after taxes

(Figure 7: Simplified bank's balance sheet and P&L statement, based on Dermine, (2015))

The following income model from Copeland, Koller, and Murrin (1994) shows the direct links between a bank's balance sheet and its P&L statement (see Figure 8). The authors' spread model shows how a bank can generate profits by exploiting the differences between being able to charge an interest rate above the market rate for loans, whilst attracting deposits with an interest rate below the market rate.

Definition		Calculation			
	(Spread on loans) x (Loan balance)		(12% - 8%) x ($933)	=	$37.32
+	(Spread on deposits) x (Deposit balance)	+	(8% - 5%) x ($1,000)	=	+30.00
+	(Equity credit) x (Equity)	+	(8%) x ($53)	=	+4.24
./.	(Reserve debt) x (Reserves)	./.	(8%) x ($120)	=	-9.60
./.	Expenses				-48.00
=	Net profit before tax				13.96
./.	Taxes at 40%				-5.58
	Net income				**$8.38**

(Figure 8: Income and spread models, see Copeland, Koller, and Murrin (1994))

How do a bank's balance sheet and P&L statement compare with the accounts of an industrial company? The majority of the bank's assets are financial assets, whereas for an industrial company the balance sheet consists mostly of physical assets such as plant, equipment, and inventories. More importantly, a bank's balance sheet contains more leverage, ie more debt. Banks earn money with their deposits – at least in times of non-negative interest rates. Correspondingly, banks do not generate revenues but rather net interest and net fee and commission income. Finally, there is no "cost of goods sold" as such in the P&L statement of a bank: the "raw material" or "inputs" are the costs such as expenses from interest income, to arrive at net interest income. The other costs are costs of risk and, of course, non-interest expenses, which are made up mostly of HR and IT costs.

There are special issues inherent in financial assets (as opposed to physical assets). In particular, loan contracts have to be designed in such a way that they align the incentives of both the borrower and the lender, and help overcome information asymmetries (ex ante), moral hazard (ex interim), and the hold-up risk (ex post) inherent in these situations. Banks are specialists in designing and monitoring incentive-compatible loan contracts.[62] To address the special issues inherent in the borrow-lender relationship, and to reduce the cost of lending, banks have developed various forms of loan agreements. These loan agreements rely on different forms of personal and material collateral agreements, as well as on affirmative and financial covenants.

Moreover, there are special risks inherent in financial liabilities and leverage, particularly due to the incentives created by debt -that is, deposits and bonds (as

62 Freixas and Rochet (2008), pp 24–30, provide a recent summary of the corresponding literature on the borrower-lender relationship.

opposed to equity).[63] The special nature of demand deposits that can be withdrawn instantly (as a means of limiting the banks' moral hazard) makes banks vulnerable to runs.[64]

Banks play an important role in the economy and make money by putting their balance sheets to work and providing useful services. But how do they create value for shareholders?

How banks create value for shareholders? – Bank valuation and strategic value drivers

The concept of shareholder value has attracted a lot of criticism lately, especially with regard to the behavior of banks before the Great Financial Crisis. Dermine (2015) summarizes the discussion on shareholder value as follows: "In a competitive economy with a well-functioning political system that acts to correct market imperfections, it can be concluded that the maximization of shareholder value enhances public welfare."[65] Long-term shareholder value can only be achieved in a stable society, with satisfied customers, a loyal client-base, and a good reputation with stakeholders.

According to Dermine (2015), the (fundamental) valuation formula for banks decomposes the equity value of the balance sheet- and interest rate-driven banking services into four different components: (1) the liquidation value of the current balance sheet (bonds, loans, and deposits), (2) the franchise value of loans and deposits, (3) the value of the operating expenses, and (4) the tax penalty (because a small portion of the balance sheet is equity funded). In addition, there is an equity value for fee-based banking services.

A number of economic and strategic factors exist that affect a bank's equity valuation, such as economic growth, the level of nominal interest rates, credit spread levels, and other market movements. Furthermore, barriers to entry can shield banks from competition and prevent financial innovation from providing substitutes for traditional banking products and services. The level of taxation, the regulatory regime, and the cost of compliance also influence shareholder-value, along with economies of scale and scope, the existence of implicit or explicit government guarantees, and more broadly speaking, changes in the legal system and governance standards.

Directly or indirectly, these factors affect RoE and the ability of the bank to

63 Admati and Hellwig (2013) discuss the incentives of debt contracts.

64 Diamond and Dybvig (1983) show that banks provide insurance to depositors against liquidity shocks and that banks are vulnerable to bank runs.

65 See Dermine (2015), p 127.

grow. Banks work with leverage in the form of deposits, bonds and other forms of debt to increase RoE. The higher the leverage, the higher the RoE given a certain level of RoA. However, leverage is not necessarily in the interest of the general public. There are high costs of distress associated with high debt levels. Depositors are, for the most part, risk-averse, and desire lower leverage: this is because equity shields them from unexpected asset impairments and subsequent losses. In general, the public also wants a higher equity component to ensure the stability and solvency of the banks. The appropriate amount of owner's equity is a function of the volatility of the asset portfolio and the level of certainty and protection demanded by depositors and the public. In theory, the more capital the bank holds, the more stable it and the banking system in general are. But this results in a lower RoE given a certain level of profitability.

Essentially, the equity value of a bank equals the current equity plus the present value (PV) of future economic profits.[66] The PV of future economic profits is, broadly speaking, a function of the future returns on equity and their growth as well as the CoE. A bank creates value if the RoE exceeds the CoE. The CoE is determined by the risk-free rate, ie cost of government bonds, plus a risk premium. The capital asset pricing model (CAPM) shows that the risk premium on shares is the product of the market premium and the beta of the shares.[67] The market risk premium is the difference between the expected return on the overall stock market and that on government bonds. The beta of a stock measures the extent to which expected returns on a stock change relative to the expected returns of the entire stock market portfolio. Because the banks' balance sheets have high leverage and are exposed to the economic cycle, their beta is typically larger than one. In other words, the performance of bank stocks is cyclical, they tend to outperform the market in economic upswings and underperform it in downswings.

The risk premium on bank shares is typically higher than the risk premium on assets, because the risk premium on bank shares contains both a premium for the riskiness of the assets and the amount of leverage. In theory, this premium should cause the CoE to go up with more leverage (less equity) and to come down with less leverage (more equity), leading to lower RoE targets for the banks with less leverage. The overall cost of capital for banks, however, is not as indifferent to the amount of leverage as might be suggested by the pure Modigliani-Mill theorem. In reality, the tax-deductibility of interest paid on bank deposits and debt, and implicit or explicit government guarantees for bank deposits and debt

66 See Dermine (2015), p 64.
67 See Sharpe (1964) and Lintner (1965).

distort market prices in such a way that they create an incentive for higher leverage.[68]

In summary

Financial markets in general, and banks in particular, perform vital functions – the real economy would not work without their proper functioning. European financial systems are historically based more on banks than on capital markets – that is why we need to rehabilitate the banks if we want to have economic growth or else allow for more (institutional) financial innovation. Banks are special institutions – the amount of leverage held against more or less illiquid financial assets makes them inherently vulnerable to runs. Bank deposits and bonds can suddenly become information-sensitive if rumors exist about possible impairments of the bank's assets. And since they are, in many cases, interconnected through the interbank (directly) and financial markets (indirectly), a run on a single bank can be contagious for the entire financial system. Hence there is need for regulation, supervision and additional safety nets.

68 See Admati et al. (2010) for a discussion of the cost of bank equity in the context of the banks' capital regulation.

Chapter 4: Banks' specialness – and the need for regulation, supervision, and safety nets

"He who seeks to regulate everything by law is more likely to arouse vices than to reform them. It is best to grant what cannot be abolished, even though it be in itself harmful. How many evils spring from luxury, envy, avarice, drunkenness and the like, yet these are tolerated – vices as they are – because they cannot be prevented by legal enactments."[69]
Benedict de Spinoza, Dutch-Jewish philosopher

"Not everything that can be counted, counts; not everything that counts can be counted."
attributed to Albert Einstein, German-born theoretical physicist

This chapter takes an in depth look at regulation, supervision, and safety nets. Why can't we just rely on the market discipline from the monitoring of depositors and institutional investors to do the job of maintaining the stability of banks and the financial system? What else, other than market failures, justifies the need for government intervention through regulation and supervision? And last, but not least, what are the limits of government intervention?

Why do we need to regulate and supervise the banks? Market failures and the need for bank regulation and supervision

In the ideal framework of a market-based economy, the case for government intervention through rule making (regulation), monitoring the behavior of individual banks, and enforcing compliance with the rules (supervision) is based on market failures. Government intervention through regulation and supervision, in other words, should lead to a better outcome for society.

The causes behind market failures in banking are:

(1) asymmetries inherent in any transaction between a bank and its customers because banks are opaque and typically better informed about their risks than their (retail) customers,

69 See de Spinoza (2016), p 149.

(2) by negative externalities because bank failures can not only affect depositors but also affect the stability of other financial intermediaries and the financial system at large (financial stability is in fact a public good), and
(3) the abuse of a dominant market position such as a monopoly or as part of a (narrow) oligopoly.[70]

Market failure due to asymmetric information arises from the fact that customers are less well informed than the financial institution. Individual customers are unable to properly assess the safety and soundness of a bank which holds their deposits, or to adequately monitor its behavior. Over time, however, banks have an incentive to engage in risky lending activities because the excess spread generated by these activities accrues to the shareholders, who typically have limited liability. Therefore, in cases where loans are not repaid, the losses in excess of the equity capital buffer in the bank accrues to the depositors. The private sector can use a mechanism such as a professional association to discipline members if they violate the code of conduct. However, because of the amounts of money at stake and the long-term nature of the relationship between depositors and their banks, this kind of mechanism does not work in the financial system.

Market failure due to externalities arises from the fact that the failure of a bank not only affects the bank itself but may also lead to contagion effects as depositors question the safety and soundness of other banks. Rumors about large losses at one specific bank can, and do, trigger a run on other banks' deposits as well. The liquidity, and subsequently the solvency, of other banks may be threatened if they are forced to liquidate illiquid assets at fire-sale prices in order to meet the withdrawals of their depositors. In turn, this fire sale of illiquid assets can both put pressure on market prices and lead to a decline in asset prices, thereby impacting the (perceived) solvency of a bank.

The purpose of banking regulation is to address the issues of asymmetric information and externalities by increasing the safety and stability of the banks. Accordingly, rules and regulations focus on minimum standards for capital, liquidity (short-term and long-term), and internal control mechanisms. Microprudential supervision is a four-stage process[71]:
(1) licensing, authorization, or chartering of banks;
(2) monitoring of the ongoing health and conduct of banks;
(3) sanctions or the imposition of penalties in case of non-compliance; and
(4) crisis management in case of a bank failure.

70 See Dermine (2015), p 435 for an overview of the economics of banking regulation.
71 Compare Lastra (2006).

The rules are typically set as thresholds or minimum standards in terms of capital and liquidity requirements or internal controls. A violation of these minimum standards may trigger sanctions or ultimately lead to the withdrawal of the bank's license and its closure. In the wake of the Great Financial Crisis of 2007–2009, governments have tightened banking regulation. Using the agreements reached by the Basel Committee on Banking Supervision (BCBS) – most recently under the heading of Basel III – as their basis, authorities in the EU (primarily through the Capital Requirements Directive (CRD) IV and the Capital Requirements Regulation (CRR)) have increased capital requirements, established new liquidity and funding requirements, and set new standards for governance and risk management. In addition to the minimum requirements for capital and liquidity (Pillar I), the Basel framework also relies on a supervisory review of the banks' Internal Capital Adequacy Assessment Process (ICAAP) (Pillar II) and the public disclosure requirements for regulatory ratios and other factors, leading to greater transparency towards stakeholders (Pillar III).

Macro-prudential supervision, in contrast, looks at the financial system at large.[72] It aims to limit system-wide financial distress. The ultimate objective is to avoid a loss in output (GDP reduction). In contrast to micro-prudential supervision, this form of supervision looks at the development of correlations and common exposures across financial intermediaries and markets over time. Furthermore, it takes into account the fact that risk can also be endogenous within a market, because risk is dependent on the collective behavior of market participants. Macro-prudential supervision, in this elaborate form, did not really exist before the 2007–2008 crisis. The Financial Stability Board (FSB) now implements this supervision at the global level, and the European Systemic Risk Board (ESRB) implements it at the European level.

Last, but not least, the abuse of market power can lead to market failure in banking. In a perfect market, no single bank would have sufficient market power to affect the market significantly. Market failure due to market power is therefore usually due to monopoly (one overly dominant bank) or oligopoly situations that consist of only a few banks. The exercise of market power by a bank or banks can be detrimental to customers because of higher fees for banking services, higher interest rates on loans, and less interest on their deposits. In addition, market power gives incumbent banks less of an incentive to reduce their cost base. Monopoly and oligopoly situations in banking can occur because of economies of scales and scope as well as network effects. That is why banks are also subject to anti-trust legislation and jurisdiction.

72 See Borio (2003) for a framework of macro-prudential regulation and supervision.

How can we prevent bank runs? The case for additional safety nets

Even if banks are financially sound and stable, they are vulnerable to bank runs as depositors over-react to rumors.[73]The undefined maturity of the deposit contract enables depositors to withdraw their deposits with immediate effect. In addition, the sequential service constraint of any banking operation can lead to a build-up of visible queues in front of bank branches (and/or via remote devices and the internet) that turn a bank run into a self-fulfilling prophecy. But bank runs can also happen – less visibly to the public but much faster – in the wholesale funding or interbank markets. A bank can quickly run through its liquidity buffer and be forced to sell illiquid loans at a discount, which endangers the overall solvency of the institution even if the loan portfolio is not impaired. Such a bank run, and a possible subsequent failure of the bank, is clearly socially uneconomical. Therefore, further frameworks need to be put in place to increase the confidence in the banking system and prevent wasteful bank runs. These are:
(1) deposit insurance,
(2) lender of last resort facilities and,
(3) when faced with acute systemic crisis, explicit government guarantees and public-led bail-outs.

Deposit insurance was introduced first in the US in 1933 with the Glass-Steagall Act. The Federal Deposit Insurance Corporation (FDIC) was implemented to address the problem of recurring bank runs in the Great Depression. The FDIC is a federally-owned institution that currently secures private deposits up to USD 250,000 per person per bank. Deposit insurance exists in other countries as well. Typically, the banks pay a premium to a deposit insurance company; in exchange, their depositors are insured up to a certain limit. Flat-rate insurance premiums present moral hazard problems because they give banks an incentive to transfer risk. A risk-related insurance premium typically depends on the deposit-to-asset ratio and the volatility of assets.[74]

In the EU, deposit insurance is the subject of a directive that requires each member state to provide for deposit insurance, with a minimum deposit coverage of EUR 100,000 per depositor per bank. The contribution of the bank is a maximum of 0.5 percent of covered deposits. If this sum, and the additional contributions of the other member banks are insufficient to repay depositors of a failed bank, the EU allows alternative borrowing from all other deposit insurance

73 See Diamond and Dybvig (1983) for a model of bank runs and the stabilizing effects of deposit insurance.
74 Compare Merton (1977).

institutions within the EU. Duly verified claims by depositors must now be paid within a period of seven days after the claim has been made.

The local central bank can play a role in the avoidance of the wasteful liquidation of the banks' loan portfolios, and in preventing financial panic, by stepping in as the lender of last resort to solvent banks or by providing liquidity to the market as a whole (through open market operations). This is against a pledge on their assets (collateralized lending).

The market interventions of the Fed in the wake of 11th September, 2001, and the global financial crisis of 2007–2008 as well the simultaneous interventions of the ECB are the most recent examples of the "lender of last resort principle" at work. Freixas et al. (2006) precisely define the function of the lender of last resort as:

> *"the discretionary provision of liquidity to a financial institution (or the market as whole) by the central bank in reaction to an adverse shock which causes an abnormal increase in demand for liquidity which cannot be met from an alternative source."*[75]

Finally, if deposit insurance and the central bank's lending can neither halt a bank run nor prevent it from affecting other banks, then there are public-led bail-outs and explicit government guarantees as an ultimate backstop. In the case of Northern Rock, this UK retail bank faced a bank run in the Autumn of 2007 at the beginning of the Great Financial Crisis. When the bank run did not stop despite (albeit inadequate) deposit insurance and emergency lending by the Bank of England, the Treasury Department ultimately stepped in to nationalize the bank. In the case of public-led bail-outs and explicit government guarantees, it is the taxpayer – indirectly via the government budget – who supplies capital and funding to the banks – not the common deposit insurance fund nor the central bank via its balance sheet.

How do we prevent contagion? Safeguarding the stability of the financial system

The failure of one bank can affect other banks and, indeed, the entire financial system, as happened in the recent Great Financial Crisis. In particular, very large, "too-big-to-fail" institutions, or more broadly speaking, systemically important financial institutions (SIFIs) can affect the system. A government led bail-out of systemically relevant banks that involves asset purchases, government guarantees, and recapitalizations can test the limits of the sovereign state as well. This is particularly the case if their debt sustainability is already stressed, as is the case

75 See Freixas et al. (2006), p 64.

with most sovereigns in the aftermath of the crisis of 2007–2009. SIFIs are now subject to special regulatory and resolution regimes, with a focus on increasing their loss absorbency and further reducing the probability of default. This regime also provides for the "bail-in" of shareholders and bondholders, who also have to absorb losses. The purpose of this is to lessen moral hazard and shield the taxpayer from further losses. The key issue going forward will be to implement this in such a way that contagion risk is also reduced. Bail-in debt needs to be "contagion-free". This means it needs to be clear, ex ante, which debt instrument absorbs which amount of loss.

How much regulation and safety nets do we need? Government failure and the (un)intended consequences of prudential regulation and safety nets

But regulation, supervision and safety nets do not always increase the safety and soundness of banks, and the financial system in general. They can have unintended consequences and can lead to a misallocation of resources, increase the cost of providing financial services, and prevent financial innovation. These consequences can also be the result of political capture.[76]

The design of regulation and its requirements can also prevent the rule of law from working. If there are too many rules, and a lack of consistency in both the rules and their application, the rule of law does not always work.[77] Increased regulation can also encourage banks to transfer activities into unregulated areas, thereby creating new fragilities and risks with respect to the safety and soundness of the system at the boundaries.[78] Regulation should not, therefore, focus solely on banking institutions themselves, but rather on banking functions, in order to close the door on this kind of arbitrage.

Banking regulation can also create barriers to entry that undermine competition and protect banks from financial innovation. Consequently, the cost of running the financial system – including the cost of regulatory compliance – may be higher than otherwise necessary. The cost of compliance can become a source of economies of scale for larger institutions and give them a competitive advantage over their smaller competitors. This is especially the case where the enforcement of regulations does not take into account the nature, scale and

76 Compare Stigler (1971).

77 Compare Ferguson (2014) for a discussion of the importance of the rule of law for the rise of Western economies.

78 Compare Brunnermeier et al. (2009), Appendix: The Boundary Problem in Financial Regulation, pp 63–69.

complexity of a bank or financial institution. Furthermore, supervisors may not always be incentivized – for instance due to political pressure or lack of a readily implementable rescue plan – to enforce regulation appropriately and to close down banks which are clearly failing. In fact, supervisory action itself may trigger a bank run. Finally, regulation and supervision can create a false sense of security and encourage riskier behavior by market participants than might otherwise be the case.[79]

The safety nets created to protect the financial system from misconduct and the resulting regulatory loopholes create moral hazard and have the potential to undermine market discipline. Deposit insurance gives depositors less of an incentive to monitor the bank's asset portfolio and behavior. The existence of a lender of last resort can also lead to moral hazard: firstly, by encouraging the risky behavior of lenders; but also by allowing regulatory forbearance if access to the support fails to discriminate against technically insolvent banks. In addition, government bail-outs can lead to increased expectations of future bail-outs for depositors and bond holders, thereby lowering the cost of funds for the systemically important institutions; this works like an implicit guarantee or state subsidy and, at the margin, encourages leverage and risk taking thereby distorting competition.

In summary

Because of the nature of their assets and liabilities and the amount of their leverage, banks are both special and fragile. Even micro-prudential regulation cannot make them totally safe. Macro-prudential supervision and additional safety nets are needed to ensure financial stability. Such a regulatory and supervisory regime, though, may in turn increase moral hazard and a false sense of security, whilst also undermining market discipline and accountability. It follows, therefore, that there is a need to avoid over-regulation and leave enough room for market discipline. In addition, there is a need to put less burden on the presumably strongest player on the field, the sovereign.

79 See Peltzman (1976).

Part II – European banking and finance in less troublesome times

Chapter 5:
Re-engineering of European banking

"The Commission would ask the Council ... to set itself the following aims: ... the intensification of efforts to smooth the way for the gradual emergence of a common market in banking, both from the point of view of conditions of entry to the market and from that of the coordination of measures on prudential control and the establishment of harmonized accounting procedures."[80]

Commission of the European Communities (1983)

"The study confirms that if Europe is to get the most out of its large home market the internal frontiers must truly disappear and be free of administrative complications between Member States. All barriers have to be removed, otherwise the last remaining barriers may, on their own, be sufficient to keep the markets segmented and to smother competition."[81]

Commission of the European Communities (1988)

"The completion of the single market will link national economies much more closely together and significantly increase the degree of economic integration within the Community."[82]

Committee for the Study of Economic and Monetary Union (1989)

In the 1980s, the objective of financial integration moved high up on the agenda of European policy-makers. The Commission (1983) of the European Communities recognized that the "specifically financial dimension of European construction is at present underdeveloped and fragmentary". This contrasted with the achievements in other fields of European integration. Let us first look at the broader drivers and specific objectives of financial integration in Europe, as well as the decision-making approaches and legislative tools used. Subsequently, we will analyze in more depth the key milestones of banking integration, with a special focus on the First and Second Banking Directive (1977 and 1988 respectively), as well as the Financial Services Action Plan (FSAP). Again, we will do this with a view to uncovering fault-lines that would remain hidden during

80 Compare Commission of the European Communities (1983), pp 20–21.
81 See Commission of the European Communities (1988), p 6.
82 Compare Committee (1989), p 10, item 10.

less turbulent times, and which only came to the forefront when crisis was hitting.

Integrating European markets...also in finance

At the beginning of the 1980s, the European banking system was severely fragmented. Directive (73/183/EEC) provided for the abolition of restrictions on freedom of establishment, and freedom to provide services in respect of self-employed activities of banks and other financial institutions. However, (the threat of) capital controls in many countries continued to severely limit cross-border banking. Moreover, with the exception of Germany, the UK and the Benelux countries, the banking sectors in most other member states were heavily regulated, with a large set of restrictions constraining their activities. Regulations included control of interest rates, capital controls, branch restrictions, foreign bank entry restrictions, and restrictions on insurance services, to name but a few. In addition, in some member states reserve requirements put in place to facilitate monetary policy were fairly onerous: consequently, interbank and money markets were largely underdeveloped.

The post-war period of industrial development and growth was followed by the oil crisis and the break-down of the Bretton Woods Agreement. This led to a slowdown in economic growth in Europe in the 1970s. GDP growth rates in the European Community fell from 5 percent in the 1960s to 3 percent during 1974–79, and to 1 percent at the beginning of the 1980s. Story and Walter (1997), remarked that "while the United States created 15 million and Japan 4 million net jobs from 1973 to early 1980s, none were created in Europe."[83] Europe clearly needed a strategy to boost its economic development.

As a result, the European Commission began to promote the concept of the Internal Market (later Single Market). As part of the completion of the Internal Market, the Commission proposed the creation of a unified market for banking services, based on mutual recognition and a single banking license.[84] This path proved to be more difficult than anticipated, given that different member states had different financial systems, with different legislations, histories and traditions. In fact, with respect to banking policies, there were fundamental tensions between:

---

83 See Story and Walter (1997).

84 Compare Commission (1985), item 102, pp 27–28: "The Commission considers that it should be possible to facilitate the exchange of such "financial products" at a Community level, using minimal coordination of rules (especially on such matters as authorization, financial supervision and reorganization, winding up, etc.) as the basis for mutual recognition of Member States of what each does to safeguard the interests of the public."

(1) the objectives of (i) liberalization of financial services, and (ii) achieving a more efficient banking systems through market entry and increased competition at the European level and,
(2) the absolute need for (i) prudential supervision and (ii) accountability for financial stability at the national level (deposit insurance was still organized nationally).

And there were also more fundamental differences among member states in terms of the role of the state more generally:[85]
(1) In a *liberal market economy* like the UK, there is less emphasis on heavy regulation by the state, and more emphasis on self-regulation of firms.
(2) In a *coordinated social market economy* like Germany, there is likely to be more coordination and government intervention.
(3) In *state-influenced market economies* like France, the state is inclined to intervene whenever it sees the need to reshape the economic environment for competitive reasons.

Acknowledging these fundamental tensions and deep-seated differences helps us to understand why the process of re-engineering and integrating European banking has proven to be so difficult. When it comes to the integration of markets, there are two basic decision-making approaches, (1) the supranational approach and (2) the inter-governmental approach. In the supranational approach, decision-making power is transferred to an international institution.[86] In the inter-governmental approach, an international institution merely acts as coordinator and the national governments retain their full sovereignty. In the institutional set-up of the EU, both types of integration approaches exist:
(1) the *European Commission* with its 28 Commissioners, one from each member state, is the most independent EU institution. It has the right to initiate legislation.
(2) the *European Council*, consisting of ministerial representatives from each member state, may request legislation. When the Council meeting comprises the minsters of economics and finance, it is also referred to as Ecofin. Decisions on financial policy are mainly taken by a qualified majority of votes, which are based on population size.
(3) the *EU Parliament*, which is directly elected by the people of the EU member states every five years, and which can also request legislation. Under the "co-operation procedure", the EU Parliament has the right to amend or even

85 Compare Bande (2012), pp 31–32.
86 Compare de Haan et al. (2015), chapter 3, pp 83–89, on the European institutions and legal instruments.

reject legislation. This is as opposed to the "consultation procedure", where it merely gives its opinion. Under the "co-decision procedure", acceptance by the EU Parliament is necessary.

(4) the *European Court of Justice* consists of 28 judges (one judge per member state) and 9 advocates-general. As the supreme court of the EU, the Court of Justice gives a coherent and uniform interpretation of Community law and ensures compliance by member states.

Legislative measures in the EU are proposed by the European Commission and – in the case of nearly all measures regarding financial integration – are adopted by the co-decision procedure. There is an important distinction between Regulations and Directives:

(1) *Regulations* are binding in their entirety and directly applicable in all member states. They promote full integration.
(2) *Directives* must be incorporated in the national law of each member state generally by introducing or amending national laws, within a deadline of 18 or 24 months after publication. They are, for the most part, implemented in a different way by each member state.

With respect to the financial services industry, the EU often opted for Directives that left the door open for incomplete harmonization. Let us look specifically at the First and Second European Banking Directives, and the issues embedded in the principles of home country control, minimum harmonization and mutual recognition of banking regulation and supervision.

First and Second European Banking Directives – home country control, minimum harmonization and mutual recognition

The First Banking Directive (77/780/EEC) on "The Coordination of Laws, Regulations and Administrative Provisions Relating to the Taking Up and Pursuit of the Business of Credit Institutions" marked the first important step towards the integration of banking markets and the liberalization of capital movements in the EU. The objective of this Directive was to allow banks in the European Community to set up branches throughout the European Community, with branch supervision remaining primarily with the home country of the parent bank, as opposed to the host country. In addition, the Directive established a Bank Advisory Committee, consisting of national supervisors, to help coordination of legislation among member states.

Despite the introduction of the "home country control" principle several important obstacles to the establishment of branches in other member states remained:

(1) *Host country authorization:* each European bank wishing to establish a branch in another member state still had to be authorized by the host country;
(2) *Host country supervision and restriction of the range of activities:* the host country also maintained supervision and the right to restrict the range of permitted activities;
(3) *"Endowment" capital requirement for branches:* the branches would have to be provided with capital as if they were new banks.

Given these obstacles, European banks had little incentive to branch out into other member states. In fact, all member states, except the UK, required branches to maintain a capital endowment. Notwithstanding these obstacles, the First Banking Directive paved the way for further initiatives of the European Commission to integrate European banking markets.

The inability of the European member states to agree on a common set of regulations, coupled with the political emphasis on completing the Single Market, prompted the development of a new approach towards integration. While most international agreements had used the national treatment principle, which ensures the equal treatment of firms operating in one country, the new approach was built on the principles of minimum harmonization, mutual recognition, and home country control:

(1) *Minimum harmonization:* this involved the "minimum harmonization" of essential aspects of banking regulation – as opposed to "full harmonization" of all aspects of banking regulation. The latter had proved to be practically impossible, as member states were not willing to change the institutional arrangements with their banks. There was certainly hope that, over time, this new approach would ultimately lead to more convergence in the regulatory and supervisory frameworks.
(2) *Mutual recognition:* the principle of "mutual recognition" of supervisory practices was based on a European Court of Justice decision in the case of "Cassis de Dijon"[87], which was then used by the Commission in the 1985 White Paper to promote financial integration in the Community.[88] It was also consistent with the Commission's open market philosophy in that it fostered competition among different national regulatory regimes.

---

87 See EC Commission versus Germany, 205/84, ECR 3755; in this case the European Court of Justice established that Germany could not prohibit the import of liquor that was lawfully produced in France only because the degree of alcohol was too low for it to be deemed liquor under German law.

88 See Commission of the European Communities (1985), item 102, p 27.

(3) *Home country control:* the new approach also included an evolved "home country control" principle: all activities of banks and other financial institutions carried out through branches in host countries would be supervised by the competent authorities of the home country.

The new approach was incorporated into the Second Banking Directive (89/646/EEC):

(1) *Home country control:* most importantly, the Directive called for home country control of solvency on a consolidated basis, including the foreign branches. "With regards to the latter", as Dermine (2002) points out, "the host state retains the right to regulate a foreign bank's activities…to the extent that such regulation is necessary for the protection of public interest."[89]

(2) *Minimum harmonization:* the Second Banking Directive called for harmonized capital adequacy and large exposure rules, and supervisory control of banks' permanent participation in the non-financial sector. Subsequently, the Commission tackled the harmonization and reinforcement of capital adequacy in two steps: firstly, by developing a common position on the definition of own funds of credit institutions[90]; and secondly, by proposing a minimum solvency ratio of 8 percent.[91] The Commission's risk-asset-based approach was very similar to the approach developed by the Committee on Banking Regulations and Supervisory Practices in Basel, then also known as the Cooke Committee, named after its chairman Peter Cooke, a Bank of England official. The minimum harmonization of EU bank regulation was building on the common ground of harmonized bank accounting rules, that had been established previously.[92] The new capital adequacy and large exposure rules came into effect in 1992. While they helped to ensure an internationally level playing field for EU banks, the Basel recommendations also introduced the zero percent risk-weighting for OECD government bonds into the EU (and later the Eurozone) which would later become the Achilles heel of the European financial system in the recent crisis.

(3) *Mutual recognition on the basis of a single banking license:* the most revolutionary feature of the Directive was the concept of a single European banking license, based on an agreed list of "banking activities". This license provided the "passport" for European banks, through which they could receive the benefit of mutual recognition. In other words, regardless of whether

89 See Dermine (2002), p 5.

90 See Directive on the own funds of credit institutions (89/299/EEC) of 17th April, 1989.

91 See Directive on solvency ratio for credit institutions (89/647/EEC) of 18th December, 1989.

92 See Directive on the annual accounts and consolidated accounts of banks and other financial institutions (86/635/EEC) of 8th December, 1986.

> headquartered in a member state or a non-EU country, once a bank had received a license in one member state, it could do business – via branches or direct cross-border services – in all member states. The single banking license deregulated European banking geographically and in terms of product. By the end of 1992, member states were required to abolish the host country authorization of branches; endowment capital requirements were also gradually eliminated. In addition, the Directive established universal banking throughout Europe, because the list of "banking activities" not only included commercial banking but also sales & trading, underwriting, portfolio management and advisory services. All in all, it set in motion a process of deregulation, as member states with more narrowly-scoped banking licenses had to allow competition from other European banks with a broader range of services.[93]

Ten years later, on the eve of the introduction of the Euro in 1999, what had been the impact of the First and Second Banking Directive on European banking?

The single banking license had been created to reduce the regulatory costs of operating in different countries. Nevertheless, a striking feature of European cross-border banking integration was that it took place more often via subsidiaries, and not via branches, as one would have anticipated. Analyzing ECB data as of 1999, Dermine (2002) finds that there were in total 450 branches and 363 subsidiaries for banks from the European Economic Area (EEA) countries, while the order was reversed for banks from non-EEA countries with 312 branches and 372 subsidiaries.[94] He concludes that the single banking license is an illusion. Despite the fact that "passporting" does not apply to subsidiaries – they are considered local banks in each country – there are tax and other economic reasons for banking groups to continue to operate via subsidiaries. In fact, subsidiaries allow the ring-fencing of certain activities and provide additional strategic flexibility as they could be listed (and funded) separately (and locally). After the 1986 Big Bang in London, the City had become the global hub for investment banking and a lot of banks chose to conduct the capital-intensive sales & trading activities via branches, that allowed them to keep the regulatory capital in their respective home country.

The European integration process led to an elevated level of M&A transactions in European banking. Over the period 1990–1999, out of a total of 2,549 transactions, more than 76 percent were "internal" country deals, as Figure 9

93 See Zavvos (1989), p 575.

94 See Dermine (2002), p 20. It should be noted that in 1992, the countries of the European Free Trade Association (EFTA), with the exception of Switzerland, joined the European Economic Area. This implies that the EEA countries also accept European banking legislation.

shows. Such domestic mergers led to a massive consolidation process in many European countries. The overall number of credit institutions in the EU declined from 12,256 in 1985 to 9,285 in 1997.[95] The key drivers of this M&A wave were efficiency gains that were mostly achieved in domestic transactions, but also in capital markets activities.

# of deals	1990	1991	1992	1993	1994	1995	1996	1997	1998	1999	Total	
within-border/ within-industry	51	181	174	137	159	132	157	123	141	181	**1.436**	**56%**
within-border/ cross-industry	25	47	48	45	60	70	70	59	36	59	**519**	**20%**
cross-border/ within-industry	24	28	31	31	41	56	49	61	62	52	**435**	**17%**
cross-border/ cross-industry	10	16	11	9	15	16	17	21	25	19	**159**	**6%**

(Figure 9: M&A in European Banking, 1990–1999, Number of deals classified by country and sector of target firm, Group of Ten (2001), p 347)

Key cross-border mergers formed large regional banking groups, such as (i) the Dutch ING Group, with the acquisition of banks in Belgium (BBL) and Germany (BHF Bank), (ii) Nordea AB, with the merger of four Scandinavian banks: Nordbanken (Sweden) acquiring Merita (Finland), Unidanmark (Denmark) and Christiana (Norway), and (iii) the German HypoVereinsbank with the acquisition of Bank Austria-Creditantstalt which owned banks in Austria and Central and Eastern Europe.

The emergence of large cross-border banking groups points to the risk of (1) cross-border spill-overs in general and (2) "too-big-to-fail" issues arising, specifically for smaller home countries:[96]

(1) *Cross-border spill-overs:* in the event of a banking crisis, the cost of a bail-out as the ultimate back stop would remain with the home country, in line with the responsibility for supervision and deposit insurance, although this would also affect financial stability in the host countries as well, resulting in disputes about burden-sharing.

(2) *"Too-big-to-fail" issues:* in addition, a small home country might find it difficult altogether to shoulder the costs of the bail-out of a large, complex banking group. In a nutshell, the home country control principle suffers from significant drawbacks. Their resolution would require some form of

95 Compare ECB (1999).

96 Compare Dermine (2015), p 450, for the pros and cons of the home country control approach.

coordination between home and host country authorities, if not outright centralization of supervision at the European level.

The emergence of cross-border banking groups in Europe also required an enhanced cooperation and information sharing among supervisors. As Padoa-Schioppa reports, by the end of 1997, 78 bilateral Memoranda of Understanding (MoUs) had been signed between the various EEA banking supervisory authorities.[97] The MoUs defined commitments and procedures for the supervisory process including on-site inspections. Even more demanding than supervision under a bilateral MoU was the multilateral approach, ie a group of supervisors working collectively "as one consolidated supervisor" or supervisory college. Questions remain, as to whether the supervisory colleges were as effective as one supervisor within a single country, given the different cultural backgrounds and supervisory traditions represented.

Financial Services Action Plan (and Basel II)

The European Council of Cardiff in 1998, underlined the importance of further financial market integration as a political priority. It was realized that monetary union would not complete the single financial market by itself. In fact, as Figure 10 shows, the market share of foreign banks was still low in the major EU countries. Consequently, the Commission published a communication entitled "Financial Services: Building a Framework for Action" which set out a series of measures to strengthen financial integration in Europe. Ultimately, this led to the launch of the FSAP in 1999, with a view to building a single market for financial services.

The purpose of the FSAP was to remove regulatory and market barriers that limit the cross-border provision of financial services and the free flow of capital within the EU, and to create a level playing field among market participants.

The FSAP had four specific objectives, (1) the creation of a single EU wholesale market, (2) open and secure retail banking & insurance markets, (3) the developments of state-of-the-art prudential rules and supervision, and (4) optimal wider conditions (essential fiscal rules) for an optimal single financial market. Key Directives under the FSAP include

(1) *the Markets in Financial Instruments Directive* (2004/39/EC) which targeted the creation of a single wholesale market

97 See Padoa-Schioppa (1999).

	From EEA countries		From Third countries		Total		
% of total assets	Branches	Subsidiaries	Branches	Subsidiaries	1983	1988	1999
Austria	0.7	1.6	0.1	1.0	n/a	n/a	3.3
Belgium	9.0	19.2	6.9	1.2	33.9	35.2	36.3
Finland	7.1	0.0	0.0	0.0	n/a	n/a	7.1
France	2.5	...	2.7	...	10.1	13.5	9.8
Germany	0.9	1.4	0.7	1.2	1.0	1.8	4.3
Ireland	17.7	27.8	1.2	6.9	27.0	21.4	53.6
Italy	3.6	1.7	1.4	0.1	2.6	3.0	6.8
Luxembourg	19.4	65.7	1.4	8.1	n/a	91.0	94.6
Netherlands	2.3	3.0	0.5	1.9	10.7	13.0	7.7
Portugal	2.5	6.8	0.1	1.0	n/a	4.2	10.5
Spain	4.8	3.4	1.6	1.9	7.3	11.0	11.7

(Figure 10: Market share of foreign banks in 1999 (as a percentage of total assets), Dermine (2002), p 59)

(2) *the Distance Marketing Directive* (2002/65/EC) aimed at protecting retail customers buying financial products and services via telephone, internet, fax or post
(3) the *Capital Requirements Directive* (CRD) which laid down new capital adequacy rules for banks and was based on the 2004 Basel II Capital Accord
(4) the *Savings Directive* (2003/48/EC), which established an automatic exchange of information on interest on savings received, to combat cross-border tax evasion on savings income.

In 2004, the EC concluded that the FSAP had been delivered on time, with 40 out of 42 measures being adopted before the 2005 deadline. As Frits Bolkestein, Member of the EC in charge of the Internal Market, Taxation and Customs concluded in his 2004 address to the European Parliament:

> *"Many of the key FSAP measures have only just entered into force or have yet to do so. However, the FSAP already acts as a catalyst for change. Financial markets are becoming organized on a cross-border basis – businesses are looking for pan-European solutions."*[98]

The FSAP also represented a major change in the approach to further integration, as it pushed for more explicit harmonization of rules and more involvement of EU institutions. The new EU policy framework was based on a complex multi-level system of EU rule-making and enhanced cooperation be-

98 Compare Bolkestein (2004), p 2.

tween national supervisors, represented – in the case of banking – in the pre-existing but reformed Banking Advisory Committee. Despite the completion of the FSAP ahead of time, the institutional set-up at the EU level was still deficient in several aspects:

(1) *Regulatory and supervisory fragmentation:* a single framework for regulation and supervision was lacking; supervision was still fragmented, despite (or because of) the complex system of reporting between supervised entities and home and host supervisors;
(2) *Fundamental differences in underlying law:* there was lack of European (private) contract law and there were significant divergences in consumer protection legislation among the member states;
(3) *Weak cooperation among supervisors:* the cooperation among supervisors was non-binding in nature. The Banking Advisory Committee, as the name suggests, had only an advisory function with regards to technical issues. The implementation of supervision was still carried out by different national governments.

As Frits Bolkestein (2004a) summarized in terms of lessons learned from FSAP implementation process:

> *"A single financial market remains a goal worth striving for. Along the way, there may be second-best outcomes – reflecting the complex and multi-dimensional rule- making at EU level. But, the question that we need repeatedly to ask ourselves is whether there is any alternative to working together. Faced with the continued internationalization of financial markets, is regulatory and supervisory autarky a realistic option?"*[99]

In Summary

Re-engineering of European Banking moved higher on the European political agenda in the 1980s and was seen as an important condition for the completion of the Internal Market. As barriers to entry were gradually removed by EU legislation, so banks began to branch out and make cross-border acquisitions. Wholesale banking markets, including money markets, began to integrate more quickly than the market for retail banking services. Progress in banking integration was uneven, as some countries, particularly the larger economies, namely France, Germany, and Italy were still resisting banking integration. The regulatory and supervisory framework remained fragmented. The introduction of the Euro would, hopefully, further accelerate financial integration in Europe.

99 Compare Bolkestein (2004a), p 5.

Chapter 6: One market, one money – (too) many banking systems

"As concerns banking, it is a clear conclusion that the introduction of a single currency will not only make the creation of a single market irreversible, but that it will, besides the obvious fall in revenue from intra-European currencies trading, alter fundamentally the nature of several businesses. The will be particularly the case in the money and capital markets. ... it will reinforce the competitiveness of European banks in the capital markets of third countries such as those of the United States."[100]

Jean Dermine, Professor of Banking and Finance at INSEAD, (1996)

"In the presence of ... excessive risk-taking on the part of financial intermediaries, there is a possibility that problems faced by financial intermediaries in one region of the Eurozone could spread rapidly to financial intermediaries located in other regions of the Euro area. In such circumstances, there could be an increase in financial market volatility... as well as in the frequency of financial distress..."[101]

Wim Duisenberg, former President of the ECB, (2001)

The introduction of the Euro in 1999 eliminated currency risk and provided a further push for financial integration, primarily in terms of money and capital markets, and less so in terms of retail banking. Despite the full Europeanization of monetary policy, banking politics remained a national prerogative. In fact, the ECB, unlike most other central banks, was originally established as a pure-play monetary institution with no supervisory role in the banking sector.

In 2007, nearly a full decade after Eurozone leaders took the decision to launch the single currency, few of those in power were ready to accept the idea of a looming financial crisis. The benign conditions of the economic cycle at that time had lasted longer than over any other period in the last century[102], leading to a false sense of security. Some political and business leaders – not to mention regulators – were too young to have experienced a true recession; others, perhaps, chose not to "talk down" the economy. True, shortcomings in macro-

100 See Dermine (1996), p 56.
101 See Duisenberg (2001), p 60.
102 See UK Office for National Statistics (2017).

economic surveillance and policy coordination were recognized; but what many political leaders failed to grasp were the potential impacts of changes in both banking technology and globalization which had occurred since the last recession. It was, therefore, difficult for many EU political leaders to comprehend just how rapidly a crisis in one part of the world ie the US, could – and would – spread to other economies, and that Europe could very quickly turn from "a pole of stability for the global economy"[103] to a major source of financial instability.

Let us look at financial integration and European banking with the single currency, in order to deepen our understanding of how hidden fault-lines and vulnerabilities were able build up underneath the surface and eventually fracture the global financial system.

Europeanization of monetary policy, banking politics a national prerogative

During the 1980s, discussion in Europe was again focused on monetary integration in Europe. [104] It was argued that in order to reap the full benefits of the Internal Market, exchange rate risks and related transaction costs should be considerably reduced, by the introduction of a common currency.[105]

The creation of an Internal Market also brought with it the removal of capital controls: this unleashed economic centrifugal forces that ultimately required the reorganization of European monetary and currency frameworks. Without the option of capital controls, weaker countries (due to a lack of adequate currency reserves for currency market interventions) could only try to stop speculative capital flows by raising interest rates relative to the interest level set by the Deutsche Bundesbank. This came at a huge cost, as it inevitably meant slowing down the domestic economy. In fact, as the trilemma of international macroeconomics states, an economy cannot simultaneously have fixed exchange rates, an independent monetary policy, and allow capital to flow freely (see Figure 11). Theoretically, the trilemma tells us that we must choose one side of the triangle.[106] As Brunnermeier et al. (2016) emphasize, France – as "a desirable

103 See Almunia in European Commission (2008), p 1.

104 The first proposal for the creation of an economic and monetary union was presented by a commission chaired by Pierre Werner, the then Luxembourg Premier, as early as 1970. The proposal, also known as the Werner Plan, included a roadmap for the creation of a monetary union over a period of 10 years; compare Werner (1970).

105 See also the Study by the European Commission: "One Market, One Money" (Emerson et al., 1992).

106 See Mundell (1962).

reflection of the state's ability to impose discipline on disorderly markets"[107] – historically had a preference for fixed exchange rates, whereas Germany was traditionally more focused on "flexible exchange rates, in an international setting, with open capital markets"[108]. Both positions could only be reconciled if monetary policy was moved to a pan-European level.

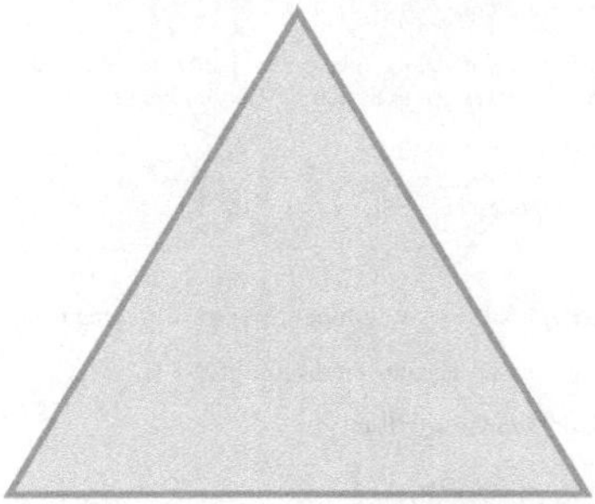

(Figure 11: Trilemma of international macroeconomics, Brunnermeier et al., 2016, p 75)

There have been two schools of thought on how to achieve monetary integration in Europe: (1) the "locomotive theory", representing a monetarist position, and, (2) the diametrically opposed "coronation theory", representing an economistic position.[109] According to the "locomotive theory", the common currency should be introduced early and function as a facilitating device for additional economic and political integration of Europe. France was the strongest proponent of this theory. On the other hand, the "coronation theory", supported by the German federal government, proposed that a common currency should only be introduced when economic and political integration had been successfully implemented.

In June 1988, at its summit in Hannover, the European Council decided to establish a committee, chaired by Jacques Delors, which would propose concrete steps leading to Economic and Monetary Union (EMU). The committee presented its report a year later.[110] Subsequent negotiations eventually led to the 1992 Treaty on European Union, signed in Maastricht. The UK – for domestic political reasons – was given an opt-out clause.

Many of the suggestions of the Delors committee found their way into the

107 Compare Brunnermeier et al. (2016), p 82.
108 See Brunnermeier et al. (2016), p 82.
109 Compare Fichtner and Koenig (2015), p 378.
110 Compare Committee (1989).

1 Stage One starting 1 Jul 1990	Complete freedom for capital transactions
	Increased co-operation between central banks
	Free use uf the ECU (European Currency Unit, forerunner of the €)
	Improvement of economic convergence
2 Stage Two starting 1 Jan 1994	Establishment of the European Monetary Institute (EMI)
	Ban of the granting of central bank credit
	Increased co-ordination of monetary policies
	Strengthening of economic convergence
	Process leading to the independence of the national central banks, to be completed at the latest by the date of establishment of the European System of Central Banks
	Preparatory work for Stage Three
3 Stage Three starting 1 Jan 1999	Irrevocable fixing of conversion rates
	Introduction of the euro
	Conduct of the single monetary policy by the European System of Central Banks
	Entry into effect of the intra-EU exchange rate mechanism (ERM II)
	Entry into force of the Stability and Growth Pact

(Figure 12: The three stages leading to EMU, ECB (2017))

Maastricht Treaty, including a three-stage approach leading to EMU (see Figure 12) and adherence to a fixed time-table. In fact, the introduction of the single currency was to have been completed by 1st January, 1999 at the latest. The Maastricht Treaty also reflected the compromise which the Delors report attempted to strike between the "coronation theory" and the "locomotive theory", by emphasizing the need for an absolute minimum of economic convergence prior to introducing the new currency. The key convergence criteria referred to relative levels of inflation and interest rates, exchange rates, public deficit (must not exceed 3 percent of GDP) and government debt (must not exceed 60 percent of GDP, unless diminishing and approaching the target level at a satisfactory pace).[111] At the same time, it also called for the speedy establishment of a European central bank. However, delays in the convergence process caused by economic shocks would mean that the tight time schedule would be barely able to accommodate viable adjustments. Since it was the responsibility of the heads of governments themselves to monitor compliance with the criteria, there was a clear conflict of interest that undermined the credibility of the convergence process and made the implementation process vulnerable to political set-backs and speculative attacks:

(1) *Stage one:* the first milestone was the abolition of capital controls on 1st July, 1990. Only in the event of large, speculative movements could the European

111 Current-account deficits and foreign debt liabilities were not among the convergence criteria.

Commission authorize capital controls. Ratification of the Maastricht Treaty was difficult in several member states and put the establishment of an EMU in jeopardy: a referendum in Denmark in 1992 resulted in an outright rejection of the Treaty, and France adopted it with the thinnest of majorities. As long as monetary policy continued to be fragmented, the liberalization of capital movements would remain on a collision course with the construction of the European Exchange Rate Mechanism (ERM). Faced with concerted speculative attacks, member states such as Italy and the UK, whose currencies were overvalued, were forced to leave the ERM. The UK also rejected membership of the single currency. In July of 1993, speculation ultimately forced European governments to widen the range of potential ERM fluctuation to plus or minus 15 percent.

(2) *Stage two:* despite these hiccups, the EMU process entered its second stage on 1st January, 2004, with the establishment of the European Monetary Institute (EMI), the predecessor of the ECB. In early May, 1998, the European Council decided that, based on the convergence-criteria that were outlined in the Maastricht Treaty, 11 of the then 15 EU members could join the Eurozone.

(3) *Stage three:* On 1st January, 1999, Europe entered a new era with the adoption of the single currency. At the time of writing, 19 out of the 28 EU member states have adopted the Euro and delegated both their national monetary sovereignty and monetary policy to the ECB[112] However, in 1999, whilst monetary policy-making was centralized at the European level, economic and fiscal policies remained largely the prerogative of national governments and were merely subject to the contractual provisions for monitoring and coordination contained in the Maastricht Treaty. These provisions were specified in more detail in the 1997 Stability and Growth Pact (SGP) which prescribed preventive and corrective measures in the event of excessive fiscal deficits, and required the Eurozone members to adhere to strict fiscal discipline. As Solbes concluded in 2001 (two years after the launch of the common currency), "all member states have made significant progress in reducing their public sector deficits"[113]. He went on to say that: "for the Eurozone as a whole, the public sector deficit was about 1.5 percent of GDP in 1999, and in the meantime, had fallen below 1.0 percent of GDP."

The introduction of the common currency clearly brought important benefits for the Eurozone[114], by:

112 And the Euro is also used in five countries outside the EU: Monaco, San Marino, Vatican City, Saint-Pierre-Et-Miquelon (two islands off the east coast of Canada), and Mayotte (island north of Madgascar).

113 See Solbes (2001), p 70.

114 See de Grauwe (2014), chapter 3, pp 53–69.

(1) reducing transaction costs through the elimination of the costs of currency exchange, which was estimated at 13 to 20 billion Euros per year at the time,
(2) improving allocation efficiency by reducing price uncertainty,
(3) eliminating shocks from extreme exchange rate movements, that had plagued EU member states in the past,
(4) increasing price transparency, thereby increasing competition, ultimately benefitting consumers, and
(5) becoming a global reserve currency which would help the development of the financial sector in the Europe.

As labor mobility in Europe was limited by multiple barriers, it is unlikely that the EU in its entirety constituted an optimum currency area.[115] Let us look at the factors affecting member states considering joining the EMU as, clearly, membership brings not only benefits but also costs.

Membership costs result from the fact that a member state joining monetary union relinquishes an important policy instrument to deal with (asymmetric) economic shocks:

(1) *Loss in monetary sovereignty:*[116] a member state loses the ability to conduct national monetary policy which previously allowed them to – at least temporarily – correct for underlying differences with respect to other countries. These differences in labor markets, legal and tax systems, as well as trading and government spending patterns do not disappear completely with the creation of a monetary union and can lead to differing levels of national competitiveness, ie different price and output levels (and qualities). Without the ability – again, at least temporarily – to devalue the currency, a country can only regain competitiveness by reducing both wages and prices. This is often more painful than a devaluation of the currency, and is therefore regarded as both a cost and a disadvantage of joining a monetary union.
(2) *Government debt in the EMU is Euro denominated:* Another cost factor is that government debt is no longer issued in the national currency but in Euros. EMU members lose the ability to guarantee that the outstanding stock of government debt will always be repaid. This means that if the credibility of the common currency suffers – and this might well be beyond a single member state's control – refinancing of government debt is made more difficult, ultimately threatening the financial viability of the member state's

115 For an exposition of the theory of optimum currency area compare de Grauwe (2014) and also the original, Nobel-prize winning article by Mundell (1961).

116 Minting, printing, managing and safeguarding a currency is indeed one of the prerogatives of the sovereign. "Sovereign" is indeed the name given to English gold coins that King Henry VII. had minted in 1489.

budget. This can lead to a liquidity crisis forcing national governments into severe austerity measures in the midst of a recession.

Given that the specific costs of relinquishing monetary sovereignty vary from country to country, and also depend on the exact economic profile of other union members, not all members have the same interest in giving up their national monetary sovereignty at the same pace:

(1) *Different speeds in joining the EMU:* in fact, monetary unification in Europe better suits the economic interests of individual countries if they can proceed at different speeds.

(2) *Adjustment to external shocks within EMU:* even member states that are net gainers from accepting the Euro take a risk by joining the union. The risk is that after a large economic shock, such as a financial crisis, they find it more difficult to adjust, having relinquished monetary sovereignty.

(3) *Enlargement of the EMU:* the enlargement of the Eurozone to potentially include 27 countries (taking account of Brexit) can change the cost benefit equation for some member states which are currently members.

Therefore, member states which joined the EMU on 1st January, 1999, took a significant risk. This risk was not visible during more benign periods but crystallized when external economic shocks were hitting home during the Great Financial Crisis. These shocks also exposed the inherent fragility of the EMU as an incomplete monetary union[117], ie a currency union with a single central bank and monetary policy making, but without full banking and budgetary union.

Swift integration of money markets (especially in the wholesale domain), but protracted integration of retail banking markets

Let us now examine what the introduction of the common currency did to the integration of financial markets, specifically money, bond, equity markets and banking services:

(1) *Swift integration of money and interbank markets:* the introduction of the common currency in 1999, in combination with TARGET, swiftly led to full integration of money markets. The ECB applied one single rate when lending to all banks. In January 1999, the dispersion of the Euro overnight rates across member states fell from 15 to 5 basis points, the variation amongst banks becoming greater than between countries. The daily average volume

117 Compare de Grauwe (2014), chapter 5, pp 101–118, on the fragility of incomplete monetary unions.

of payments in the TARGET system rapidly reached EUR 1 trillion. But, as Padoa-Schioppa (1999) observed with tremendous foresight, "the ever stronger interbank and payment links clearly increase the possibility of financial instability spreading from one country to another".[118]

(2) *Full integration of government bond markets but only partial integration of those for corporates:* government bond markets integrated fairly quickly, as spreads among different member states tightened across the board. In fact, between 1999 and 2008, differences in interest rate levels between different member states narrowed from several hundred basis points to just 50. Corporate bond markets did not integrate in a similar pattern, as differences in accounting and governance legislation, as well as other underlying laws, prevailed. Overall, an increase in the number of market participants operating in the same currency increased liquidity and helped to reduce the cost of capital.

(3) *Limited integration of equity markets:* the introduction of the Euro also led to a certain level of integration in equity markets by reducing the home bias of investors, as they could avoid exchange risk when investing. Nevertheless, differences in tax and accounting laws prevented many European firms from seeking a stock-market listing outside their home country. These sorts of issues make it difficult for investors to compare the values of firms incorporated in different member states. Similarly, changes in local tax legislation can affect the value of firms incorporated in that country. So, while exchange rate risk might disappear for investors, there will always be a specific country risk premium attached to shares.

(4) *Incomplete banking integration:* banking integration, however, remained incomplete. Wholesale, ie corporate and investment banking activities, benefitted from the continuing integration of bond markets, as did equities markets, although to a lesser degree. However, integration of retail banking markets progressed very slowly (see Figure 14). This was due mainly to differences in tax laws, private contract law, consumer protection laws but also differences in culture and language.[119]

Financial integration is not just the inevitable consequence of introducing a common currency: it is also desirable, in that it results in increased risk sharing.[120] Investors in a member state hit by a negative economic shock can retain their incomes at a relatively high level if they have, for example, diversified their

118 See Padoa-Schioppa (1999).

119 Compare Walkner and Raes (2005) of a comprehensive analysis of obstacles to cross-border banking integration in the EU.

120 See de Grauwe (2014), pp 232–235 for a discussion of the (risk) sharing benefits of financial integration.

investments across the Eurozone. As a consequence, of course, residents in other member states would see their income increase less. Financial markets in the US allow for more risk sharing among regions compared with the EU. According to Marinheiro (2003), US capital markets redistribute 48 percent of asymmetric shocks in output that occur at the state level, as opposed to the EU-15 capital markets, that only achieved a shock redistribution of 9 percent in 1999.[121] In other words, without financial integration, if the GDP of Italy declines by 15 percent, only 1.4 percent are redistributed across Europe.

Therefore, financial markets integration in the Eurozone is even more important in the absence of budgetary risk sharing, as it exists in the US.

Increased financial integration, however, whilst facilitating improved risk sharing also increases the risk of contagion. Risk sharing and risk of contagion are two sides of the same coin. As Padoa-Schioppa (1999) observed, banks operating "in increasingly integrated capital markets…will be exposed to shocks originating beyond their national borders".[122] This was confirmed in a recent analysis by Hale and Obstfeld (2014). They demonstrated that, since the launch of the common currency, banks in the core of the Eurozone increasingly borrowed in financial centers such as the UK and the US, and invested in sovereign as well as private (real estate) debt issued by the European periphery. They conclude that "the Eurozone contributed not only to the big net current-account deficits of the peripheral countries, but to inflated debt liability and asset positions for core Eurozone countries"[123]. These imbalances proved to be major fault-lines that broke open in the aftermath of the Great Financial Crisis.

ECB – a pure-play monetary institution, no supervisory role

With the introduction of the common currency, member states delegated monetary policy to the ECB – a pure-play monetary institution, with hardly any supervisory role at that time. The design of the ECB, which is enshrined in the Maastricht Treaty, followed the German role model of a central bank focused on the single objective of price stability, and with strict political independence (as opposed to the Anglo-French model, which favors a more politically dependent central bank, pursing multiple objectives):

(1) *Objective of price stability:* the Maastricht Treaty is very clear on the "primary objective of price stability" in Article 105 (1) which also adds: "Without prejudice to the objective of price stability, the ECB shall support

121 Compare Marinheiro (2003).
122 Compare Padoa-Schioppa (1999).
123 See Hale and Obstfeld (2014).

the general economic policies in the Community with a view to contributing to the achievement of the objectives of the Community as laid down in Article 2." Article 2 mentions "a high level of employment", but this is clearly seen as a secondary objective. The ECB specifies the objective of price stability as inflation "below but close to 2 per cent in the Eurozone in the medium term".[124]

(2) *Political independence:* the principle of political independence is firmly anchored in Article 107: "when exercising the powers and carrying out the tasks and duties conferred upon them by this Treaty…neither the ECB nor a national central bank, nor any member of their decision-making bodies shall seek or take instructions from Community institutions or bodies, from any Government of a member state or from any other body." The political independence is further guaranteed by the fact that the statutes of the ECB can only be changed by a revision of the Maastricht Treaty, which would require unanimity among all EU member states.

The ECB and the National Central Banks (NCBs) of the Eurozone countries make up the European System of Central Banks, in short Eurosystem. The ECB is responsible for monetary policy decision and the NCBs are responsible for its implementation through open market operations (see Figure 13 for an overview of monetary policy instruments). In addition, it sets reserve requirements and executes asset purchase programs. As per Article 105 (2), the Eurosystem, in its entirety, is also responsible for foreign exchange operations, the holding and management of the official foreign reserves of the EU member states, and the operation of the payment system.

The Maastricht Treaty is also explicit on the principle of decentralization, as far as regulatory and supervisory powers are concerned. Article 105 (5) states that "The European System of Central Banks shall contribute to the smooth conduct of policies pursued by the competent authorities relating to the prudential supervision of credit institutions and the stability of the financial system." The ECB was originally only allowed to regulate or supervise financial institutions in special circumstances and with a unanimous vote in the European Council (compare Article 105 (6)). However, in line with Article 105 (4) the ECB must be consulted on any draft community or national legislation in the fields of banking and supervision. And, according to its own statutes, the ECB can provide advice on its own initiative on the scope of community legislation in these matters.

In summary, central banking and supervision in the Eurozone were separated, functionally and geographically. To remedy for this double separation in

124 Compare ECB (2011).

	Monetary policy operations	Liquidity provision	Liquidity absorption	Maturity	Frequency
Open market operations	Main refinancing operations	Reverse transactions	–	One week	Weekly
	Longer-term refinancing operations	Reverse transactions	–	Three months	Monthly
	Fine tune operations	Reverse transactions	Reverse transactions	Non-standardised	Non-regular
			Several fixed term deposits		
		Foreign exchange swaps	Foreign exchange swaps		
	Structural operations	Reverse transactions	Issuance of ECB debt certificates	Standardised/ Non-standardised	Regular and non-regular
		Outright purchases	Outright sales	–	Non-regular
Standing facilities	Marginal lending facility	Reverse transactions	–	Overnight	Access at discretion of counterparties
	Deposit facility	—	Deposits	Overnight	Access at discretion of counterparties

(Figure 13: ECB Monetary policy instruments, ECB (2011))

light of the increasing importance of cross-border banking (groups), Padoa-Schioppa (1999) argued for "the establishment of smooth co-operation between the Eurosystem and the national banking supervisors", and that "the system of national supervisors needs to operate as effectively as a single authority when needed".[125] As integration of European banking and financial markets progressed, the importance of smooth cooperation amongst national banking supervisors and with the Eurosystem - based on exchange of supervisory information - was increasing.

While the ECB had no direct responsibility in banking supervision it clearly had a vital interest in a stable and efficient banking sector. In fact, financial stability and a well-functioning banking system are critical for targeting inflation, and for the smooth transmission of monetary policy. Differences in bank health across countries in Europe could potentially hamper the smooth transmission of monetary policy as Kashyap and Stein (1997) emphasized before the launch of the common currency.[126] Angeloni and Ehrmann (2003) found early "evidence that the transmission through banks has become more potent…because of EMU".[127]

125 See Padoa-Schioppa (1999).
126 See Kashyap and Stein (1997).
127 Compare Angeloni and Ehrmann (2003).

The Euro@10 – not much to complain about (at the time)

At the beginning of 2008, the Eurozone celebrated the tenth anniversary of the decision by European leaders to launch the Euro. As Joaquin Almunia, the then EU Commissioner of Economic and Monetary Affairs, explained in the foreword to the "EMU@10" edition of the "European Economy", this was a reason to be proud:[128]

> *"Economic and Monetary Union and the Euro are a major success. For its member countries, EMU has anchored macroeconomic stability, and increased cross-border trade, financial integration and investment. For the EU as a whole, the Euro is a keystone of further economic integration and a potent symbol of our growing political unity. And for the world, the Euro is a major new pillar in the international monetary system and a pole of stability for the global economy."*[129]

While the "EMU@10" report mentioned some challenges for the EMU, the Commission still did not see the crisis coming. On the contrary, the report maintained that "ten years into its existence, the Euro is a resounding success", "the Euro has acted as a powerful catalyst for financial market integration", and "the Eurozone has become a pole of stability for Europe and the world economy". The Commission apparently did not see major risks to financial stability. In fact, the report claimed that "today, once again, the Eurozone appears protected (!) from the worst of the present financial turbulences"[130]. Clearly, political leaders at that time were aware of such turbulences but were unable to accept their severity. The EU Commission (2008) proposed a three-pronged reform agenda solely targeted at improving macroeconomic stability in the currency block, namely:

(1) better fiscal policy co-ordination across the economic cycle and budgetary surveillance under the SGP's preventive arm;
(2) enhancing the Eurozone's international role commensurate with the reserve status of the currency and
(3) strengthening the governance of the EMU.

It would take the financial tsunami on the horizon to catapult financial stability concerns, and banking union, to the top of the political agenda in Europe. The ECB Financial Stability Review of December, 2007, while noting that "the risks to the Eurozone financial system stability had materially increased", also pointed

128 See European Commission (2008).
129 Compare the Foreword in European Commission (2008).
130 See European Commission (2008), p 5; exclamation mark added.

out that "there are several mitigating factors" and "there were signs that the turbulence in money and credit markets were subsiding (!)".[131]

In the spring of 2008, early warning signs were noted by the ECB, but not correctly interpreted, as they were looked at from a financial integration perspective rather than a financial stability point of view. An increase in dispersion in EONIA lending rates in the middle of 2017, against the background of increasing EUREPO rates was – timidly, but correctly – interpreted as an "increase in variability in credit risk", that had entered the interbank market. While it was noted that "since July 2007, Eurozone sovereign spreads vis-à-vis the German benchmark have increased substantially"[132], sovereign risk was seen as playing only a "very (!) small" role "in explaining differences in bond yields across countries"[133].

What is now clear is that, in the wake of the introduction of the Euro and the integration of financial markets, fault-lines had been developing in the European banking sector, that an ineffective and politically-influenced supervisory framework failed to detect:

(1) *Slow integration, remaining fragmentation:* as Figure 14 demonstrates, third country ie non-EU banks – via branches and subsidiaries – slowly increased their market share in the EU to close to 30 percent by 2006. This average masks the importance of these foreign banks in the eastern European member states. In fact, the eastern part of the EU probably benefited more from third-country-bank entry in terms of higher growth than any other region.[134] Overall, however, due to the remaining barriers to entry in retail banking, the European banking system remained fragmented.

(2) *Increasing leverage:* banks were allowed to play the leverage game and significantly expand their balance sheets. In particular, the balance sheets of not only the largest banks in the Eurozone (such as Deutsche Bank), but also those in the UK and Switzerland, experienced rapid growth (see Figure 15). This made the banks vulnerable to financial shocks.

(3) *Growing dependence on volatile wholesale funding:* increased leverage was funded in the volatile wholesale markets. As Figure 16 shows, less than half of the balance sheets of the largest banks in the Eurozone were funded by deposits from the public. This dependence on wholesale funding was also much greater in the Eurozone than in the US. Collateralized wholesale funding in the Repo markets increasingly allowed for widening maturity mismatches – liquidity risks were beginning to build up.

131 See ECB (2007), pp 17–18.
132 See ECB (2008), p 13.
133 See ECB (2008), p 14; exclamation mark added.
134 See Allen et al. (2011) for a comprehensive discussion of cross-border banking issues in Europe.

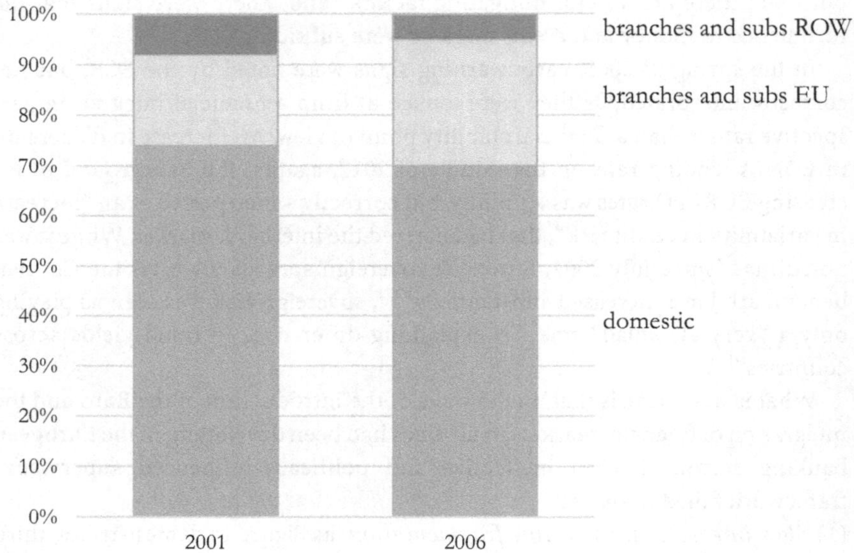

(Figure 14: Average share of foreign establishments in total domestic bank assets in EU-15, Commission (2008))

(4) *Sizeable cross-border exposures:* a significant amount of wholesale funding was used to finance the growth in cross-border exposures. In fact, in 2008, the share of foreign assets on the balance sheets of the major European banks was very high, with 82 percent for Deutsche Bank (mostly Europe and the US), 64 percent for Santander (mostly Latin America), 62 percent for UniCredit (mostly CEE), 41 percent for BNP Paribas (Europe and the US) and 29 percent for Société Générale (mostly CEE).[135] The largest banks were extremely vulnerable to external shocks.

In Summary

On the eve of the Great Financial Crisis, the Eurozone was operating with one monetary unit, but (too) many different banking systems. Monetary union, driven by liberalization of capital controls, was celebrating its 10th anniversary: "EMU@10". It was, however, incomplete – with a weak contractual budgetary union, no political union – and a decentralized bank supervision architecture. It had been serving as the locomotive for integration of financial and banking

135 See Allen et al. (2011).

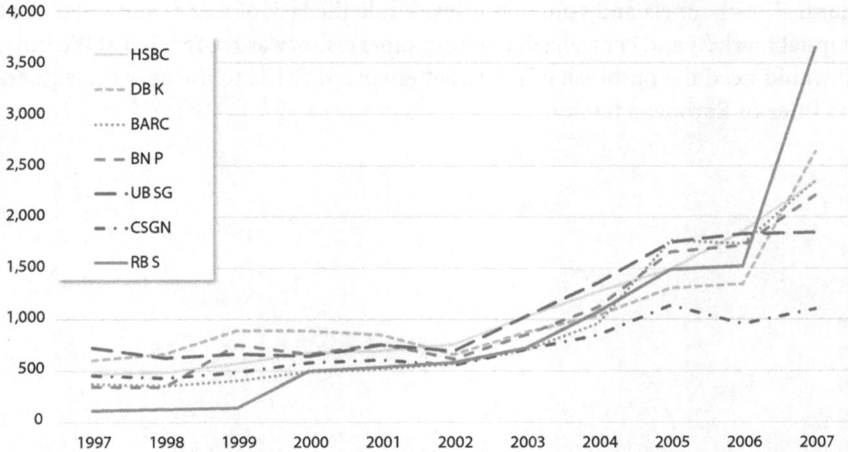

(Figure 15: European banks' balance sheets 1997–2007 (total assets, USD billion))

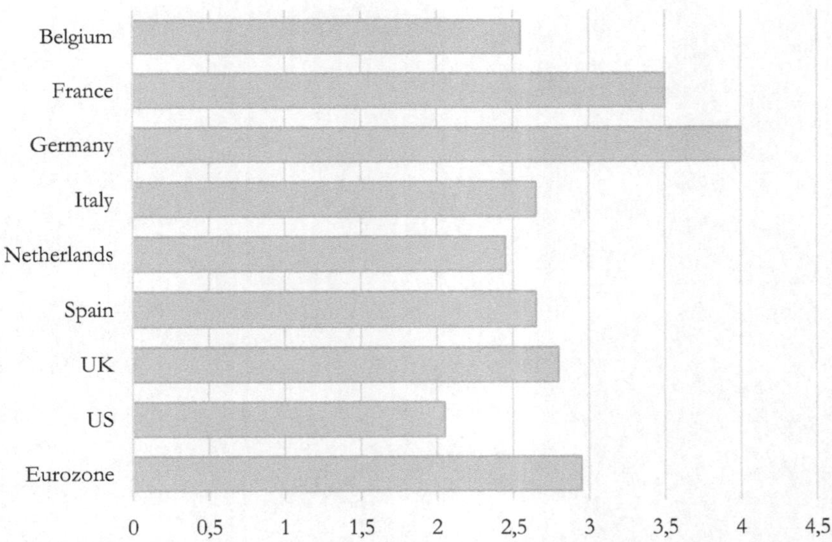

(Figure 16: Ratio of bank's total assets to deposits (top five banks in each country) in 2007, Source: Bankscope, Eurostat)

markets, with tangible benefits for the economy. The European banking landscape, despite significant progress, remained fragmented. And the increasing integration of banking and financial markets not only meant increased cross-border lending and reduced cost of capital, but also new risk concentrations, contagion channels and vulnerabilities. While the lack of macro surveillance of capital markets and centralized banking supervision was recognized at the time, it would need the outbreak of the Great Financial Crisis to uncover the vulnerabilities in European banking.

Part III – Crisis hitting and multiplying

Chapter 7: From “turbulences” to the Great Financial Crisis

“In the current crisis, as in past crises, we can learn much, and policy in the future will be informed by these lessons. But we cannot hope to anticipate the specifics of future crises with any degree of confidence.”[136]

Alan Greenspan, former Chairman of the Federal Reserve Bank, 17th March, 2008

“In mid-2007 we started to see the backlash. The start of the financial turmoil was sudden but not unexpected. The financial system as it worked over the past decade – with its flawed incentives and the overly complex products and with global imbalances as its macroeconomic backdrop – was no longer sustainable. The asset cycle turned, the weaknesses were exposed and investors suddenly lost confidence. After years of exceptional risk appetite and high profits, the pendulum swung in the opposite direction, as markets became extremely sensitive to financial risk.”[137]

Jean-Claude Trichet, former President of the ECB, 12th June, 2009

When the global financial crisis hit, the European financial system was not yet fully integrated. Whilst the Eurozone had centralized its monetary policy in the ECB, banking politics and supervision remained largely a national prerogative. Banks had been using the introduction of the Euro to expand, (1) across borders in the Eurozone, and (2) internationally via branch openings and mergers and acquisitions. Wholesale markets and, in particular, the money markets, were increasingly integrated, while retail banking markets still remained fairly fragmented. Against this backdrop, how did the US subprime mortgage crisis evolve into a global financial crisis that severely affected European banks? What were the gateways of the contagion? Where in Europe did we see the first turbulences? And what was the first line of defense? Most importantly, how did a global liquidity crisis morph into a full-fledged financial crisis of historic proportions?

136 See Greenspan (2008).
137 See Trichet (2009).

How could the US subprime crisis so severely affect European banks? Weak risk underwriting, long-intermediation chains, and the European banking glut

The literature documents well the origins of the financial crisis and the global economic downturn that it caused.[138] Beginning in the late 1990s, increases in house prices in the US began to accelerate. According to the Case-Shiller index, between 1996 and 2006 house prices in the US increased at an average rate of 17 percent per year (see Figure 17). House prices peaked in June, 2008, when delinquencies began to signal the bursting of the housing bubble (see Figure 18).

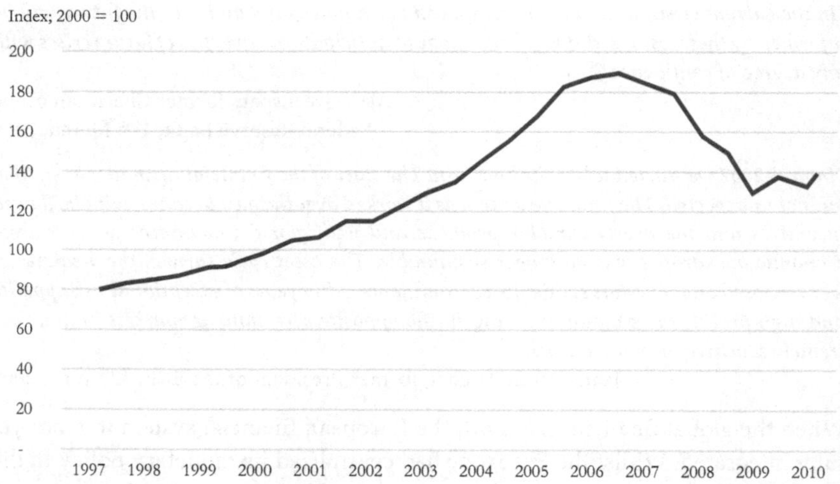

(Figure 17: S&P Case-Shiller Index (1997–2010), see Acharya and Richardson (2009))

The growing housing bubble was accompanied by a significant increase in private debt. In fact, the ratio of total consumer debt to home values increased from 56 percent in 1985 to 68 percent in 2005, and finally to 89 percent in late 2008.[139]

From a macro-economic perspective, low interest rates encouraged the US housing bubble. The Fed had adopted a relaxed interest-rate policy to counter deflationary pressures after the burst of the dotcom bubble in 2001. In fact, it kept the Federal funds rate down to 1 percent until 2004.

In addition, capital inflows from emerging markets, particularly from Asian

138 Compare for example Acharya and Richardson (2009) for a comprehensive documentation and analysis of the causes of the financial crisis.

139 Compare Acharya et al. (2009), pp 14–16.

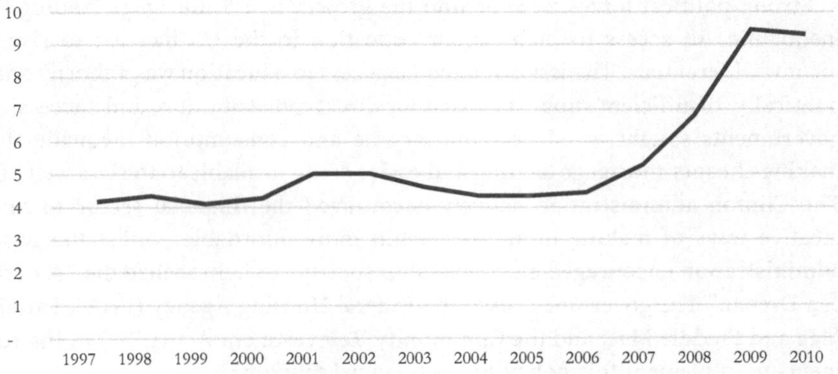

(Figure 18: US mortgage delinquency rate (1997–2010), see Acharya and Richardson (2009))

countries, kept long-term interest rates low. These countries bought US securities to peg their currencies to the US dollar, thereby supporting their export competitiveness. Moreover, they were building up funds of US securities, especially US Treasury bills, to hedge against a rapid depreciation of their currencies, as had happened during the Asian financial crisis of 1987. Oil-rich countries followed the lure of the US dollar as the leading global reserve currency, and invested a significant amount in USD denominated securities, a phenomenon which is also referred to as the "Global Savings Glut."[140]

These low interest rates fueled a boom in mortgage lending. Mortgage lending in the US – contrary to many other European countries – is typically based on variable interest rates and is a non-recourse loan. In other words, borrowers benefited from low interest rates and appreciating house prices, which allowed them to refinance their first mortgages and take out second mortgages. However, they also ran the risk of a sudden increase in interest rates, above all, those borrowers with very low or irregular incomes and low FICO (Fair Isaac Company) credit scores. The non-recourse nature of the US mortgages distinguishes them from most European mortgages and creates different incentives when house prices decline. If US borrowers cannot afford the payments anymore they can "hand back the keys" to the bank and vacate their homes, owing nothing. The bank would then sell the house to limit its loan losses. If many houses are put on the market at the same time, house prices will decline.

140 Bernanke (2005) was the first proponent of the 'Global Savings Glut' thesis.

Strong political forces were behind the growth in US mortgage lending:[141] inequalities in access to high-caliber education in the US had led to rising income differentials. The issue of unequal access to education was a thorny one, politically. Insufficient support existed for direct redistribution, and successive governments sought to address the income and consumption inequality by making cheaper mortgage lending and easier credit available to the less well off. The Clinton administration actively encouraged the financial sector to find creative ways of making home ownership more affordable; whilst the Bush administration encouraged an "ownership society" to help realize the "American Dream." The government used the Federal Housing Agency (FHA), Fannie Mae and Freddie Mac, and the Community Reinvestment Act (CRA) as instruments to implement this policy in the financial markets.

A transformation of the banking business model also spurred the growth in mortgage lending. The traditional hold-to-maturity business model of lending, in which aggregate lending capacity was capped by the balance sheet capacity of the banks, was rapidly being replaced by the originate-to-distribute business model. In this new model, loans were pooled in special purpose vehicles (SPVs), tranched into rated securities, and then resold to investors, a process called securitization (see Figure 19). Whilst securitization was originally used as a risk management tool to transfer risk off the balance sheet of the "originator" bank and out of the banking system per se, more than 50 percent of all securitizations ended up on the balance sheets of other banks and brokerages. Credit risk transfer thus worked at the level of the individual bank but not at the level of the overall banking system.

In many cases, the role of the banks was reduced to the short-term warehousing of the mortgage loan, and the structuring and placement of the securitizations. Most of the action took place outside the banking sector. Even originators who specialized in mortgages had "too little skin" in the game because their business model was built on origination and servicing fees, and only the very first payment defaults got pushed back to them. In addition, there was a conflict of interest at the level of the rating agencies, who were paid by the issuers to rate the securities. This lack of proper incentives for all market participants contributed to a deterioration in lending standards and the rise in subprime mortgage lending. This form of mortgage lending comprised of borrowers with lower FICO scores, lower documentation standards (including self-certification of income), and higher combined loan-to-value ratios. In 2005 and 2006, subprime mortgage origination ran up to USD 600 billion, more than 20 percent of

141 Compare Rajan (2010), chapter 1: "Let Them Eat Credit", for an account of the political process and pressures supporting the surge in subprime lending in the US.

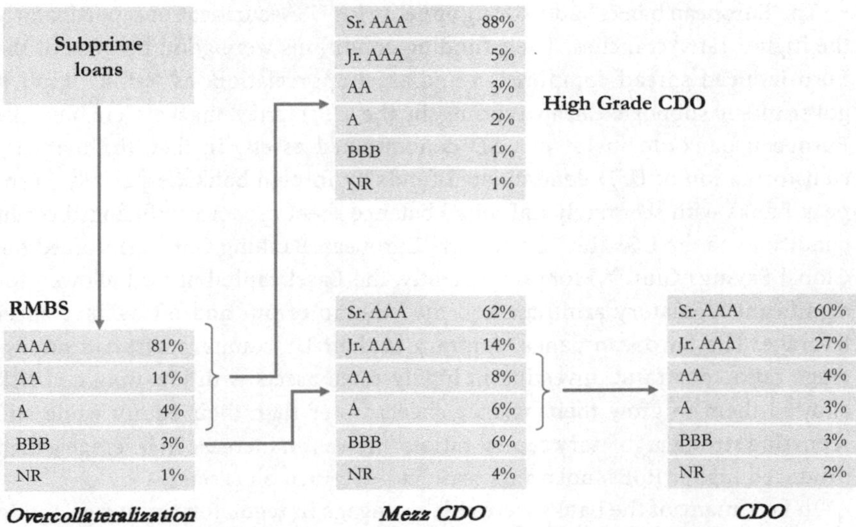

(Figure 19: Securitization, see Acharya and Richardson (2009), Figure 3.1, p 105)

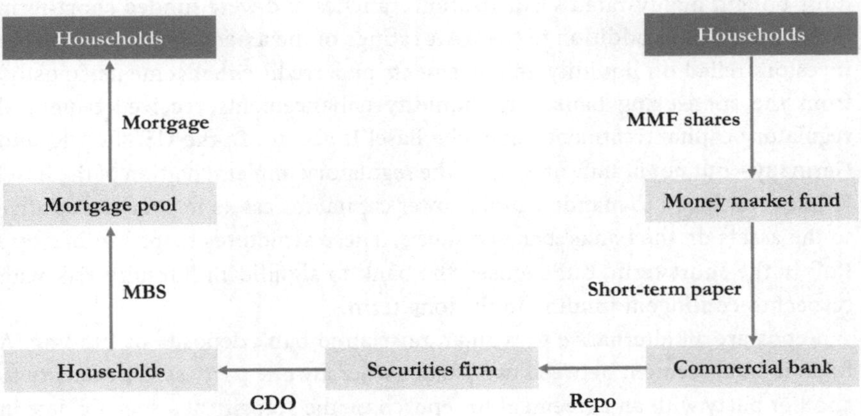

(Figure 20: Long intermediation chain, see Adrian and Shin (2010), shown in de Haan et al. (2015), p 33, Figure 1.8))

the total mortgage origination, and more than 80 percent of the subprime origination, was sold into securitizations.

The securitization model not only led to a deterioration in lending standards: it also lengthened the intermediation chain and opened the door for other investors and non-US banks (European banks in particular), to gain exposure to the US (subprime) mortgage market (see Figure 20). In fact, the distinction between traditional banking and trading all but disappeared.

The European banks had a strong appetite for US securitizations, particularly the higher rated tranches. Their funding conditions were good because of the Euro-induced spread compression and asset appreciation, as well as implicit government support. Cheap funding in the US money markets enabled the European banks to invest in USD denominated assets. In fact, the maturity transformation of USD denominated funds by foreign banks, especially European banks with seemingly unlimited balance sheet capacity, influenced credit conditions in the US. The "Global" or "European Banking Glut" reinforced the Global Savings Glut.[142] More importantly, the Basel capital accord allowed for significant regulatory arbitrage and the buildup of on- and off-balance sheet leverage. The European banks, contrary to their US counterparts, had no leverage ratio constraint. Investing in highly-rated assets with low-weighted risk allowed them to grow their balance sheets faster than their equity while still reporting strong regulatory capital ratios.[143] It was an increase in leverage which produced higher RoEs, not an increase in the return on assets.

In fact, many of the banks were able to engage in regulatory arbitrage and to set up conduits consisting of so-called off-balance sheet Asset-Backed Commercial Paper (ABCP) or Structured Investment Vehicles (SIVs).[144] These conduits bought highly-rated securitization tranches and were funded short-term (see Figure 21). In addition to the AAA ratings of the assets, commercial paper investors relied on liquidity enhancements and credit enhancements (mostly) from the sponsoring bank. The liquidity enhancements received beneficial regulatory capital treatment under the Basel II accord. In the US, the UK, and Germany – but not in Italy or Spain – the regulatory implementation of the Basel II rules continued to mandate much lower capital for assets in conduits relative to the assets on the banks' balance sheets. These structures helped to increase RoE in the short-term, but exposed the bank to significant liquidity risk with respect to contingent funding in the long term.

Repos are an alternative to regular, unsecured bank deposits or funding. A Repo is an agreement between two parties whereby one party sells a security to another party with an agreement to repurchase the security at a specific date in the future for a price fixed today. In other words, a Repo is a kind of collateralized deposit or securities financing instrument and the Repo market is a short-term security financing resource. The growth in this market in the run up to the crisis

142 See Shin (2011).

143 Compare Noeth and Sengupta (2010), pp 463–468, for a summary of the "Global Banking Glut" argument.

144 Acharya and Schnabel (2010) provide a detailed analysis of how ABCP conduits set up by commercial banks contributed to spreading the US subprime crisis to the European banks.

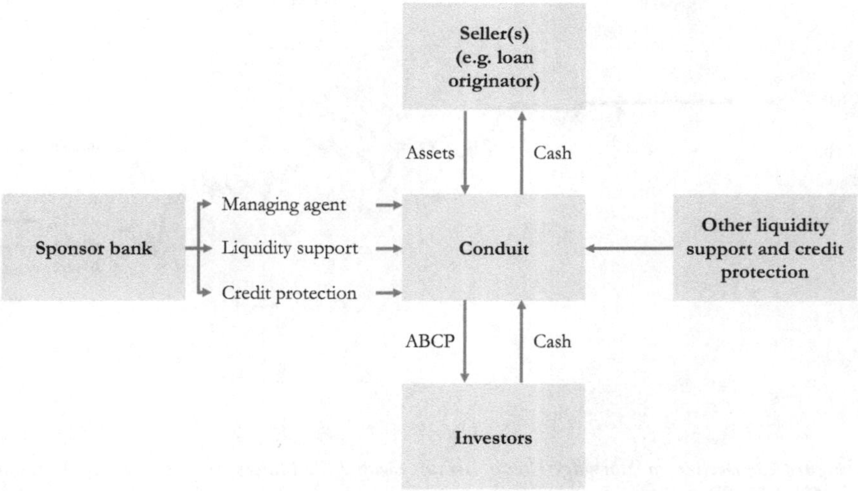

(Figure 21: Conduit/SIV structure, see Black and Fisher (2008), Graph 1, p 2)

also contributed to the build-up of leverage, mainly on the balance sheet of the global investment banks.[145]

The reversal of fortunes began in the subprime market in February 2007: as house prices began to fall, and interest rates began to rise, delinquencies and defaults increased rapidly. This was particularly the case in the subprime mortgage segment where the weakest borrowers were to be found. The value of securitizations backed by such mortgage loans began to fall. Leveraged derivative claims on these securities began to decline even more. Firstly, the lower rated tranches of the ABX price index began to fall. This index is based on a basket of 20 Credit Default Swaps (CDSs) referencing asset backed securities containing subprime mortgages of different ratings. In June of 2007, the index for the AAA tranches began to fall as well (see Figure 22).

The decline in the ABX indices reflected subprime-related losses in the underlying securitizations and a mounting wave of downgrades. On 4th May, 2007, UBS had to shut down its US-based internal hedge fund Dillon Read after suffering around USD 125 million in subprime-related losses. Later that month, Moody's, the rating agency, put 62 tranches across 21 US subprime deals on "review" for a possible downgrade. Against the backdrop of rising subprime delinquencies and defaults and serial downgrades, two hedge funds run by the US brokerage firm Bear Stearns had trouble meeting margin calls in June, 2007, forcing the Bear Stearns to inject USD 3.2 billion to protect its reputation.

145 See Adrian and Shin (2010).

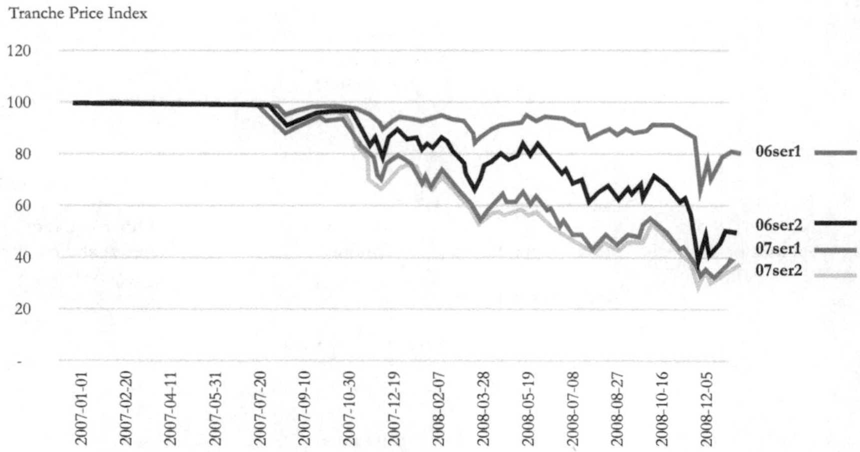

(Figure 22: Decline in Mortgage Credit Default Swap ABX Indices, see Acharya, Richardson (2009), p 22, Figure P11)

Where did we see the first turbulences in the Eurozone financial system? Liquidity in the interbank money market as the "canary in the coal mine"

Amid widespread concerns about how to value structured products and an erosion of trust in the reliability of ratings, the market for short-term ABCP began to dry up. As conduit investors refused to roll over their paper, many sponsoring banks had to draw on their liquidity guarantees. Moreover, because they had to take even more commercial paper onto their books, they were ultimately forced to consolidate the securitized (and deteriorating) assets of the conduits on their own balance sheets. As they began to sell assets there was more pressure on market prices, and the negative asset price "spiral of doom" accelerated. Investors tried to cover their losses by selling other assets, other markets were affected, and the financial crisis spread from the subprime credit markets to other structured credit products, including more liquid asset classes such as high yield and corporate bonds and equities. Spreads were widening, volatility was increasing, and there was a flight to quality across the board, as investors began to mistrust the banks and pile into safer assets such as US treasury bonds and Bunds.

When and where did the subprime crisis reach Europe? Not surprisingly, it first hit the banks in those countries where the regulatory regime had allowed a significant amount of leverage in off-balance sheet vehicles, especially Germany and the UK. A small German bank, IKB that was partially owned by KfW, the

German-government-owned development bank, was the first European victim of the crisis. In July 2007, its conduits "Rhineland" and "Rhinebridge" were unable to roll over ABCP, and IKB was not able to provide the promised liquidity line. After hectic discussions over a weekend, a EUR 3.5 billion rescue package involving KfW and some private banks was announced. IKB was later sold in October 2008, to Lone Star Holdings. Similarly, Sachsen LB ran into trouble with its Dublin-based "Ormond Quay" conduit, and needed to be bailed out by the regional government of Saxony. Other large, internationally active banks in the US and Europe survived the run in the ABCP market but suffered significant losses.

In August of 2007, a run started on the assets of three SIVs of the French bank BNP Paribas. The run was so severe that on the 9th August, BNP Paribas had to suspend redemptions. This event sent shock waves through the ABCP market, as investors came to realize that these short-term vehicles were not necessarily safe. Indeed, because these conduits held significant amounts of subprime related securitization tranches and other assets of questionable credit quality, they were rather opaque and difficult to value.

As the mistrust among the European banks increased - no one really knew how much, and where, subprime and structured product exposure was held - liquidity in the interbank market evaporated. The increased rollover risk - ie funding liquidity - had shown up in significantly widening spreads between unsecured versus secured funds.

The spread between unsecured versus secured funds in the interbank market became a fear gauge and reflected the heightened mistrust among banks (see Figure 23). In hindsight, it performed like a "canary in the coal mine", a very sensitive early warning instrument. Interbank deposits had become information sensitive, a bank run had started to gain momentum amid rising subprime delinquencies and defaults, continuing downgrades of mortgage-backed securitizations and mounting write-downs of structured products on banks-balance sheets.

Spill-overs from the US subprime crisis hit the European banks rather unevenly. Most exposed were the larger, globally active banks from Germany, the Netherlands, the UK, and Switzerland. Spanish and Italian banks were not as exposed because their regulators had not allowed the same level of regulatory arbitrage and build-up of the maturity mismatch and leverage in the ABCP conduits.

In response, and in close cooperation with the Fed, the ECB began to flood the market with liquidity in August 2007, thereby stabilizing highly vulnerable financial markets. This step demonstrates classical lender-of-last-resort behavior. The ECB managed to satisfy all existing demands for liquidity at the policy rate, and also relaxed conditions with regard to the length of tender operations and

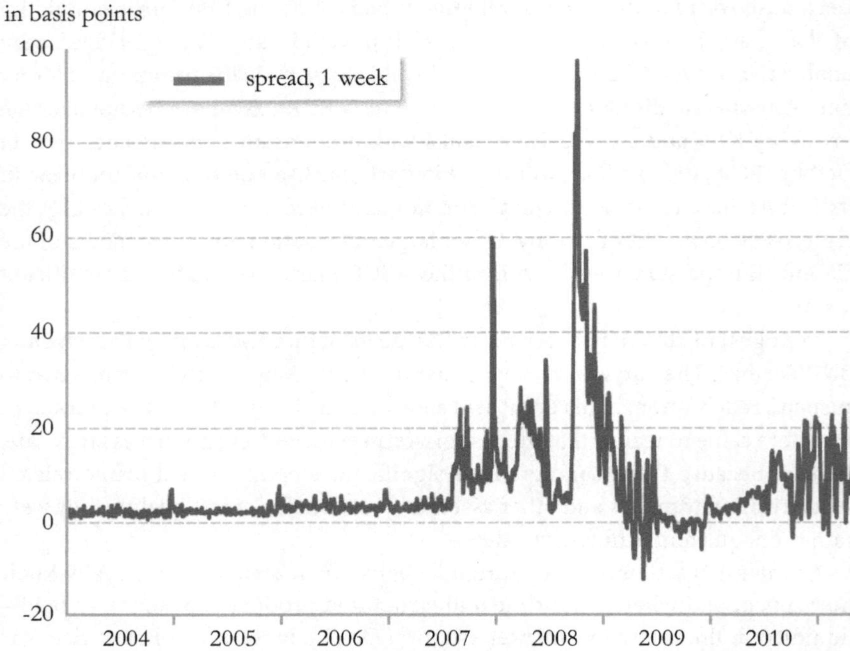

(Figure 23: Interbank Money Market – Unsecured versus Secured Funds, see Kotz (2011), Figure 1, p 99)

the eligibility of collateral (see Figure 24).[146] Moreover, in view of the tensions in the USD funding markets, on which a lot of European banks had heavily drawn, the ECB entered into a swap agreement with the Fed in December 2007. This agreement allowed the ECB to provide USD funding to European banks against Euro denominated collateral.

Liquidity troubles or solvency issues? Following the falling dominos in the global financial system

The US subprime crisis set in motion a highly negative liquidity spiral. As funding and market liquidity began to dry up, leveraged investors were forced to unwind their positions. This process caused more losses and higher margins and haircuts, which in turn exacerbated the funding problem. A loss spiral arose for leveraged investors because a decline in asset values eroded their net worth

146 Compare Kotz (2010) for a detailed account of the ECB's crisis response.

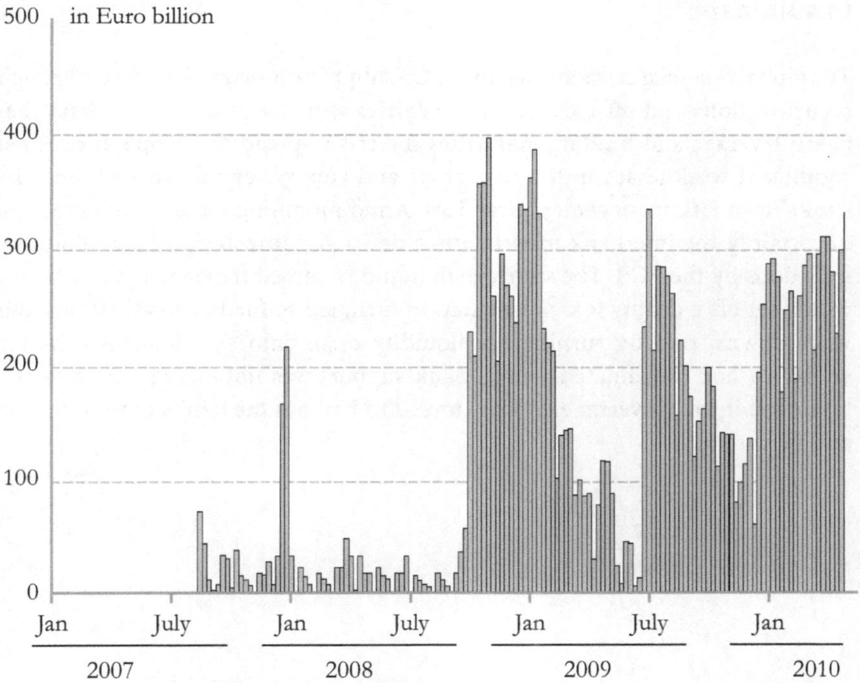

(Figure 24: The Response of the ECB – MRO Allotment, see Kotz (2010))

faster than their gross worth. Margins and haircuts spiked with large price drops leading to a general tightening of lending and the emergence of a vicious circle.[147]

This vicious circle became very pronounced in the global Repo markets, where significant volumes of securities were refinanced short-term, on a secured basis. [148]A decline in the value of collateral led to an increase in the haircut and was, therefore, equivalent to the withdrawal of cash. The owners of the securities were either forced to sell them at a loss or find additional sources of unsecured funding, which were clearly scarce in such an environment of high uncertainty and increased volatility. Liquidity troubles were becoming solvency issues. The weakest, most leveraged banks, and other financial institutions in this environment faced a choice between illiquidity and insolvency. The lender-of-last-resort was overrun and (for insolvent banks) out of mandate. As turbulences turned into a full-blown financial crisis all eyes turned to the government for backstops.

147 Compare Brunnermeier (2009) for a detailed account of the global liquidity crisis.

148 See Gorton (2009) for an analysis of the developments in the USD 1.6 trillion global repo market.

In summary

The global financial crisis started in the US subprime mortgage market. Through securitizations and off-balance sheet vehicles with significant mismatches between leverage and funding maturities the crisis spread to Europe. It exposed significant weaknesses in the regulatory and supervisory framework and the banks' own risk management practices. Amid mounting losses and increasing uncertainty the interbank market broke down and forced significant liquidity injections by the ECB. The shortage in liquidity forced the banks to sell assets, which set off a deadly loss spiral that, in turn, led to further devaluations and write-downs, thereby turning the liquidity crisis into a full-blown solvency crisis. Ad hoc coordinated central bank support was not enough to prevent a total meltdown. Governments were forced to bail out the banks both in the US and in Europe.

Chapter 8: Mopping up – containing the crisis

"What we know about the financial crisis is that we do not know very much."
attributed to Paul A Samuelson, American economist and Nobel Prize winner

"September and October of 2008 was the worst financial crisis in global history, including the Great Depression"
Benjamin S Bernanke, former Chairman of the Federal Reserve Bank, (2010)

The culmination of the Great Financial Crisis in the Autumn of 2008, raises many questions: why did the safety net provided by the central banks as lenders of last resort not hold? When did the global liquidity crisis turn into a solvency crisis? Why did Lehman Brothers fail? Why did the US government have to come to the rescue of AIG, and ultimately the entire financial system? How was the big bail-out organized in Europe, and to what extent did the approach differ from the approach taken in the US?

Why did the US government have to come to the rescue of the financial system? The failure of Lehman Brothers, the rescue of AIG, and the big bail-out

In the aftermath of the closure of the BNP Paribas' conduits, the short-term funding markets, specifically the commercial paper and Repo markets began to freeze up. These markets only really began to function again when central banks on both sides of the Atlantic injected liquidity into the system. The central banks were able to ease the immediate liquidity concerns fairly quickly, but they were neither able to restore the transparency of the financial markets', nor to address solvency concerns at the same pace. Private markets cannot function without pertinent information, reporting, and disclosure to both market participants, and to the relevant regulators and supervisors. The general level of uncertainty in the market increases significantly when investors are in the dark as to which financial institutions are vulnerable to subprime losses, and to what extent those losses might affect their solvency. As this lack of transparency in the financial market increases it sows the seeds of a systemic crisis.

The end of 2007, and early 2008, was characterized by a continual series of announcements about subprime lenders going bust, significant write-downs by financial institutions, and news about mono-line insurance companies approaching bankruptcy. By early 2008, the banks had ceased to trust one another, and had switched from unsecured to secured overnight borrowing.[149]

Three defining events during this time confirmed that these counterparty risk concerns were valid: (1) government support for the acquisition of Bear Stearns by J.P. Morgan, (2) the bankruptcy of Lehman Brothers and (3) the big bail-out of AIG.

During the week of 10th March, 2008, a wholesale bank run had started on Bear Stearns, the fifth largest US investment bank. Bear Stearns was the smallest of the major investment banks, but had a great deal of leverage, and was extremely vulnerable to the subprime mortgage market. Over the weekend the government helped to engineer J.P. Morgan's purchase of Bear Stearns by guaranteeing USD 29 billion of subprime-backed securities. Bear Stearns was systemically important for several reasons: it generated significant counterparty risk for other market participants, because of its major role in the USD 2.5 trillion Repo market; it was one of the largest hedge fund prime brokers on Wall Street; and it was a large participant in the trillion-dollar US CDS market.

The rescue of Bear Stearns initially calmed the markets. That is, until they began to turn their attention to the next problem in line: Lehman Brothers, the fourth largest investment bank in the US, behind Goldman Sachs, Morgan Stanley and Merrill Lynch. On 29th January, 2008, Lehman Brothers had reported its 2007 results, with record revenues of USD 60 billion, and record earnings of more than USD 4 billion. During January, 2008, the stock price averaged in the mid-fifties, implying a market capitalization of USD 30 billion. Less than eight months later, on 10th September, 2008, the stock closed at less than USD 4, down 95 percent. Over the weekend of the 13th-14th September 2008, the US Treasury, the New York Fed and the Securities and exchanges Commission (SEC) made last-ditch attempts to coordinate the rescue of Lehman Brothers, involving the CEOs of other leading financial institutions, all of which failed. On 15th September, Lehman Brothers was forced to file for bankruptcy. It was the largest bankruptcy ever filed, and was a turning point in the global financial crisis.

149 Acharya et al. (2009) provide a complete timeline on pp 51–56. Also, refer to the final report of the National Commission on the Causes of the Financial and Economic Crisis in the United States (2011).

With the benefit of hindsight, what were the key reasons for the failure of Lehman Brothers? The Lehman failure, unlike Bear Stearns's near-failure, was caused by the rapidly declining economic and market environment. But as the Report of the examiner to the bankruptcy court in the southern district of New York discloses, the negative consequences of Lehman's failure to its shareholders, creditors, and the financial system at large were clearly exacerbated for the following reasons:
(1) Lehman's highly leveraged investment banking business model;
(2) serious errors of judgment by Lehman's management in terms of market timing, concentration risk, and maturity mismatches;
(3) concealed balance sheet manipulations that were not adequately questioned by the financial auditors;
(4) inadequate attempts by Lehman to mitigate the situation; and
(5) the inadequate response of government agencies, who should have better anticipated and mitigated the outcome.[150]

As Bernanke, the then Chairman of the Fed, summarized in 2010, at the end of his testimony before the Committee on Financial Services of the US House of Representatives:

> *"First, we must eliminate the gaps in our financial regulatory framework that allow large, complex, interconnected firms to operate without robust, consolidated supervision...Second, ..., we need a new resolution regime...ensuring that the failing firm's shareholders and creditors take losses, and its management is replaced."*[151]

The following are more in-depth contributing factors to Lehman's failure that provide important insights:[152]
(1) *Significant maturity-mismatch:* Lehman had USD 400 billion of assets, and corresponding liabilities mostly in the short-term Repo market, but with only USD 25 billion in capital reserves. Lehman, not unlike other investment banks at the time, followed a high risk, high leverage, high maturity-mismatch business model that necessitated the full confidence of its counterparties. If the short-term Repo counterparties lost confidence in Lehman Brothers and refused to roll-over its daily funding, Lehman would be unable to fund itself.
(2) *Outsized subprime mortgage exposure:* in 2006, Lehman's management team decided to "double down" on subprime residential mortgages in a declining market, an event which significantly increased its principal risk and which

150 Compare Valukas (2010).
151 Compare Bernanke (2010), pp 3–4; Calello, Ervin (2010) describe how a bail-in resolution of Lehman might have worked.
152 See Valukas (2010), pp 2–27 for a summary.

deliberately breached its internal risk limits and controls. The focus had shifted from the "moving" to the "storage" business. The senior management team side-lined or dismissed any managers who advised against this shift in strategy.[153] At the same time, the team failed to recognize the speed of the decline in the residential housing market, as well as the spill-over into other markets where Lehman had significant exposure. This was particularly true with respect to commercial real estate and leveraged lending. Lehman's losses, of USD 2.8 billion and USD 3.9 billion in the first two quarters of 2008 respectively, fueled a rapid loss in market confidence. The losses were a direct result of their strategy.

(3) *"Repo 105":* Lehman's standing in the funding market was critically dependent on its counterparty rating, which in turn – against the backdrop of deteriorating asset quality – was critically dependent on reported net leverage and liquidity numbers. To avoid further downgrades, Lehman Brothers used an accounting device called "Repo 105," which permitted Repo transactions at the end of a quarter to be treated as sales rather than financing. None of Lehman's peers resorted to this sort of tactic. At the end of Q2 2008, the Repo 105 volume stood at USD 50.4 billion, equivalent to a 1.8 point "improvement" in reported net leverage ratio. In addition, the fact that their reported liquidity pool included a substantial portion of difficult to liquidate or otherwise encumbered assets was neither disclosed to the rating agencies nor to the market. By 12th September, 2008, two days after it publicly reported a USD 41 billion liquidity pool, the pool contained less than USD 2 billion of liquid assets.

(4) *External audit failures:* the financial auditors Ernst & Young failed to adequately question the accounting and reporting practices of Lehman and, more importantly, did not adequately question the Repo 105 transactions.

(5) *"Too little, too late":* the actions to stop origination, de-risk the balance sheet, and increase capital were unsuccessful. Attempts to sell subsidiaries, such as the asset management arm Neuberger Berman, and even efforts to sell the firm itself to a stronger player such as the Korea Development Bank (KDB), Bank of America, or Barclays proved insufficient and were "too little, too late." "Lehman should have done more, done better."[154]

(6) *Failed government rescue:* the US government, represented by the Treasury, alongside the New York Fed (a main creditor and provider of liquidity under the recently created broker-dealer facility), and the SEC (the primary su-

153 As Valukas (2010) reports on p 46 based on press reports, Madelyn Antoncic, Chief Risk Officer (CRO), and Michael Gelband, head of the Fixed Income Division (FID) had been removed because of their opposition to the build-up in risky and illiquid assets.

154 Valukas (2010), p 14.

> pervisor of the firm), tried to facilitate a last-minute acquisition of Lehman Brothers by Bank of America and Barclays. But the government had no authority to directly recapitalize the investment bank, nor did sufficient assets exist to support a large enough funding line from other banks or the Fed.

The failure of Lehman sent shock waves through the financial system, not only in the US, but also globally. The systemic risk and its spill-over crystallized in several different forms as markets declined, counterparty risk was amplified, and uncertainty increased. On 15th September, 2008, the Dow Jones closed over 500 points down, as market participants liquidated positions and ran for cover.

The markets realized that if, contrary to their expectations and despite the rescue of Bear Stearns, Lehman Brothers could fail, a similar fate might also befall other investment banks. These concerns led to the sale of Merrill Lynch to Bank of America, and a classic run on Goldman Sachs and Morgan Stanley, that was only stopped by massive government intervention.

Money market funds suffered losses on their holdings of Lehman commercial paper and were "breaking the buck," – that is, dropping below par. This led to a significant run on money market funds and resulted in the drying up of both the commercial paper and Repo markets, for which money market funds are the largest source of funding. The government ultimately had to guarantee all money market funds so as to stop the run.

Over 100 hedge funds used Lehman as their prime broker and relied largely on Lehman for financing. As a consequence of the Lehman bankruptcy, a lot of hedge fund assets that had served as collateral for this financing were "frozen." Hedge funds became unsecured creditors to the bankruptcy estate and suffered significant losses.

The Lehman bankruptcy also put pressure on the prices of securitized residential and commercial real-estate assets, because the market expected the liquidation of many positions.

As uncertainty about the size of the potential losses rose and market participants ceased to trust each other's solvency, the interbank markets froze. Thus, all Lehman counterparties suffered losses as a result. "The entire financial intermediation activity was at risk of collapse."[155]

A particular case in point was the global insurer, American International Group (AIG). In the wake of the Lehman failure, and amid the subsequent market turmoil, AIG faced a significant jump in collateral calls. In 2008, AIG had USD 1 trillion in assets, but had lost USD 93 billion, and was ultimately rescued on 16th September, 2008, with the support of the New York Fed, the US Fed, and

155 Acharya et al. (2009), p 7.

the US Treasury. The rescue played out over several months, and involved loans, equity investments by the Treasury, and the creation of special purpose vehicles[156]. Even now, it is hard to believe the rate at which the financial system descended into chaos.

AIG's troubles primarily resulted from two different activities which both led to significant exposure to real estate. On 16th September, 2008, the cumulative losses from both activities had reached USD 50 billion, which triggered the government bail-out. The first issue concerned its subsidiary, AIG Financial Products which wrote CDSs on more than USD 500 billion of assets, including USD 78 billion on multi-sector collateralized debt obligations (CDOs). The counterparties were other financial institutions across the globe. By 16th September, 2008, AIG's multi-sector CDS portfolio had lost more than USD 33.9 billion. However, due to the specific swap agreements, AIG had only posted USD 22.4 billion of collateral, leaving counterparties with USD 11.5 billion of exposure.

The second set of activities that contributed to the losses was AIG's securities lending business. AIG was lending out the securities of its life insurance companies to finance the outright purchase of residential mortgage-backed securities (RMBS) and real-estate related CDOs. By the end of 2007, AIG had loaned USD 75 billion of securities, with 65 percent of the lending proceeds invested in mortgage-backed securities. The total losses amounted to at least USD 21 billion.

As a result of these two activities, the business profile of AIG had changed. Instead of an "insurance company like" and "safe" portfolio of liquid bonds and stocks, funded by stable long-term liabilities to policyholders, the company's financial profile had become more "bank-like." Its portfolio now contained significant maturity mismatches and roll-over risks on the liability-side, and exposure to structured, illiquid RMBS and CDOs on the asset side. This transformation was the result of serious business misjudgments, significant risk management failures and governance shortcomings, as well as gaping regulatory holes.

Without a government rescue, AIG's situation would have greatly impaired the solvency of the insurance subsidiaries. The CDS counterparties would have suffered significant losses, and AIG would have had to liquidate a substantial number of assets in a disorderly manner. This liquidation would have added to the overall fragility of market participants, who were already occupied with the fallout from the Lehman failure.

"Too-big-to-fail" had become a reality in the US and elsewhere.

The US authorities were forced to rescue financial institutions to prevent a

156 Compare McDonald and Paulson (2014) for an analysis of the CDS and securities lending operations of AIG.

systemic meltdown. AIG was awarded an emergency loan from the government in exchange for an 80 percent ownership stake. The two main agencies in the residential mortgage market, Fannie Mae and Freddie Mac, were put into receivership and taken over by the government. The government announced a USD 700 billion facility to buy troubled RMBSs from financial institutions – the Troubled Asset Relief Program (TARP).

The financial system continued to change rapidly. Wachovia divested its banking subsidiaries to Citigroup; and the FDIC sold Washington Mutual's assets and liabilities to J.P. Morgan, after the Office of Thrift Supervision (OTS) shut it down and placed it in FDIC receivership.

In addition to TARP, which the US government used to prop up banks and car companies, the government also created an array of other programs. As of 30th April, 2011, the US government had committed about US 12.2 trillion, or over 70 percent of GDP. Of these commitments, it had spent USD 2.5 trillion, but had also collected more than USD 10 billion in dividends and fees.[157] These commitments reinforced the link between the government and its banks. The fiscal position of the government deteriorated as the severe recession (and loss in tax revenues which resulted) pushed the debt-to-GDP ratio beyond 100 percent. The US lost its AAA rating, as a direct consequence of the Great Financial Crisis.

All in all, deposit insurance was unavailable, and therefore unable to stop the run in the wholesale markets: the lender-of-last resort facilities of the Fed, initially only available to bank holding companies, could not deal with the solvency issues that resulted from mark-to-market and write-down losses on real-estate assets. The US government scrambled to fully underwrite its implicit guarantees so as to avoid a systemic meltdown.

How did the Great Financial Crisis escalate in Europe? And how did the European governments react to the global bank run that followed the failure of Lehman?

How did European governments react to the global bank run? Hypo Real Estate, a special case in point

The US crisis forced the hand of European governments to bail out their banks:

(1) the failure and subsequent nationalization of its banks almost caused the Icelandic government to fall;

(2) Switzerland had to bail out UBS;

157 See The New York Times (2011) for an overview of the "Government's Total Bailout Tab".

(3) in the UK, authorities were forced to nationalize Northern Rock early on in the crisis, and to restructure Bradford & Bingley, while taking significant direct stakes in two large institutions, RBS and Lloyds-HBOS;
(4) in the Benelux, the authorities were forced to bail out Fortis, ING, and Dexia;
(5) in Germany – having already rescued IKB and Sachsen LB in 2007 – the government had to bail out the private sector banks Hypo Real Estate (HRE) and Commerzbank. The German government was also forced to bail out HSH Nordbank, Nordeutsche Landesbank, and wind down Westdeutsche Landesbank (WestLB).

French president Nicolas Sarkozy presented a concerted action plan at the Eurozone summit in October, 2008, that became the management plan for the European financial crisis. Coordination at the Eurozone level was of particular importance to avoid deposit flights from a country with a government backstop to another with none, or only weak government support. The final declaration of the summit introduced an action plan with three aims:[158]
(1) *"Ensuring appropriate liquidity conditions for financial institutions"* referred to the welcoming of the easing of monetary policy by the European Central Bank (ECB) and other central banks in cutting interest rates and providing long-term financing;
(2) *"Facilitating the funding of banks, which is currently constrained"* referred to government guarantees of banks' senior debt issuance;
(3) *"Providing financial institutions with additional capital resources, so as to continue to ensure the proper financing of the economy"* referred to Tier 1 capital injections and the urging of national supervisors "to implement prudential rules also with a view to stabilizing the financial system."

The case of HRE is worth a closer look, to better demonstrate how the Lehman Brothers failure led to banking failures in Europe.[159]

HRE was a specialized commercial real estate lender that had recently expanded into public sector lending through the ill-timed acquisition of Depfa Bank in 2007. The combined balance sheet had more than EUR 400 billion in assets and liabilities that were supported by only EUR 8 billion in capital reserves: their leverage was thus over 50 times their reserves. In addition to the significant leverage, HRE's business model demonstrated extreme maturity mismatches. Moreover, the extent to which HRE was hit by the crisis raised questions as to the adequacy of its internal risk controls and governance, in particular with regard to liquidity risk management.

158 See Eurozone Summit (2008).
159 Compare Moenninghoff and Wieandt (2011) for a detailed account of the HRE case.

One immediate effect on HRE of the bank run in the interbank and Repo markets was that the run triggered a liquidity crisis at its wholly-owned Irish subsidiary Depfa, whose business model consisted of public sector lending, mostly to government. Its highly-rated, long-term assets were funded short-term, mostly in the Repo market. The Basel II regulations required minimum capital, allowing for significant maturity mismatches and significant leverage (see Figure 25). When "the music stopped", the asset side was frozen with sizeable Fair Value losses, and there was no funding available to roll the maturities on the liability side. Increasing collateral calls on derivatives, mounting requests by rating agencies for additional coverage on pooled collateral to sustain bond ratings, and the rapid draw-down of liquidity facilities made matters worse.

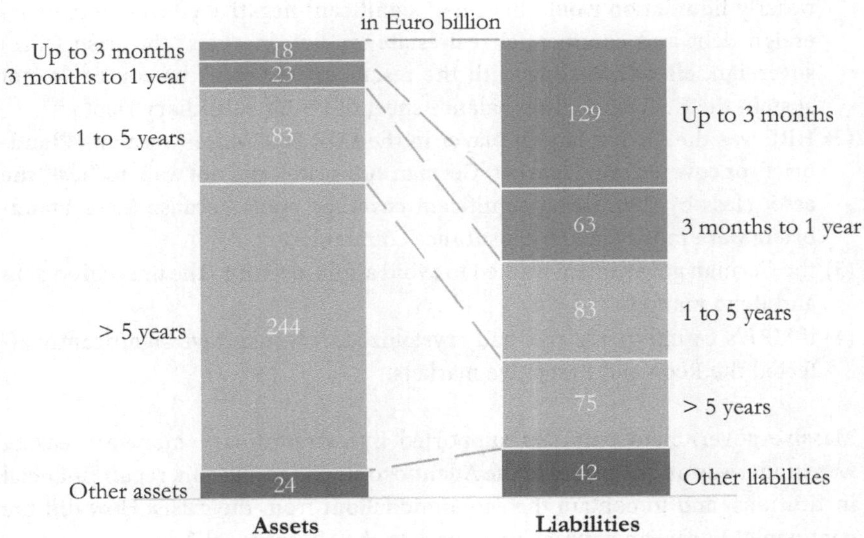

(Figure 25: HRE Group's IFRS Q3 2008 balance sheet by maturities, in Euro billions)

At the same time, the decline in the commercial real-estate market led to a solvency crisis in HRE's other core business. After years of profitability, HRE reported a loss of EUR 5.5 billion for the fiscal year 2008, wiping out most of its capital. In the following quarters, LLPs continued to weigh heavily on the bank's P&L and capital positions.

The Emergency Liquidity Assistance (ELA) facilities of the Deutsche Bundesbank ultimately rescued HRE. The ELA facilities grew into a EUR 50 billion collateralized loan facility provided by a consortium of German banks and insurance companies, with a EUR 35 billion built-in government guarantee. The total liquidity support, once a special law had been enacted, reached a maximum of EUR 102 billion in the first quarter of 2009. The solvency crisis was also solved with the support of the German government. Total recapitalization needs reached EUR 10 billion. As a consequence, HRE was nationalized in 2009. Significant parts of its balance sheet were hived off into a government sponsored bad bank scheme, FMS Wertmanagement. In particular, the assets transferred involved large portfolios of public sector exposure to Greece and other countries on the EU periphery, which had been affected by the Eurozone sovereign debt crisis of 2009. These assets also included troubled commercial real-estate exposures in the European periphery and the US.

So why was HRE rescued? HRE was both deemed "too big" and "too interconnected" to fail:

(1) HRE's balance sheet was comparable in size to that of Lehman and a disorderly liquidation would have had significant negative effects on the sovereign debt and commercial real-estate lending markets: the Irish (Eire) sovereign, already dealing with the rescue of its "own" banks, could not sustain the EUR 220 billion balance sheet of HRE's subsidiary Depfa.[160]
(2) HRE was the second largest player in the EUR 800 billion German "Pfandbrief" or covered bond market; German authorities did not want to "test" the asset class by liquidating significant coverage pools because these Pfandbriefe were mostly held by insurance companies.
(3) the German government wanted to avoid a spill-over into the unsecured debt and Repo markets.
(4) if HRE's counterparty risk had crystallized, it would have significantly affected the Repo and derivative markets.

Massive government bail-outs supported by extraordinary monetary easing were underway on both sides of the Atlantic to stop the bank run, repair financial institutions, and to contain the economic fallout from the crisis. How did the continental European approach compare to the US approach?

How do the European and US reactions to the crisis compare? Swift recapitalization versus protracted forbearance

Both sides of the Atlantic witnessed unprecedented levels of government involvement in the financial sector. Looking into the abyss, governments took ad hoc action, and pushed comprehensive rescue programs through the respective

160 It was agreed at a European level that home countries would be responsible for the rescue operations including for the Euro-area subsidiaries.

legislative bodies in record time. Measures included capital injections, debt guarantees, direct lending, and asset guarantees and purchases. The total committed direct assistance to the financial sector between 2007 and 2009 amounted to over USD 20 trillion across the globe, 74 percent of GDP in the US, 86 percent of GDP in the UK, and 18 percent of GDP in the Eurozone (see Figure 26).[161] The recession was contained – when compared to what the world had experienced in the Great Depression of the 1930s – but these actions significantly constrained the governments' fiscal flexibility, because rescue programs, lower tax revenues, and spending for counter-cyclical measures pushed up government debt to the equivalent of GDP across the board (see Figure 27).

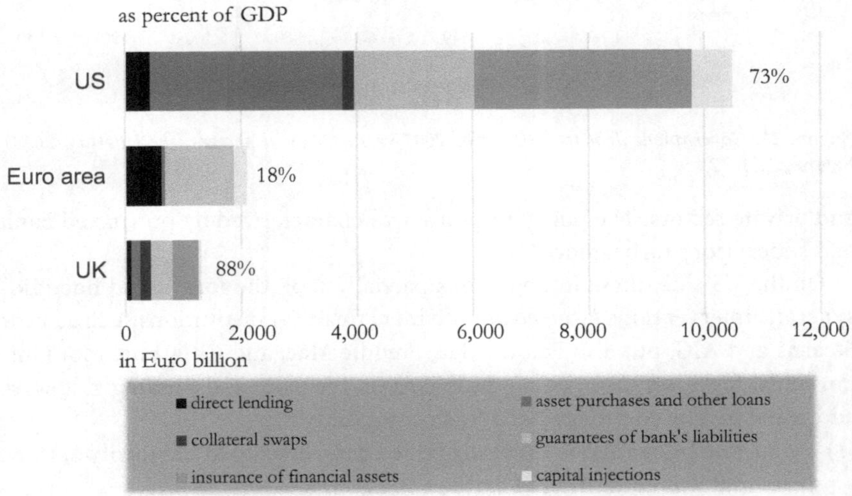

(Figure 26: Official support for the financial sector, 2007–2009, in USD billions, in percent of GDP, see Huertas (2014): Figure 2.1., p 12)

The role models for the policy response were the last financial crises in the Nordics, in particular, the Swedish banking crisis of 1989. Each of these crises were characterized by a single, sharp recession. Policy responses in the Nordics were quick, involved decisive recapitalization of the banks and – in the case of Sweden and Finland – splitting off troubled assets into bad banks. These policies facilitated a rapid recovery. The opposite case – and one to be avoided – was the Japanese financial crisis of the 1990s. The Japanese crisis also had its origins in the liberalization of banking sectors and a credit -real estate asset bubble. It lasted a decade, and was characterized by a prolonged period of weak economic performance and the buildup of a significant debt overhang in both the public

161 See Huertas (2014), pp 11–12.

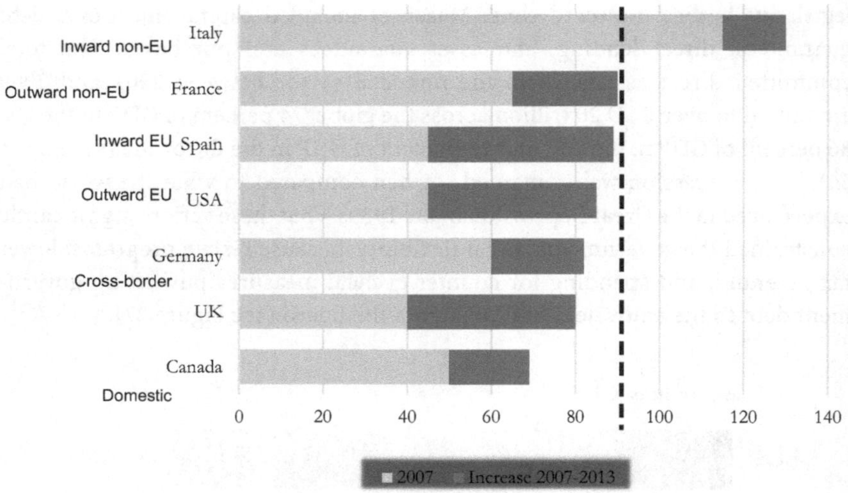

(Figure 27: Government debt-to-GPD ratios 2007 versus 2013 in percent, see Huertas (2014): Figure 2.2., p 12)

and private sectors. The policy response was characterized by protracted bank and supervisory forbearance.[162]

On the US side, these interventions partially took the form of ad hoc idiosyncratic interventions targeted at individual financial institutions such as Bear Stearns and AIG, but also Fannie Mae, Freddie Mac, and Citigroup. More importantly, however, the systemic problems on the asset and funding side were addressed in a three-pronged approach consisting of:

(1) a loan guarantee scheme for newly issued bank debt up to a maturity of three years that was administered by the FDIC;
(2) a mandatory bank recapitalization scheme undertaken by the US Treasury, in which the Treasury purchased preferred equity stakes in the largest banks; and
(3) a funding facility for commercial paper operated by the Fed.[163]

In Europe, especially in France, Germany, the Benelux and the UK, government support became crucial when traditional sources of funding dried up. The size of the interventions varied greatly between countries and was determined by the size of the local banking system relative to the economy. The intervention was higher in countries such as the UK, where there is a large financial services

162 Compare Bank of England (2009), Box 3, pp 21–23, for a summary and comparison of the recent financial crises in the Nordics and in Japan.
163 Compare Acharya and Sundram (2009).

industry, whose institutions were severely hit by the crisis. The interventions were much smaller in other countries such as Italy (only 0.6 percent of GDP), where the banking system was less vulnerable to the immediate crisis. Programs were mostly set up in a system-wide way, primarily in the form of debt guarantees and recapitalizations for banks. Measures targeted at bank assets were less common.[164]

On both sides of the Atlantic, government measures were successful in helping to stabilize the markets. The rescue packages widely contributed to reducing the banks' probability of default, as measured by the CDS spreads: in particular, capital injections proved to be effective. The issuance of bank debt without guarantees began to pick up. Lending volumes remained low though, as the recession affected the overall demand for lending.[165]

The European response was different, however, not only in that it varied by country and slightly lagged behind the US in terms of timing, but also because it was characterized by:

(1) critical bank recapitalization programs that were voluntary;
(2) lengthy bank-specific state aid proceedings by the EU's Directorate General (DG) Competition;
(3) ineffective stress tests with weak sovereign backstops and a lack of a common European backstop;
(4) continued supervisory and bank forbearance, sowing the seeds for an extended banking crisis; and
(5) lack of effective coordination of rescue measures with fiscal and monetary policies across Europe.

The following is a more detailed look at these five critical differences:

(1) The capital injection program in the US targeted all leading banks. These banks were reportedly "not given a choice" as to participation. The government invested via preference shares with a 5 percent preferred dividend for the first three years, and 9 percent thereafter. These terms were deemed to be below market at the time.[166] Banks could only repurchase the preference shares if they had issued enough stock of their own. The injection of public funds was not accompanied by many real restrictions on the banks. However, most of the European recapitalization schemes were "voluntary in nature," such as in the UK or Germany, where banks had to apply for government capital injections and automatic access to these programs was not possible.

164 Compare Panetta et al. (2009) for a first assessment of financial sector rescue programs.
165 See IMF (2009) for an early assessment of the effectiveness of government interventions during the financial crisis.
166 Compare Acharya and Sundram (2009) for a detailed discussion.

Moreover, major restrictions on the operations of the banks provided significant disincentives for banks to apply.

(2) In the US, unlike in the Eurozone, rescue measures were not subsequently subject to a review by the anti-trust authorities. In the eye of the storm, financial stability took priority over competition policy because of a clear recognition of the value of the positive spill-over from stronger banks on the entire sector and broader economy. This can be seen as a continuation of the policy response to the Great Depression, which led to a discontinuation of most standard competition policies in banking in order to foster financial stability. The US recapitalization program deliberately targeted the largest and most systemically relevant banks. Rescue measures erred on the side of wealth transfers to the banks. In contrast, the EU required all individual rescue programs be subject to a mandatory review by DG Competition. The rescuing government had to negotiate with DG Competition on behalf of the rescued bank over "adequate" restructuring measures and behavioral constraints, to compensate for the potential anti-competitive effects of state aid. These proceedings dragged on – not only because DG Competition was overwhelmed with requests in 2009 – and created significant uncertainty. The banks in question could not really access public equity or funding markets as long as the extent of government support was unclear, and the extent of the business they were required to restructure or sell had not been ascertained. The proceedings also led to a thinner recapitalization, as DG Competition was trying to limit state aid to the greatest extent possible, with a tacit threat to force further restructurings on the rescued bank.[167] As Beck et al. (2010), observe, where recapitalization plans were offered for "voluntary sign-up, banks that are marginally capitalized, but not under immediate threat, may not sign up, in the hope that future plans will be less restrictive."[168]

(3) As a consequence, the stress tests applied to the respective banking industries had different effects. In the US, the 2009 stress test by the Fed was tough on the largest banks if they were in the recapitalization program. In fact, the Fed used the stress test to determine when the government's preferred stock could be bought back. Only if the bank's capital base was strong

167 Compare Beck et al. (2010).

168 See Beck et al. (2010), p 53. On p 54 they go on to point out that "forcing banks that are still solvent and have received state aid to sell assets to 'compensate' for the state aid risks creating further downward pressure on some very fragile markets for banking assets." …"Similarly, trying to use the state aid vetting process as a tool to turn back the clock on bail-out decisions and force certain banks to downsize, or even liquidate, in the belief they should not really have been aided in the first place, would not only be inefficient, but also very risky."

enough was the bank allowed to buy back the preferred shares held by the Treasury. In most cases in Europe, the sequence was the reverse: the industry-wide stress tests identified holes that the banks had to close with capital increases, which were difficult to execute without backstops; going back to the sovereign was fraught with many political problems.

(4) The resulting continuation of a negative spiral of bank and supervisory forbearance exacerbated the structural problems in the European banking sector. When benchmarked with the US, "the European record before and during the crisis appears to feature a considerable degree of regulatory forbearance": national supervisors in the Eurozone area appear to have been far less inclined to shut down and liquidate distressed banks than the FDIC, which acquired a reputation for swift and efficient bank resolution.[169] Overcapacity and "zombie lenders" made it more difficult for "healthy" banks to earn their cost of capital; weakly capitalized banks and competition from "zombie lenders" that were "gambling for resurrection" are the root causes for today's banking crisis in Europe.

(5) The effectiveness of monetary easing and fiscal programs was arguably higher in the US, because they could be transmitted through a healthier and stronger banking sector to the real economy. Policy coordination proved more difficult in Europe. Lending to the real economy picked up faster in the US than in Europe.

All in all, thanks to a better policy mix and coordination with a clearer focus on restoring financial stability and repairing the balance sheets of the largest intermediaries, the US banking sector seems to be in better shape today than the European banking sector.

In summary

The failure of Lehman Brothers accelerated and spread the bank run that was going on in the unsecured interbank and Repo markets. The central banks, as lenders of last resort, could no longer stem the tide. Governments all over the world had to come to the rescue of over-leveraged financial institutions with significant funding mismatches and weak risk management. Taxpayers' money was necessary to prevent a total meltdown of the financial system and to mop up the pieces. The massive government bail-outs stabilized the system and put the global economies back on track. But they also reinforced the idea of "too-big-to-fail." The US's crisis response – despite all the ad hoc crisis management re-

169 See Pagano (2015), p 35.

quired – seemed to have been faster and more coordinated across policies with a clearer priority on financial stability.

The failures and shortcomings in the financial system that became apparent in the financial crisis subsequently triggered an unprecedented wave of regulatory and institutional reforms on both sides of the Atlantic. In Europe, even more crisis management would be required to deal with what is referred to as the "Euro Crisis." The longer term political consequences of the Great Financial Crisis, however, are only becoming evident now.

Part IV – Crisis becoming existential

Chapter 9: Early lessons drawn: shackled by principles?

"This confidence, taken for granted in well-functioning financial systems, has been lost in the present crisis, in substantial part due to its recent complexity and opacity...weak credit standards, misjudged maturity mismatches, wildly excessive use of leverage on and off-balance sheet, gaps in regulatory oversight, accounting and risk management practices that exaggerated cycles, a flawed system of credit ratings and weakness of governance."[170 171]

Group of Thirty, Consultative group on international economic and monetary affairs, January, 2009

"In spite of some progress, too much of the European Union's framework today remains seriously fragmented. The regulatory rule book itself. The European Union's supervisory structures. Its crisis mechanism."[172]

The High-Level Group on Financial Supervision in the EU, February, 2009

"I have too often observed the limits of coordination. It is a method which promotes discussion, but it does not lead to a decision."

Jean Monnet, French political economist and diplomat, quoted by Bini Smaghi, Member of the Executive Board of the ECB (2009)

In October, 2008 – while national governments and central banks on both sides of the Atlantic were acutely focused on dealing with the Great Financial Crisis, and attempting to contain the economic fallout – the EU finally began to draw some early lessons from the crisis: by addressing the supervisory fragmentation in Europe. It was recognized that the supervisory framework had "not allowed the EU to identify and/or deal with the causes of the current financial crisis"[173]. Micro-prudential regulation and supervision of banks alone had been unable to maintain financial stability, largely because it did not recognize the problem of systemic risk arising through interconnectedness and contagion.

170 Compare Group of Thirty (2009), p 13.

171 One might add the systemic maturity mismatch of the European banking sector in terms of USD as another vulnerability that was not uncovered.

172 See High-Level Group (2009), p 3.

173 See EC (2008a).

In October, 2008, the EC invited Jacques de Larosière to lead a High-Level Group of experts, which was mandated to identify the causes of the crisis in Europe and "make proposals...to establish a more efficient, integrated and sustainable European system of supervision"[174]. Let us look at the recommendations of the de Larosière Group and their implementation. And let us further investigate how reluctant government bail-outs and lengthy restructurings in Europe, shackled by state aid rules, have inadvertently strengthened the "devilish nexus" between bank and sovereign solvency, thereby paving the way for the ensuing sovereign debt crisis in the Eurozone.

The de Larosière report – a new framework for macro- and micro-prudential supervision and effective crisis management

The de Larosière report was delivered to the President of the European Commission in February, 2009.[175] It clearly identified macro-economic issues – ample liquidity, low interest rates, global imbalances, ie excess of desired savings over actual investments, increase in leverage, failures in risk assessment and management, underestimation of structured credit risk by the rating agencies, corporate governance failures, and regulatory, supervisory and crisis management failures, as causes of the Great Financial Crisis.

With regard to supervisory and crisis management failures, the report summarized its findings as follows:

> *"Taken together, these developments led, over time, to opacity and a lack of transparency. This points to serious limitations in the existing supervisory framework globally, both in a national and cross-border context. It suggests that financial supervisors frequently did not have, and in some cases, did not insist on getting, or received too late, all the relevant information on the global magnitude of excess leveraging; that they did not fully understand or evaluate the size of the risks; and that they did not seem to share their information properly with their counterparts in other Member States or with the US."*[176]

To promote financial stability in Europe, the de Larosière report recommended establishing a European system of supervision and crisis-management, consisting of a new European Systemic Risk Council (ESRC), later called the European Systemic Risk Board (ESRB), and three new European Supervisory Authorities (ESAs), one for the banking sector, the European Banking Authority

174 Compare EC (2008).
175 High-Level Group (2009).
176 See High-Level Group (2009), pp 10–11.

(EBA), one for the insurance and occupational pension sector (EIOPA)[177] and one for securities sector (European Securities and Markets Authority (ESMA)[178]. Figure 28 gives an overview of the "European Framework for Safeguarding Financial Stability" which existed at that time.

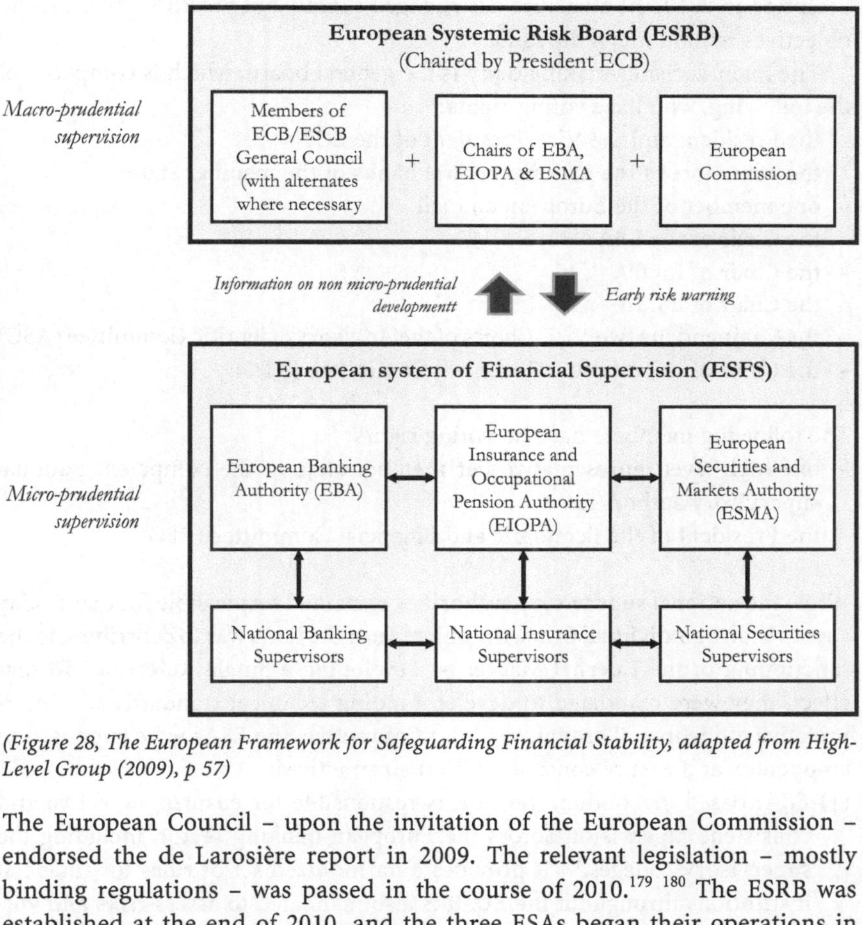

(Figure 28, The European Framework for Safeguarding Financial Stability, adapted from High-Level Group (2009), p 57)

The European Council – upon the invitation of the European Commission – endorsed the de Larosière report in 2009. The relevant legislation – mostly binding regulations – was passed in the course of 2010.[179] [180] The ESRB was established at the end of 2010, and the three ESAs began their operations in January, 2011.

The ESRB, like its US counterpart, the Financial Stability Oversight Council

177 Originally called European Insurance Authority (EIA) by the High-Level Group.

178 Originally called European Securities Authority (ESA) by the High-Level Group.

179 See Regulations (EU) Nrs 1097/2010 (ESRB), 1096/2010 (ECB, ESRB), 1093/2010 (EBA), 1094/2010 (EIOPA), 1095/2010 (ESMA) and Omnibus Directive 2017/78/EU.

180 Also, see EC (2009).

(FSOC), was, and still is, responsible for the macro-prudential oversight of the European financial system, and the prevention and mitigation of systemic risk. The ESRB makes assessments and, where appropriate, issues warnings and recommendations. The ESRB had – and still has – an advisory-and-warnings role with no legal authority and is, in fact, not even a separate legal body. Since its inception in 2010, the structure has changed slightly but the ERSB mission and objectives remain much the same.

The main decision-making body is the general board, which is composed of the following, who have voting rights:
- the President and the Vice-President of the ECB
- the governors of the national central banks of the member states
- one member of the European council
- the Chair of the EBA
- the Chair of EIOPA
- the Chair of ESMA
- the Chair and the two Vice-Chairs of the Advisory Scientific Committee (ASC)
- the Chair of the Advisory Technical Committee (ATC)

The following members have no voting rights:
- one high-level representative per member state of the competent national supervisory authorities
- the President of the Economic and Financial Committee (EFC)

While the national supervisory authorities remained responsible for day-to-day supervision of individual firms, the objective of the ESAs was to contribute to the functioning of the Internal Market by developing a Single Rulebook. To that effect, they were mandated to develop binding technical standards and interpretative guidelines. Through the Joint Committee, the ESAs were supposed to co-operate, and ensure consistency in their practices:

(1) *EBA:* based in London, the EBA is responsible for ensuring effective and consistent supervision across the European banking sector, including the supervisory colleges.[181] It provides a harmonized set of rules for financial institutions throughout the EU. It is also mandated to assess risks and vulnerabilities in the EU banking sector, including through the use of stress tests.

(2) *EIOPA:* based in Frankfurt and focuses specifically on "the protection of policyholders, pension scheme members and beneficiaries. EIOPA is commissioned to monitor and identify trends, potential risks and vulnerabilities

181 Compare EBA (2017).

stemming from the micro-prudential level, across borders and across sectors."[182]

(3) *ESMA*: which is based in Paris. In addition to its indirect supervisory powers over market participants, it also exercises direct supervisory powers over financial players with a pan-European profile such as credit rating agencies and trade repositories.[183]

The great novelty of the new supervisory structure was that the member states had managed to agree to transform the previous advisory committees – in the case of banking, the Committee of European Banking Supervisors (CEBS) – into supranational authorities, which had the legal right to bypass national supervisors and to regulate market participants directly. However, since the Supervisory Board of CEBS was composed of representatives from national supervisory authorities, it seemed unlikely from the very start that CEBS would use this authority very often.[184] Moreover, the standards and guidelines developed still needed to be separately endorsed by the European Commission. On 1st January, 2011, the EBA succeeded CEBS, taking over all of its existing and ongoing tasks and responsibilities.

At the heart of the debate at the time, was the role of the ECB in prudential supervision. Bini Smaghi (2009), and Issing (2009), both ECB board members, took opposing views on the projected role of the ECB. Bini Smaghi (2009) argued for a stronger supervisory role for the ECB, because of its institutional track-record and informational synergies between central banking and supervision.[185] Issing (2009), however, formerly on the board of the German Bundesbank and very much imbued in its conventions, warned against a stronger role for the ECB in supervision. He claimed that mandating the ECB "with micro-prudential supervision could undermine its independence" and weaken its present mandate, "which is primarily the maintenance of price stability".[186] Issing's position prevailed in the de Larosière report.

The de Larosière report was clearly a political trade-off and is – among other things – rightly criticized for:

(1) separating macro- and micro-prudential supervision;

(2) keeping the three ESAs de facto apart, despite the establishment of a joint Steering Committee; and

182 See EIOPA (2017).
183 Compare ESMA (2017).
184 Compare Donnelly (2011).
185 See Bini Smaghi (2009).
186 See Issing (2009), p 442.

(3) the lack of bank bail-out and restructuring regime cum funding at the EU level.[187]

Onado (2009) identified "seven sins of omission" regarding macro-prudential supervision in the de Larosière report:[188]

(1) *Too narrow scope of macro-prudential supervision and lack of intervention rights:* the key risks – especially systemic risk – do not come from macro-economic developments and general trends in financial markets, but from common exposures of large global banks to the same risk factors, which makes financial risk more and more endogenous.[189] This calls for a need for broader intervention rights and closer collaboration of macro- and micro-prudential supervision in the case of large global banks. This was not fully implemented in the new supervisory structure.
(2) *No responsibilities in matters of macro-prudential relevance:* the clearing and settlement infrastructure, usually the responsibility of central banks, should not (only) have been supervised by ESMA but should also have moved into the focus of the ESRB, and the ECB in particular, as it was (and remains) a potential source of financial instability itself.
(3) *Risk of important issues "falling between two stools":* there was a risk that important issues would "fall between the cracks" when macro-prudential analysis was undertaken by the ESRB, and supervision of individual banks remained with the national competent authorities.
(4) *Only advice and warnings, limited intervention rights:* the macro-prudential supervisor needed "not only a voice, but also teeth". Would warnings and recommendations for remedial action be enough? The "act or explain" mechanism would expect those warned "to act unless inaction could be adequately justified"[190]. This, and reliance on public disclosure to increase the effectiveness of warnings, was unlikely to ensure timely implementation of remedial actions.
(5) *No clear role for the ECB in terms of financial stability:* even though there were many compelling reasons why the ECB should play a leading role in macro-prudential supervision, and add financial stability to its mandate, its role in the new supervisory framework was limited. Originally, the president of the ECB did not even have a casting vote on the ESRB board (although this is now the case) and, at the time, did not have any authority vis-à-vis national supervisors.

187 See Laano (2009) and Vives (2009).
188 See Onado (2010), pp 64–69.
189 See Borio (2003).
190 See EC (2009a), p 5.

(6) *Limited independence of the ESRB:* membership of a representative of the EC (with voting power) in the ESRB, and allowing finance ministries to be represented indirectly, cast doubts on the political independence of the ESRB.

(7) *Access to information:* the ESRB did not have a clear mandate for instigating a common database for macro-prudential supervision and would have to rely on the ESAs to furnish the information needed. The ESRB would, therefore, potentially be flying blind, without even the power to define the reporting requirements for the national supervisors. In fact, as Bini Smaghi (2009) reports, supervisory authorities in some countries, such as Germany and Austria, withheld information from other European authorities on the grounds of confidentiality and data protection.[191]

Micro-prudential supervision and regulation, despite the three newly-created ESAs, remained very much fragmented, and segmented along national lines, so very much at odds with the objectives of the Internal Market and the common currency. Onado (2010) highlighted two specific issues:[192]

(1) *No explicit role for the ECB in supervision:* there was no explicit role for the ECB in micro-prudential supervision, and no other body with clear responsibility for coordinating decisions across national supervisors with respect to large cross-border banks.

(2) *No harmonization of supervision:* the de Larosière report ducked the issue by choosing a compromise which would have support from the main EU member states, but which made the decision-making process much more cumbersome, if not impossible. The ESAs had responsibility for rules and regulations, but their implementation remained the responsibility of national supervisors. In other words, supervision was not going to be fully harmonized and the ESAs had no authority to take clear decisions, especially in crisis situations.

Although the addition of a macro-prudential layer of supervision was an important step in the right direction, the ESRB solution was far from a state-of-the-art supervisory framework. And while the ESAs were clearly designed to improve the coordination of regulation and supervision in Europe, they did not provide a comprehensive "battle plan". Moreover, a comprehensive European crisis management and resolution framework was still way over the horizon. The de Larosière report lacked specificity, and the EC (2009) merely asked the European Council to "support the acceleration of work" to "strengthen the EU's

191 Compare Bini Smaghi (2009).
192 See Onado (2010), pp 67–71.

financial crisis management/resolution system".[193] Overall, the complexity of the supervisory framework had increased significantly, adding further layers (and, therefore, additional costs), without any significant benefits at the micro-prudential level. As Bande (2011), puts it, provokingly "the outcome of the reformation was again a hodgepodge of rules and responsibilities, which still leave the European institutions with little (idea) of what they can do and which leave intact the powers of the member states to take decisions."[194]

No bail-out, no restructuring – principles not upheld (for good reasons?)

The outbreak of the Great Financial Crisis also demonstrated another acute deficiency: the lack of a comprehensive crisis management framework. The EU had been pushing for financial integration for more than 20 years but had not created a commensurate crisis management framework. The ECB was the "only game in town" but could not help with solvency issues. As the de Larosière report diagnosed, "in the absence of a common framework for crisis management, member states were faced with a very difficult situation. Especially for the larger financial institutions, they had to be prepared to react quickly and pragmatically, to avoid a banking failure".[195] Fonteyne (2007), from the perspective of the IMF, had already concluded before the outbreak of the crisis, that an agreement was missing on "a credible and cost-efficient EU-level exit framework for systemic cross-border banks, supported by further harmonization and improvements in national crisis-resolution frameworks."[196]

In fact, national supervisors and national governments were left alone in dealing with their failing banks. This lack of a centralized crisis management framework, again, was not consistent with the requirements of the common currency. It led to a patchwork of ad hoc rescue plans and packages across Europe, and gave the banks in those countries, where the domestic administrations were most skillful in designing a rescue plan compatible with the European state aid framework, an advantage.

When the crisis was hitting hard, the principles of "no government intervention" and "no bail-out" could no longer be upheld. On the one hand, politicians complained about the privatization of gains and the socialization of losses, on the other hand, the financial crisis forced their hand and required

193 See EC (2009), p 16.
194 Compare Bande (2012).
195 See High-Level Group (2009), p 12.
196 Compare Fonteyne (2007), p 15.

decisive bail-out and restructuring action. In the past, national governments and politicians had relied on banks to finance economic growth, thereby helping to increase tax revenues, which in turn were needed to fund growth in government budgets. Now, the same governments – and the same politicians – under political pressure from the public, which was looking for scapegoats for the crisis, had to do a "U-turn" in their public stance towards the banks. Bank (and banker) bashing was suddenly very fashionable. This change in stance did not happen, however, without a loss in credibility for the political establishment, contributing to the rise in populism, and voter migration to the extremes, mostly to the far right of the political spectrum.[197]

When national governments began to bail out their banks, the European Commission could no longer uphold a strict ban on state aid. In fact, at its meeting in 2008, the European Council resolved that national governments could provide state guarantees to bank debt, and recapitalize banks. At the same meeting, it also endorsed a flexible interpretation of the EU's state aid framework, given the "exceptional circumstances".[198] What was the background of this unique framework? How were the underlying principles adapted during the crisis? And what was the role of the EC in the framework?

(1) *State aid framework – background:* the state aid framework is based on Article 107 (state aid control) of the Treaty on the Functioning of the European Union (TFEU) (2007). It was originally conceived to ensure a level playing field in the Single Market and prevent governments from supporting their national champions in a quest for pan-European dominance. Whilst state aid, as per Article 108 TFEU, is "incompatible with the internal market" in that it distorts competition, Article 107(2) and (3) list categories of aid that are either compatible or may be considered – by the Commission – compatible with the Internal Market.
(2) *Adaptation in the Global financial crisis:* early on, the European Commission decided that, during and after the crisis, banking rescue measures, would fall into the category of "aid…to remedy a serious disturbance in the economy of a Member State" (Article 107(3)(b) TEUF). The objective of the European Commission in the Global Financial Crisis was to strike a "balance between financial stability and competition objectives;" in other words, state aid was not forbidden, but it was limited to "the minimum necessary" to safeguard "against undue distortions of competition."[199] Although the state aid framework did not prevent government rescues per se, it posed a considerable challenge for national governments coming to the aid of their banks.

197 See Funke et al. (2015).
198 See EC (2008), p 2.
199 See EC (2009b).

The state aid framework was clearly at odds with "Crisis Management 101", which called for swift, bold action.

(3) *Role of the EC:* it is important to note that the Commission alone had – and still has – the authority to decide whether, or not, national aid is compatible with the state aid framework. It also insists on compliance with bank rescue and restructuring guidelines published in August, 2009 (!). The state aid framework, therefore, conferred extraordinary responsibility on the Commission, not only in terms of administrative discretion with regards to "compatibility of state aid", but also with regards to restructuring plans that had to be negotiated between the European Commission and the government applying for state aid approval. The European Council (after consultation with the European Parliament), did not, in fact, make use of its right under Article 109 TFEU to exempt bank rescue measures from state aid procedures altogether, and create a uniform framework.

There were two further issues with the application of the framework in the Great Financial Crisis:

(1) *Limited judicial review in the EU:* the administrative discretion of the European Commission was subject to a judicial review by the European Courts. However, the judicial review was merely limited to assessing whether the Commission has made "a manifest error of appreciation" in its economic assessment.

(2) *Lack of due process, creating significant uncertainty for stakeholders and markets:* between October, 2008 and August, 2009, the Commission published 4 successive communications on banking, in respect of (1) general principles, (2) recapitalization, (3) impaired assets and (4) restructuring aid. Although theoretically non-binding, in principle these Communications constituted an authoritative guide. They did not, however, afford "due process", as the state aid proceedings were solely conducted between the Commission and the notifying government. Representatives of the bank in question were only involved at the discretion of the Commission. Overall, the process of provisionally approving notified "rescue aid", with a final decision based on a restructuring plan that was submitted about six months later was lengthy and created significant uncertainty for both stakeholders and markets.

During the financial crisis, 20 bank debt guarantees, 15 bank recapitalization schemes, and 44 individual bank aid cases were dealt with by the EC under the state aid rules. Most member states had a national scheme. Germany and the UK had the most comprehensive national schemes, and Germany had the highest number of cases (13).[200] The total amount of state aid granted to the financial sector amounted to EUR 4.1 trillion. Only EUR 1.5 trillion, or 12.5 percent of the EU's GDP has been effectively used (see Figure 29).

	General measures	Ad hoc support	Total	Effectively used	Share	% GDP
in Euro billion	(A)	(B)	(C = A + B)	(D)	(D/C)	(D / GDP)
Debt guarantee schemes	2,747	402.8	**3,149.8**	993.6	31.5	7.9
Recapitalization	338.2	164.9	**503.1**	241.6	48.0	1.9
Support for bad asset schemes	376	54	**430**	322	74.9	2.6
Liquidity support	41.9		**41.9**	41.9	100.0	0.3
Total	**3,503.1**	**621.7**	**4,124.8**	**1,557.2**	**37.8**	**12.5**

Note: For country specific data, see European Commission (2009a)

(Figure 29: Public interventions in the EU banking sector, see CEPS (2010), Table 1, p 12, based on EC data)

All in all, the policy applied did not, in practice, result in a level playing field. On the contrary, "the end result", as the Center for European Policy Studies (CEPS) (2010) Task Force concluded, was "a more uneven playing field", and "different forms of restructuring packages, thus not necessarily only bank specific, but also country-specific". Clearly, in terms of crisis management and restructuring, there was an acute lack of a common policy framework. The state aid rules had morphed from a tool to protect competitors from unfair competition, into a tool to limit moral hazard – after the fact.

Despite the state aid restraints, bank bail-outs and restructuring put both a financial burden on national government, as well as created bail-out expectations going forward. Whilst the larger, stronger member states were hardly impacted in terms of their government debt ratings, the cost of bank bail-outs weighed heavily on the debt levels of the small, peripheral countries. The devilish credit risk link between weaker sovereigns and their banks would be at the heart of the European sovereign debt crisis that, in 2009, was looming on the horizon. But, first, let us look at the underlying dynamics of this link before we turn to the Euro crisis, which was beginning to unfold in the wake of the Great Financial Crisis of 2007–2009.

200 Numbers by mid-2010 as per CEPS (2010), pp 10–12.

...and the devilish nexus (between the sovereign and its banks)

Banks typically hold sizeable holdings of the national government bonds of their home country. At that time, the Basel regime attached a zero percent risk-weighting to OECD government bonds, regardless of their credit rating, providing a strong incentive for banks to hold such bonds, as long as there are no leverage constraints.[201] When a bank is hit by a financial crisis, it first tries to reduce its assets, to improve its liquidity position. This means a reduction in lending, which in turn leads to less investment and reduced tax revenues for the sovereign. Nevertheless, the bank will ultimately need to be bailed out by its government. This weakens the sustainability of the government debt position and impacts the value of the government bond-holdings on the bank's balance sheet, which, in turn weakens the solvency position of the bank. The "devilish nexus" is established, as banks and sovereigns will be in crisis simultaneously (see Figure 30).

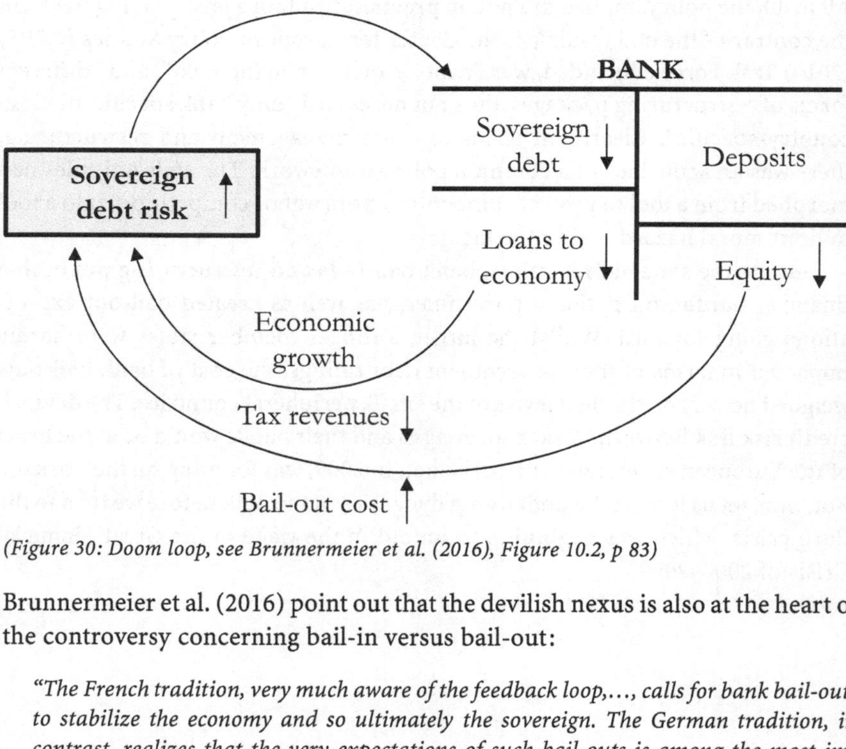

(Figure 30: Doom loop, see Brunnermeier et al. (2016), Figure 10.2, p 83)

Brunnermeier et al. (2016) point out that the devilish nexus is also at the heart of the controversy concerning bail-in versus bail-out:

> *"The French tradition, very much aware of the feedback loop,..., calls for bank bail-outs to stabilize the economy and so ultimately the sovereign. The German tradition, in contrast, realizes that the very expectations of such bail-outs is among the most im-*

201 See ESRB (2015).

portant reasons why sovereigns and banks are so closely bound together in the first place."[202]

The first EU-wide EBA bank stress-tests in 2011, shortly after the new authority had been set up, failed to detect this diabolical loop.[203] In fact, government bonds in the banking book, which is where the majority of them were held on the balance sheets of European banks, were explicitly excluded from the stress tests. Eight out of 90 banks failed the stress test – five in Spain, two in Greece and one in Austria. But several banks in the periphery such as Irish Life and Permanent or Spanish Bankia, and banks with exposure to peripheral sovereign bonds such as the Franco-Belgian Dexia passed the test, only to require a government bail-out a few months later. Consequently, the credibility of the newly-established EBA with the financial markets was immediately undermined, as the European sovereign debt crisis unfolded.

According to a later review by the European Court of auditors, the EU's banking supervisors did not have the staff or powers to successfully stress-test EU banks' resilience to financial shocks.[204] As the Internal Market Commissioner Michel Barnier commented:

"*EBA faced constraints in both available resources, and in the legal basis for the conduct of its tasks. A more pronounced increase in resources, as well as further clarifications in roles and responsibilities would enable the EBA to develop its tasks, especially around the issue of supervisory convergence…*"[205]

Europe did not seem to have learnt its lessons from the Great Financial Crisis quite yet.

In summary

Early lessons drawn from the Great Financial Crisis were incomplete in Europe, which was shackled by principles. Micro-prudential supervision was only coordinated at the level of the ESAs as national governments were unwilling to transfer supervisory authority to a central institution. Giving the ECB a bigger role in macro-prudential supervision and entrusting it with micro-prudential supervision of banks was prevented by the principle of a central bank focused solely on monetary stability. Bank bail-outs and restructurings, necessary to preserve financial stability, were held back by the state-aid framework. As a

202 See Brunnermeier et al. (2016), p 184.
203 See EBA (2011).
204 ECA (2014).
205 Barnier (2014).

consequence, bank rescues and restructurings were undertaken only half-heartedly. Nevertheless, bank rescues burdened government budgets and created the expectations of more rescues across the EU. This ultimately helped to create the devilish credit risk nexus between weaker member states and their banks, the nexus that should move to center stage in the European sequel to the Great Financial Crisis, the Euro crisis.

Chapter 10: Then come Greece and Ireland: "unnecessary, undesirable, and unlikely"[206]

"Nobody should think that another fifty years of peace and prosperity in Europe can be taken for granted. It cannot. That is why I say: if the Euro fails, Europe fails. That must not be allowed to happen."[207]

Angela Merkel, German Chancellor, 26th October, 2011

"The cost to Greece, the cost to Europe and the cost to the entire global economy may still be enough to cause Greek politicians and European politicians to pause before they pull the trigger on a Greek exit."[208]

Charles Dallara, Managing Director of the Institute of International Finance (IIF), 15th May, 2012

"...Studying the EU/IMF program... imposed on Greece in May 2010, the original sin of the crisis highlights both the nature of the problem and the difficulty in resolving it. ...Rather than help Greece, the May 2010, program was designed to protect specific political and financial interests in other member states. The ease with which the Euro was exploited to shift losses from one member state to another, and the absence of a corrective mechanism render the current framework unsustainable. In its current form, the Euro poses a threat to the European project."[209]

Athanasios Orphanides, Professor at MIT and former Governor of the Central Bank of Cyprus (2015)

As Europe was still trying to break free from its shackles and draw the appropriate lessons from the Great Financial Crisis, another crisis was looming on the horizon: the European sovereign debt crisis, in short, the "Euro Crisis". This crisis revealed the incompleteness of European monetary union, particularly the limits of the arrangements to enforce fiscal discipline at that time, and the lack of a banking union with a common crisis management mechanism. It put the spotlight on the deadly nexus that had been building up between the banks and

206 See IMF (2011), arguing that sovereign debt default in today's advanced economies is "unnecessary, undesirable, and unlikely".
207 See Merkel (2011).
208 See Dallara (2012).
209 See Orphanides (2015), p 1.

their respective sovereigns, first in Ireland, then in Spain, and later also in Portugal, Greece and Cyprus. As "money" was running for cover in the aftermath of the Great Financial Crisis, it discovered that it was no longer safe anywhere in the Eurozone: not in any bank account, nor invested in any sovereign bond. 'One money' had become 'many moneys' again – all denominated in Euros, but held in various countries and banks of different financial strengths. Capital was increasingly flowing to the largest, most systemically relevant banks, domiciled in the countries with the strongest sovereign debt ratings, thereby threatening to capsize the common currency.

Something has to give: from Greece I and European stability facilities…

In the beginning of the Great Financial Crisis, throughout 2008, and most of 2009, there was relatively little concern about European sovereign debt.[210] The focus was on the crisis management of both the ECB, which was flooding the markets with liquidity, and the respective national governments who were bailing out their banks within the cumbersome EU state-aid framework. But the financial shock of the Great Financial Crisis led to an abrupt reduction in cross-border financial flows, as liquidity was increasingly repatriated.[211] In Ireland, a banking system that had become highly dependent on the short-term commercial paper market needed to be supported by the Irish government, with an extensive two-year liability guarantee program. As the availability of cross-border funding was drying up, not only in Ireland, but also in Spain, the credit-fueled construction booms came to a sudden stop and economic activity stalled, along with prospects for tax revenues. Similarly, falling property prices resulted in large losses for the banking systems. Nevertheless, country-specific fiscal risks remained in the background at first, as both Ireland and Spain had entered the crisis with very low debt-to-GDP ratios, and sovereign spread-widening was contained. This was because (domestic) banks were continuing to hold sovereign debt as highly-rated collateral, in order to obtain access to ECB funding lines.

Towards the end of 2009, the sovereign debt crisis entered a new phase: a number of member states were beginning to report unexpectedly high deficit-to-GDP ratios. The drop in economic activity was beginning to leave its mark on the fiscal position of sovereigns. Moreover, investors were beginning to see the growing fiscal risks emanating from weak banking sectors.

210 For an overview of the Greek crisis, compare de Haan et al. (2015), pp 63–71.
211 See Lane (2012) for a detailed analysis of the European Debt Crisis.

In October, 2009, the newly elected government of Giorgos Papandreou revealed that the country had understated its debt and deficit figures for many years. It eventually became necessary for the projected budget deficit for Greece for 2009, to be revised upwards from 7 percent to 15.6 percent. These very disturbing revelations led to a significant widening of the spread of 10-year bond yields not only between Germany and Greece, but also between Germany and Ireland, Portugal, Spain and Italy (see Figure 31). In fact, the Greek spread over Bunds shot up by 300 basis points. As market sentiment further deteriorated, and concerns about economic growth and debt sustainability led to rating downgrades, first by Fitch, and then by S&P and Moody's, Greek spreads widened to almost 900 basis points in April 2010, effectively shutting Greece out of the debt markets. With an imminent roll-over crisis in sight, the Greek government had no choice but to turn to both Eurozone governments and the IMF for help.

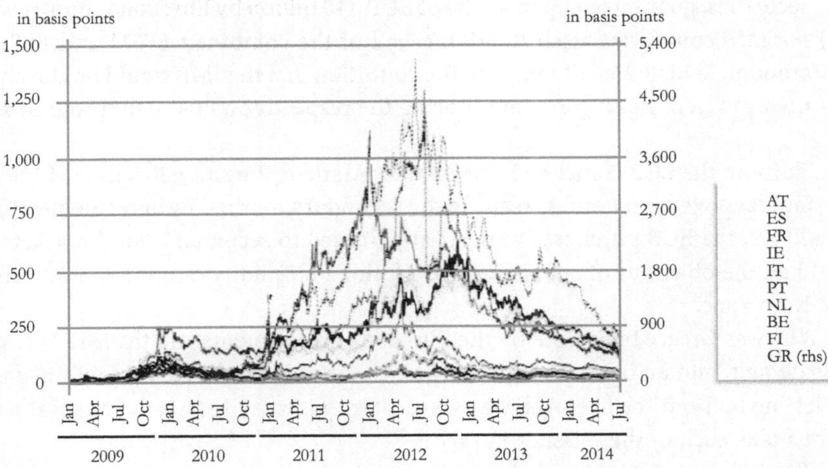

(Figure 31: 10-year government bond spreads against German Bunds, 2008–2015, compare de Haan (2015), Figure 2.6, p 63)

On 2nd May, 2010, the Eurozone countries and the IMF agreed a total rescue package (Greece I) for Greece of EUR 110 billion. The Eurozone governments agreed to provide bilateral loans totaling EUR 80 billion, to be paid out in several tranches between then and June 2013. The payout was conditional on the implementation of a fiscal adjustment program of 11 points of GDP over three years, and further structural reforms to restore competitiveness. The IMF agreed to finance an additional EUR 30 billion under a Stand-By Agreement (SBA), ie in exchange for a commitment to a structural reform program aimed at bringing the country back on the paths of financial stability and debt sustainability. The

European Commission was made responsible for both coordinating and administering the bilateral loans, including their disbursement to Greece. In spirit, at least, the "no bail-out" clause of the Maastricht Treaty had been violated.

However, this initial support for Greece proved insufficient to stabilize the markets and prevent contagion between countries. Sovereign spreads continued to widen and the Euro continued to fall against the US dollar. One week later, European leaders were forced to agree on the establishment of two additional facilities, the European Financial Stabilization Mechanism (EFSM), and a newly-created European Financial Stability Facility (EFSF); the IMF joined the two facilities with a separate commitment to complete a total package of EUR 750 billion or USD 1 trillion at the time:

(1) *the EFSM* allowed the European Commission to raise up to EUR 60 billion on behalf of the EU, to provide financial assistance to EU member states in financial difficulties.
(2) *the EFSF* set up as a limited liability company authorized to issue debt securities, guaranteed up to a total of EUR 440 billion by Eurozone countries.
(3) *the IMF* committed itself to adding half of the combined EFSM and EFSF amount, ie EUR 250 billion, with the condition that the IMF would be closely involved in designing and monitoring the respective adjustment programs.

In addition, the ECB launched its Secondary Markets Purchase Program (SMP) to stabilize sovereign bond spreads in the secondary market. By agreement with the TFEU, the ECB purchases were strictly limited to secondary bond markets, and had the objective of enhancing the depth and liquidity of bond markets in the Euro zone.

Why was Greece bailed out by the Eurozone governments and the IMF? Why was default "not an option"? Especially since the Maastricht Treaty contained a strict "no bail-out" clause? And why was austerity imposed as a strict condition? Let us take each of these issues in turn:

(1) *Fear of contagion:* essentially, Greece was bailed out because of the growing fear of contagion. Many economists, at the time, feared that a default – and subsequent debt restructuring – of Greece would further aggravate the situation not only in Portugal, Ireland, and Spain but potentially also in Italy, a situation which would ultimately overburden the financial capacities of the core Eurozone countries. Greece was also bailed out because many banks in the Eurozone had significant exposure towards Greece and other countries in the periphery (see Figure 32). The banking sector in Europe was still recovering from the losses of the Great Financial Crisis, and governments were unwilling to have to explain to the public why they had to bail out their banks yet again.

in USD million	Greece	Ireland	Italy	Portugal	Spain
Austria	104	3,193	105,097	187	5,288
Belgium	240	4,689	4,173	465	4,441
Cyprus	11,351	–	1,729	82	92
Estonia	3	–	399	–	12
Finland	2	–	1,271	59	3,014
France	1,675	15,955	41,153	7,411	28,790
Germany	5,246	62,664	266,138	3,910	58,840
Greece	–	773	4,694	10,158	1,265
Ireland	544	–	14,324	22,250	11,052
Italy	537	13,182	–	2,998	35,190
Luxembourg	7,687	3,088	28,598	2,613	8,325
Malta	382	–	890	818	166
Netherlands	4,502	5,986	25,908	13,111	19,892
Portugal	92	2,475	4,331	–	89,932
Slovakia	–	–	19,711	86	167
Slovenia	2	–	8,778	43	110
Spain	361	13,737	31,764	25,616	–

(Figure 32: Exposure of Eurozone banks to Eurozone countries, in USD million, see de Haan et al. (2015), Table 2.4, p 65)

(2) *IMF involvement:* the involvement of the IMF has been a contested issue among Eurozone governments, especially between Germany and France.[212] Involving the IMF had several advantages, including the fact that the fund followed established procedures, was well equipped, and specialized in crisis management; in other words, it brought additional firepower to the rescue operations. The involvement of the IMF also helped to "multi-lateralize" any deal, thereby taking the political tension out of the process, which was in Germany's interest. France, on the other hand, had reservations about IMF involvement, because it felt that this could create the impression that Europe was not capable of dealing with its own problems. In March 2010, after the Ecofin meeting, Germany began to actively promote the involvement of the IMF, partly because there was no trust in EU institutions to enforce adjustment, ie austerity measures. In hindsight, this was a lost opportunity to create and build up a European Monetary Fund, which would have strengthened the intra-European crisis management framework, and to maintain European sovereignty.[213]

(3) *No default and no debt restructuring:* more critical than the decision to involve the IMF both in the Greek rescue package and the financial stability architecture of the Eurozone, was the decision to provide rescue loans to Greece. Why was the route of a default, followed by debt restructuring inside the Eurozone not pursued? Obviously, the fear of contagion heavily influ-

212 See Brunnermeier et al. (2016), pp 20–24.

213 The idea of establishing a European Monetary Fund has recently been floated again by the German Ministry of Finance.

enced the decision-making process: not only in the weaker countries in the periphery, but (albeit tacitly) also in the core countries, whose banks had significant exposure to Greece and other peripheral countries (see Figure 32). As Sandbu argues convincingly, "Public and private debt restructurings could, and should, have been carried out instead, and before any rescue program."[214] Again, there was a lack of a crisis management framework – not for the banking sector this time – but for the sovereigns themselves. On the one hand, debt restructuring was the only solution in a world where there were "no bail-out" clauses, and common currency denominated debt. On the other hand, this scenario had not been provided for by the architects of the common currency. To make matters considerably worse, the prevailing Basle II regime, introduced just before the crisis, was still stipulating a zero percent risk-weighting for sovereign risk, giving the banks strong incentives to accumulate Eurozone sovereign debt, without any leverage restrictions. In other words, the Euro crisis coupled with the activation of the devilish nexus between the sovereigns and the banks was an accident waiting to happen.

All in all, Greece I and the establishment of the EFSM und EFSF proved insufficient to stabilize the market: Greece was not the only member state whose economy and banking system were negatively affected by the shock of the Great Financial Crisis.

...to Ireland (overwhelmed by a blanket guarantee)

The next domino to fall was Ireland. On 21st November, 2010, Ireland requested EU financial assistance; unlike Greece, it was not a lack of fiscal discipline and competitiveness that brought down Ireland, but a partly wholesale-funded, outsized banking sector. Let us take a more detailed look at developments in Ireland at that time.

Between 1994 and 2000, Ireland enjoyed a period of very rapid output, employment and productivity growth, establishing its reputation as the "Celtic Tiger".[215] The international recession in 2001, in the wake of the bursting of the dotcom bubble in the US, marked a turning point in the Irish economy; Ireland was particularly hard hit because a number of "dotcom" companies, exploiting low rates of corporate tax, and other economic advantages such as a relatively young workforce, had been encouraged to set up in Ireland. This enhanced economic activity was increasingly dominated by a surge in construction ac-

214 Sandbu (2015), p 266.
215 See Lane (2011).

tivity. Rising property prices, through wealth effects and rising tax revenues, fed into strong growth in private consumption and public expenditure. The growth in construction activity was fueled by a sharp increase in private credit (see Figure 33). Much of the credit boom was provided by Irish banks, which progressively funded themselves in the international wholesale markets. By 2006, there were clear signs that the property boom had passed its peak, as domestic investors were beginning to pull away from the market. Hopes for a soft landing were thwarted by turbulences in the international wholesale markets, which started to appear in 2007, and which made it increasingly difficult for Irish banks to roll over their funding. As the Great Financial Crisis was fully erupting, these developments resulted in a "triple crisis, with a severe decline in economic activity, massive losses in the banking system and rapid deterioration in the fiscal position"[216].

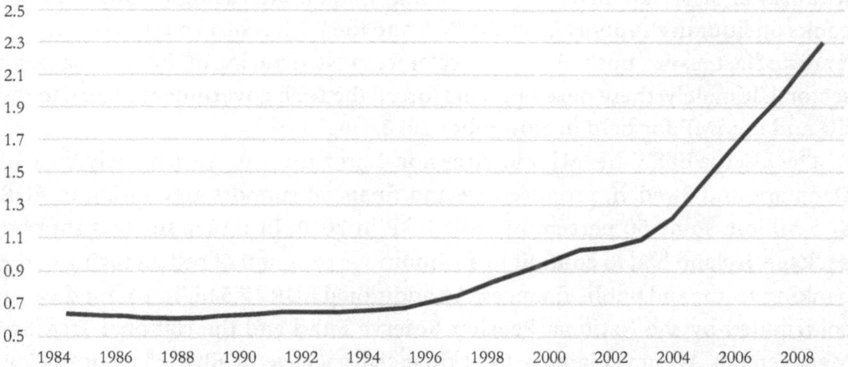

(Figure 33: Ratio of private credit to GDP in Ireland, 1984–2008, see Lane (2010), Figure 1, p 7)

As the bottom began to drop out of both the housing and the commercial real estate markets, the Irish banking sector was forced to absorb exceptional losses on mortgage lending, whilst at the same time facing a withdrawal of international wholesale funding. At this point the Irish government was forced to step in and stabilize the banking system. To alleviate the funding concerns, the government provided a two-year blanket guarantee for all deposits, senior debt and dated subordinated debt. As losses in the banking system continued to mount, the government was compelled to establish the National Asset Management Agency (NAMA), whose mandate was to buy property-related loans at market prices, ie steep discounts. This approach obliged the banks to crystallize underlying losses, and also enabled the Irish government to exclude NAMA from

216 Lane (2010), p 11.

the government debt statistics. However, under the EU state aid rules, and in accordance with the approval of the NAMA scheme by DG Competition, the discounts had to be applied on a loan-by-loan basis, resulting in significant transaction costs and a lengthy period of uncertainty. Although this "arm's length" approach had the advantage of creating transparency around the losses, it ultimately triggered even more losses in the banking system. The Bank of Ireland was the only bank which was able to raise significant new private capital; none of the other banks were successful. The Irish government was therefore forced to inject public capital into the banking sector. These capital transfers pushed the overall general government deficit to 14.5 percent of GDP in 2009, and 32 percent in 2010, triggering serious concerns about Irish public finances. The bank bail-out had proven to be a "pyrrhic victory", as it had overstretched the capacities of the Irish sovereign.[217] In addition, in September 2010, the expiry of the two-year blanket guarantee for the banking sector resulted in an increased withdrawal of private investors and, worse still, an increasing reliance of Irish banks on liquidity support from the ECB and the Irish central bank. The ECB, as lender of last resort, pushed for an accelerated restructuring of the Irish banking sector. Ultimately, these developments forced the Irish government to turn to the EU and the IMF for help in November 2010.

The EU, the EFSF, the IMF and three non-Eurozone countries, namely the UK, Denmark and Sweden, promised Ireland financial support amounting to EUR 67.5 billion, some 50 percent of Irish GDP in 2010. In return for this support package, Ireland had to commit to an ambitious program of restructuring of the banking sector and public finances. An additional EUR 17.5 billion of funds were contributed by the National Pension Reserve Fund and the National Treasury Management Agency, giving a total financial package of EUR 85 billion. How exactly was this package used?

(1) EUR 50 billion were made available to the Irish state as a funding line,
(2) EUR 10 billion were earmarked for bank restructuring, and
(3) a further EUR 25 billion were available as contingency funding, should the situation of the Irish banking system further deteriorate.

The key objective was the restructuring of the banking system through extra capital injections, more loan transfers to NAMA and loan sales to investors, as well as a further sale of non-core assets and the winding down of the Anglo-Irish Bank (AIB), and the Irish Nationwide Building Society (INBS). Subordinated bond holders had to share the burden and were not repaid in full.

All in all, unlike the Greek sovereign debt crisis, which was caused by excessive government spending and misreporting, the Irish crisis was caused by "a

217 See Acharya et al. (2014).

twin failure, with the financial regulator losing control of systemic financial risk, while fiscal policy was insufficiently counter-cyclical"[218]. When the crisis hit and financial flows shifted into reverse gear, the property bubble burst, Ireland was in no position to deal with the fallout.

...to Greece II (debt restructuring I)

The next domino to fall was Portugal. In April 2010, Portugal had to seek external financial support in the face of sluggish growth, eroding competitiveness, growing current account deficits, and pronounced credit expansion, which ultimately resulted in expanding budget deficits. The financial package agreed on 17th May, 2011, covered Portugal's financing needs up to EUR 78 billion, with EUR 26 billion coming from each of the EFSM, the EFSF and the IMF, again under strict conditionality.

At their meeting in Deauville on the French Atlantic coast in October 2010, the German chancellor Angela Merkel, and the French president Nicolas Sarkozy had agreed that, going forward, the new crisis management framework should also rely on the participation of private creditors. [219] This principle was thereafter referred to as private sector involvement (PSI). In exchange for this concession, Germany dropped its requirement for stronger ex ante controls of national budgets in the Eurozone – designed to prevent another Greece from happening. The introduction of "market-discipline" led to spread-widening in the rest of the periphery, as investors realized that Eurozone sovereign debt was not perfectly safe anymore. As a sign of mounting contagion risk, the CDS spreads of those banks which had major exposures to the so-called "PIIGS" ie Portugal, Italy, Ireland, Greece and Spain, were also rising rapidly.

Against the background of the financing needs of Ireland and Greece, and further negative developments in the periphery, the question of the size of the EFSM and EFSF moved to the forefront. The "white elephant in the room" was clearly Italy, which had over EUR 2 trillion of government debt outstanding in 2010. In June 2011, the EC finally decided to establish a permanent crisis-resolution mechanism with effect from 2013: the European Stability Mechanism (ESM). The ESM is a permanent last-resort rescue mechanism with a total lending capacity of EUR 500 billion. Whilst the EFSM had merely been a multilateral private agreement of participating states, the ESM was established as an international institution, according to Article 136 of the TFEU. Its lending capacity was augmented through participation of the IMF and non-EU countries.

218 See Lane (2011), p 31.
219 See Brunnermeier et al. (2016), Chapter 2.

During 2011, it also became obvious that Greece would require a second major rescue package. Following a further downgrade of Greece's country rating by Moody's in June 2011, market skepticism had returned: spreads of Greek sovereign debt versus Bunds once again began to exceed 800 basis points. The spreads of other countries in the Eurozone periphery also continued to widen. In mid-July, the IMF concluded that Greece's outlook "does not allow the staff to deem debt to be sustainable with high probability",[220] and ruled out a return of Greece to the international bond markets before the end of the program in 2012. At their summit in July 2011, the Eurozone countries announced several measures to alleviate the Greek debt crisis. This support was conditional on implementation of yet another austerity package and PSI. The Euro summit statement of 26th October, 2011 invited "Greece, private investors, and all parties concerned, to develop a voluntary bond exchange with a nominal discount of 50 percent on notional Greek debt held by private investors" and pledged to "contribute to the PSI package up to EUR 30 billion" as well as additional lending. On 21st February, 2012, Greece and the steering committee of 12 banks, coordinated by the Institute of International Finance (IIF), the global banking industry association, in parallel, announced to the press that a deal had been agreed.

This debt restructuring achieved significant debt relief for Greece: in fact over 50 percent of 2012 GDP, with minimal financial disruption, using a retroactive collective action clause, exceptionally large cash incentives, and official sector pressure on creditor banks in the respective countries.[221] The retroactive introduction of a collective action clause was possible because over 90 percent of the Greek debt had been issued under local law, allowing for a unilateral change in terms through a majority vote in Parliament. Hold-outs, mostly bonds issued under international law could, de facto, avoid the costly restructuring. Bonds held by the ECB were excluded from the "voluntary" debt exchange by being given a new international security number (ISIN). In the aftermath of the Greek debt restructuring, Eurozone countries agreed to issue only bonds with collective action clauses going forward, to ease future sovereign debt restructurings. After the completion of PSI, more than 60 percent of Greek sovereign debt was held by European institutions, be it the ESM or the ECB.

Even Greece II with PSI equal to a 50 percent debt relief was not enough to end the Greek drama. Amidst internal political turmoil caused by the severe austerity measures imposed by the adjustment programs, Greece fell short of achieving the required debt consolidation.

The IMF has been criticized for its involvement in the very first rescue

220 See IMF (2011a), p 30.

221 For a detailed analysis see Zettelmeyer et al. (2013).

package. Orphanides (2015), called the first rescue package "the original sin", even "a crime", committed by Germany, France and the IMF colluding to burden the Greek people with EUR 110 billion worth of debt, in order to rescue the main creditors at the time: the major German and French banks. The use of this stark rhetoric – even in academic circles – clearly demonstrates how divisive a well-intended bail-out can be.

In 2016, the Independent Evaluation Office (IEO) of the IMF published a report assessing the involvement of the IMF in the Euro crisis.[222] The report criticizes the IMF for painting too rosy a picture, and sacrificing its rigorous debt sustainability analysis on the basis of a newly-developed policy to avoid contagion. The report of the IEO shows the significant disagreement that existed at the time regarding the critical issue of debt sustainability. On the one hand, some staff members argued that "in the absence of restructuring, debt was unsustainable." On the other hand, some staff members held the view that with the right policies, and adequate financial support, Greece would be able to ensure debt sustainability without debt restructuring. This was a material division, as the internal rules of the IMF demand debt sustainability as a key requirement of an SBA of this magnitude. All in all, the IEO (2016) report concludes that "making more realistic assumptions would have materially worsened the projections of Greece's debt sustainability, but would have resulted in a more…thorough discussion of potential alternatives."[223] The IEO also concludes that the "exceptional access framework" – ultimately allowing Greece to obtain the support of the IMF without creditor burden-sharing, primarily on concerns about "systemic spill-overs" – was neither transparently introduced into the internal decision-making process nor properly analyzed.[224]

Bailing out – whom?

Greece, Portugal and Ireland were not the only member state dominos at risk of falling over: Spain and Cyprus also had to be bailed out. In both cases, the banking sector proved to be their Achilles heel. In July 2012, a EUR 100 billion program was agreed with Spain to recapitalize the ailing banking sector, which was hemorrhaging because of the bursting of a real estate price bubble. The ESM disbursed a total of EUR 41.3 billion to the Spanish government under this program. The Cypriot government also requested a bail-out in June 2012, to support its banking sector, which was grappling with its exposure to Greece. It

222 See IEO (2016).
223 See IEO (2016), p 7.
224 See IEO (2016), p 41.

was only in May 2013, that a final deal of EUR 10 billion was agreed between Cyprus, the EU and the IMF. At the time of writing, all of these member states, with the exception of Greece, have successfully exited their adjustment programs. Greece subsequently required a third rescue package of EUR 86 billion in 2015, in order to recapitalize its banking sector – after having already returned to the market with the issuance of a 5-year bond in 2014.

So, who was actually bailed out? On the face of it, the member states themselves. However, in the case of Ireland, and also of Spain, Cyprus, and later Greece, the bail-out money was, in reality, used to recapitalize the banking systems in these countries. In other words, it was the creditors of these banks, namely depositors and senior bondholders, who were bailed-out. Where bonds and deposits belonged to large insurance companies or pension funds, the bail-outs ultimately amounted to a bail-out of the insured or the pensioners thereof. All in all, the bail-out and restructuring programs amounted to a significant transfer of wealth from taxpayers to creditors and their beneficiaries. Piling up more debt and leverage on the balance sheet of the ESM (and the ECB) was politically more acceptable than writing down debt and forcing creditors to fully recognize losses. But it also meant that there is no more buffer left to absorb future financial shocks.

In summary

The "Euro crisis" was caused by a lack of fiscal discipline, diverging financial boom-bust cycles, diverging competitiveness, and the devilish nexus between sovereign debt and the banking system. Initially, politicians were reluctant to let a Eurozone sovereign default, and subsequently undergo debt restructuring. Crisis management at the European level was uncoordinated, initially relying on inter-governmental bail-out agreements, instead of building the necessary institutions and introducing market discipline right away. The bail-outs created the perception of violating the spirit (if not the substance) of the Maastricht Treaty. The IMF lost its credibility by agreeing to the first Greek bail-out. The introduction of PSI came too late. More centralized crisis management and a principled reorientation was clearly required. And banking union was needed to break the devilish nexus between the banks and sovereigns that had been at the heart of the Euro crisis.

Part V – Finishing the business, in a principled way

Chapter 11: Centralization of financial policies – if Greece (or Ireland) were Texas

"We affirm that it is imperative to break the vicious circle between banks and sovereigns."[225]

Joint Statement, Eurozone Summit on 28–29th June, 2012

"Yes Virginia, there is a European Banking Union! But it may not make your wishes come true."[226]

Martin Hellwig, German economist, (2014)

Clearly the Greek and Irish sovereign debt crises, and the corresponding fear of contagion around the Eurozone periphery, particularly in Spain, Portugal, Italy and beyond, point to deep, underlying problems in European financial architecture. The fears on the market concerning interlinkages between sovereign and bank solvency raise the question of why financial stability, financial integration, and national financial policies are not compatible. How can this trilemma be solved? Is financial disintegration, or centralization of national financial policies the answer? Moreover, despite the UK Brexit vote, as the EU obviously does not want to relinquish the benefits of financial integration, and is moving toward a centralization of financial policies, what can be learned from the experiences of the US?

Why are financial stability, financial integration, and national financial policies not compatible? The European financial trilemma

Three interlocking crises have undermined the Eurozone's financial stability:[227] a continuing economic growth crisis, a lingering sovereign debt crisis, and a protracted banking crisis (see Figure 34).

225 See Euro Area Summit (2012).
226 See Hellwig (2014).
227 Compare Shambaugh (2012) for a detailed account of Europe's three interlocking crises.

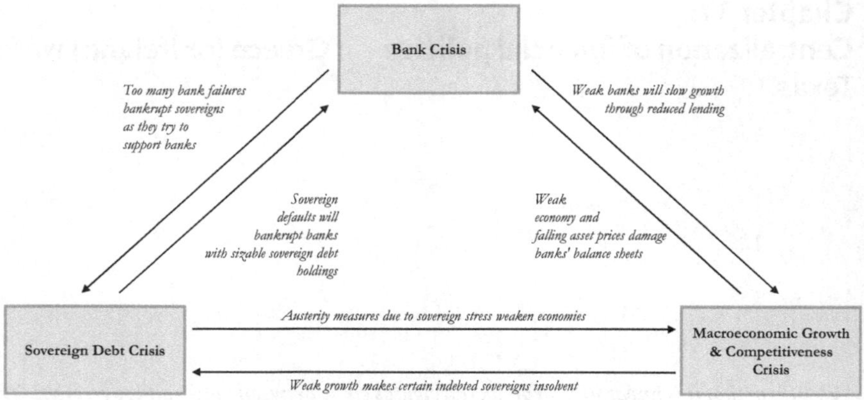

(Figure 34: Shambaugh (2012): The Euro's three crises, Figure 2, p 159)

(1) *Economic growth crisis:* the Eurozone's growth continues to be subdued, not only in the member states on the periphery (because of their cash-for-reform bail-out packages) but also in core countries such as Italy, France, and Germany. Whereas the US economy regained its 2007 GDP level in 2011, it took until April 2016, for the Eurozone to finally achieve pre-crisis GDP levels. In that month, the EU released data showing that the overall economy of the 19 Eurozone countries rose by 0.6 percent in the first quarter of the year, compared with Q4 2015. Since 2009, the US unemployment rate has followed a downward path, which has taken it to 4.3 percent at the end of 2015, whilst for the Eurozone the unemployment rate was still 10.9 percent. At the same time, the unemployment rate for the EU, ie the 28 member states, was substantially lower at 9.4 percent, due to the fact that unemployment decreased more rapidly in the non-Eurozone countries after the financial crisis. Youth (ie less than 25 years old) unemployment in the US at the end of 2015 stood at 11.6 percent, considerably less than the 22.4 percent average for the Eurozone countries, and the 20.3 percent for the 28 EU member states. However, the latter averages for 2015 are misleading: some of the member states on the periphery eg Greece and Spain were experiencing youth unemployment levels of considerably in excess of 40 percent. In Greece, the 2015 figure was 49.8 percent, for Spain 48.3 percent. Even in Italy, the ratio of young people out of work was 40.3 percent.[228]

(2) *Sovereign debt crisis:* the sovereign bond markets for debt in the peripheral countries came under pressure after the 2008 Euro-area recession. The poor growth prospects obviously added to the pressures in peripheral sovereign bond markets and led to increases in the yields and spreads over Bunds,

228 See Eurostat (2017) and Eurostat (2017a).

Germany' s sovereign debt. In fact, ever since the debt markets began anticipating a sell-off in sovereign debt at the end of 2008 (primarily by the two large-but-troubled public sector lenders HRE and Dexia), and Greece had surprised the market with serial revisions of the primary deficit in 2009, levels of sovereign spreads in the peripheral countries have remained elevated.

(3) *Banking crisis:* weak, outsized banking systems have added to the woes of the sovereign debt markets. Europe's economy is much more bank-based than the US economy. The Eurozone's largest banks are also larger relative to their home country's GDP than their US counterparts. This is mainly because they are more active both inside and outside the Eurozone, both in terms of asset and loan origination as well as funding. As the subprime bubble burst, and the run in the interbank and Repo markets started to gain momentum after the Lehman failure, the Eurozone's banks were hit hard by the crisis.

The Euro crisis exposed additional issues in the banking sectors of the periphery.[229] In Greece, ever since sovereign spreads began to widen, with rising levels of public debt, the banks were confronted with a depositor bank run at various speeds. In Ireland, the overexposure to domestic real estate that had been built up during the boom weighed heavily on the banking sector and ultimately forced the government's hands. [230] When a weak Ireland had to bail out Anglo Irish at the end of 2009, the markets finally realized that weak sovereigns and their insolvent banks "had become joined at the hip." Spreads for sovereign and bank debt across Europe started to move in tandem.[231] "Not only did financial sector stress raise sovereign spreads as before, but now sovereign weakness was being transmitted to the financial sector."[232]

In the cases of Greece and Ireland, the sovereign could not come up with the funding needed to bail out its banks. In Greece, the sovereign debt level was too high for debt market access. In Ireland, the outsized banking sector and its problems were ultimately too big for a sovereign which, up to the Great Financial Crisis, had been a poster child for the Eurozone's economic integration. With the help of the ESM and its precursor, the EFSF, as well as the IMF, the sovereigns (and indirectly the banks) in both member states were bailed out, not only for the benefit of their domestic economies, but also to avoid negative spill-over effects into the Eurozone's other banking sectors, which were weak and over-

229 See Blundell-Wignall and Slovik (2011) for "A Market Perspective on the European Sovereign Debt and Banking Crisis".
230 Compare Lane (2011) for an analysis of the Irish crisis.
231 See Mody and Sandri (2011) for an analysis for bank and sovereign spread movements in Europe during the financial crisis.
232 Compare Mody and Sandri (2012), p 4.

Exposure of banks of the area/country to the financial instruments shown in the column

	in USD million	All countries banks	Of which … European banks	German banks	French banks	Spanish banks	Italian banks	Non-EU banks	US banks
Greece	Sovereign	39,027	36,578	12,411	10,686	462	1,871	2,449	2,321
	Banks	9,692	6,696	1,842	1,583	28	191	2,996	2,487
	Non bank priv.	82,307	77,439	7,119	43,470	665	1,666	4,868	3,547
	Guarantees incl. CDS	48,580	10,057	3,106	4,411	27	355	38,523	38,460
Portugal	Sovereign	32,106	29,896	8,978	6,153	7,138	509	2,210	1,144
	Banks	36,306	33,609	12,554	6,170	5,050	1,867	2,697	2,250
	Non bank priv.	136,036	133,145	14,320	13,339	76,295	1,556	2,891	1,856
	Guarantees incl. CDS	72,838	25,778	15,628	489	5,883	1,076	47,060	46,891
Ireland	Sovereign	16,753	13,522	3,470	2,896	163	584	3,231	1,898
	Banks	78,066	63,202	21,532	9,841	1,174	4,402	14,864	11,730
	Non bank priv.	371,154	302,263	85,507	19,278	7,874	9,857	68,886	39,960
	Guarantees incl. CDS	89,935	41,869	14,852	18,453	560	3,120	48,066	46,062
France	Sovereign	254,979	173,331	31,373	–	6,610	2,420	81,648	24,927
	Banks	701,894	456,894	116,084	–	10,906	30,322	245,000	191,557
	Non bank priv.	394583	290,961	75,828	–	15,271	17,821	103,622	55,196
	Guarantees incl. CDS	477,036	120,999	35,166	–	3,550	5,349	356,037	347,166
Spain	Sovereign	106,581	86,523	29,454	30,492	–	6,394	20,058	7,633
	Banks	227,536	192,471	69,144	38,616	–	6,722	35,065	28,375
	Non bank priv.	407,573	363,969	78,867	81,784	–	16,860	43,604	30,765
	Guarantees incl. CDS	206,379	56,701	34,757	8,273	–	2,314	149,678	148,848
Italy	Sovereign	288,732	237,322	47,624	106,764	11,173	–	51,410	12,891
	Banks	164,087	138,705	48,338	44,657	4,240	–	25,382	19,110
	Non bank priv.	485,218	460,433	65,795	264,952	24,351	–	24,785	14,898
	Guarantees incl. CDS	329,403	89,001	47,045	23,367	7,092	–	240,402	237,581
Totals for above 6 countries	Sovereign	738,178	577,172	133,310				161,006	50,814
	Banks	1,207,889	884,881	267,652				323,008	253,022
	Non bank priv.	1,794,564	1,550,776	320,317				243,788	142,675
	Guarantees incl. CDS	1,224,171	344,405	150,554				879,766	865,008

(Figure 35: Cross-border exposure of banks, see Blundell-Wignall (2012), Table 3, p 13)

exposed to peripheral debt (see Figure 35). As a consequence of the recapitalization of the banks, the sovereigns were left with higher debt levels to the ESM.

This reliance on the government of the member state where the bank is located is different from the policy in the US, where the specific state location is not the determinant of who bears the costs. Bank regulation and supervision in the US take place at the national level through the Fed and the Office of Financial Stability (OFS). Bank restructuring and resolution are undertaken through the FDIC, which is backed by a credit line from the US Treasury. In addition, bail-out policies and programs, such as the 2008 TARP, were both designed and funded at the national level. In fact, Texas would not have been able to deal with its banking crisis in the 1980s: the FDIC facilitated most of its bank restructuring.[233]

The Irish crisis clearly demonstrated a "fundamental inconsistency in European monetary and financial architecture: the singleness of money and financial markets, on the one hand, and the fragmentation, along national lines, of banking supervision and banking safety nets, on the other hand."[234] At the heart of this inconsistency was the financial trilemma, namely the incompatibility of the objectives of financial stability, financial integration, and national financial policies in the Eurozone.[235] The famous monetary trilemma states that a fixed exchange rate, capital mobility and national monetary policy cannot be achieved simultaneously: only two of the three objectives can be successfully combined because financial stability is clearly a public good that benefits not only the home country but – depending on the depth of financial integration – has spill-over effects into other economies of the Eurozone. The European Currency Union resolved the trilemma with the introduction of the Euro monetary system.

For smaller countries with outsized banking systems, the national benefits of a bank bail-out may be smaller than the costs, and the benefits of the bail-out may be larger in other member states. National financial policies and financial stability are achievable if there is little, or no, financial integration. But when more financial integration and national financial policies are combined, financial stability across the Eurozone can no longer be guaranteed. To restore financial stability in the Eurozone the policy choice was now clear: give up on financial integration, or centralize financial policies, at least for the banks (see Figure 36).

233 See O'Keefe (1990).

234 Compare Angeloni (2012), p 10.

235 See Schoenmaker (2011) for a comprehensive and formal analysis of the European financial trilemma.

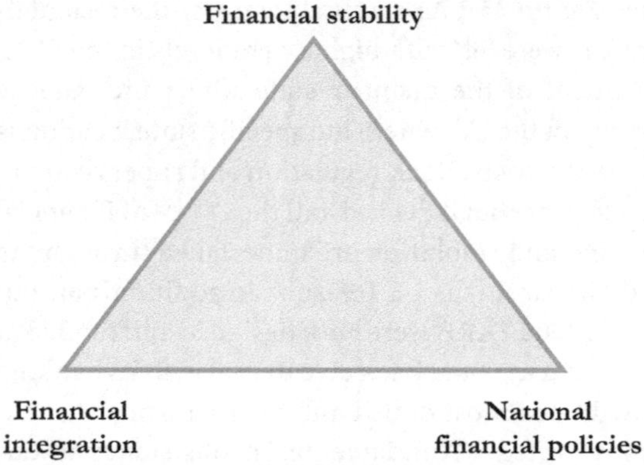

(Figure 36: The financial trilemma, Schoenmaker (2011), p 58, Fig. 1)

Financial disintegration or centralization of national financial policies? Towards a Banking Union for financial stability in Europe

What was happening in the Eurozone in the immediate aftermath of the Great Financial Crisis – and at the outbreak of the Euro crisis – was, to a certain degree, financial disintegration. Banks were deleveraging, particularly with respect to their exposure to the member states in the periphery. Cross-border deposit and lending flows were slowing down, especially from the non-distressed to the distressed countries[236], as banking supervisors in non-distressed countries began to limit cross-border deposit flows into peripheral countries within banking groups. A case in point is the Italian banking group, UniCredit, whose wholly-owned German subsidiary, HVB, began facing regulatory restrictions in terms of depositing capital with its parent, UniCredit SpA, in Italy.

This financial disintegration was happening at a point in time when cross-border flows into the periphery to spur lending and investments were most needed, resulting in a more "national" approach: financial disintegration in the form of subsidiaries and nationalism destroys intra-group banking synergies. Plus, the home country supervises the local banks, whereas the host country supervisors would look after the foreign subsidiaries, resulting in disparities in approach within the group. Additionally, there is no reaping of the benefits of financial integration, such as more efficient capital allocation, more risk-sharing, and stronger governance resulting in higher levels of investment and growth.

236 Compare ECB (2015), pp 27–35.

The centralization of national financial policies is, of course, the other option. This means moving the authority for financial policy – regulation, supervision, and bank restructuring – to the supranational European level: centralizing it, in fact – not unlike monetary policy in the common currency area. This centralization would make financial integration in the Eurozone more sustainable. In the future, banks in Greece, Ireland and Europe would be treated in the same way as the banks in Texas were treated by the US federal institutions in the 1980s. And the banking crises in those member states would not affect the credit rating of their sovereigns.

However, centralization alone is not sufficient to break the circular feedback loop between the sovereign and its banks. The Eurozone also needs to:

(1) provide regulatory incentives for removing large sovereign debt exposures from banks' balance sheets[237],
(2) the central supervisor needs to be independent enough to break with the pattern of national supervisory forbearance,
(3) a harmonization of fundamental national laws needs to be able to effectively sanction banks' misconduct and regulatory breaches, and
(4) there needs to be a large enough centralized backstop for a common European deposit insurance scheme to work as efficiently as the FDIC in policing bank and supervisory forbearance and closing down "zombie" banks, shored up by explicit or implicit government support.

If arrangements in the US had been similar to those in the Eurozone, the state of Washington would have to bear the fiscal burden when Washington Mutual collapsed with nearly USD 200 billion in deposits. Similarly, if Greece or Ireland had been Texas, a federal-level authority like the FDIC, with bank resolution powers, would have dealt with the crisis. So, what in the US regulatory and supervisory system might work for Europe going forward?[238]

What we can learn from the US in terms of centralized financial policies?

Before tracing the development of the institutional framework in the US, we must examine the 1980s, and the Texas banking crisis. The distinguishing feature of the history of banking in the 1980s was the extraordinary increase in the

237 See the recent Dutch proposal at the EU level to deal with this problem by either introducing risk-weights or limiting the exposure size relative to a bank's regulatory capital.
238 An excellent overview of the history of bank regulation in the US is provided by Barth et al. (2009).

number of bank failures in the US. Between 1980 and 1994, more than 1,600 banks insured by the FDIC were closed down or received financial assistance. The banking collapse in the period was concentrated in the southwestern states of the US, and it was particularly devastating to Texas's banking industry. Between 1980 and 1989, 425 Texas commercial banks failed, including nine of the state's ten largest holding companies. The failure of the Texas banks accelerated when the domestic energy and commercial real-estate markets experienced dramatic declines after 1985. Today, Texas, the second largest economy of the 51 US states (after California, and ahead of New York) is left without a major local bank. Comerica, which is headquartered in Dallas, is the result of the acquisition and merging of failed Texan banks in the 1980s by a group of Michigan banks. However, it is only the 14th largest US bank, as measured by the size of its balance sheet. If Greece or Ireland was Texas, a European agency, ex ante, funded by contributions from all European banks, would have restructured the banks in the two countries. Like the state of Texas, Greece and Ireland would not have had to carry the burden of their failing banking systems alone.[239]

The development of the institutional framework in the US is characterized by increasing centralization, and waves of post-crisis regulation and deregulation. After the federal charters of both The First and The Second Bank of the United States were not renewed in 1811 and 1836 respectively, the federal government was completely out of the bank chartering and regulation business, leaving it, until the Civil War, to the states themselves. Bank regulations varied greatly across different states. In addition to commercial banks, mutual savings banks[240], Savings & Loans (S&Ls)[241], and credit unions[242] – collectively sometimes also referred to as thrifts – were chartered at the state level.

Because the Civil War created great demands on the Union government to finance the war against the Southern states, Congress passed the National Currency and Bank Act of 1863–1864. This act created a new department in the

239 It is important to recall that the Savings & Loan industry suffered an even greater catastrophe in the US during this timeframe. During the 1980–1994 period, approximately 1,300 thrifts failed, leading to the demise of the FFDISL (the equivalent of the FDIC for the thrift industry) and imposed heavy costs on surviving institutions and on taxpayers, but not on the home states of the S&Ls.

240 The first mutual savings bank, the Philadelphia Savings Fund Society, was established in 1816 primarily to fill the gap left by commercial banks that avoided mortgages and smaller term deposits.

241 The Savings & Loan also started in Philadelphia. The first one, Oxford Provident Building Association, was formed in 1831. They also focussed initially on providing mortgages and savings accounts to the growing urban population.

242 Credit unions were only started in 1909, when the first union was chartered in New Hampshire. They are non-profit institutions and enjoy tax advantages over other depository institutions that allow them to charge lower interest rates on mortgages and offer higher rates on deposits.

Treasury, the Office of the Comptroller of the Currency (OCC). The OCC had the authority to charter national banks that could issue uniform currency backed by US government bonds, which made the currency superior to the currencies issued by state chartered banks. The creation of the OCC lead to a unique dual banking system, where banks could choose between a national or a state charter. This inevitably led to competition among regulators, who tried to get banks under their control by offering laxer regulation.

As the banking system in the US expanded rapidly after the end of the Civil War, the US suffered several economic downturns accompanied by numerous bank runs. The larger banks were called to the rescue of smaller banks in distress. After almost half a century of recurring banking panics, the severe panic of 1907 led to the establishment, in 1913, of the Fed as a "lender of last resort." It was modeled, to a certain degree, after the Bank of England, whose role as lender of last resort had been successful in preventing bank runs in the UK in the second half of the nineteenth century, and the beginning of the twentieth.

The next important changes to the institutional landscape took place after the Great Depression. Legislation enacted in 1933, led to the strengthening of the independence of the Fed and, most importantly, to the creation of the FDIC, which was set up to restore consumer confidence in a banking system that had been shaken by numerous bank runs. The Fed was given more independence from the executive branch, and the authority of the seven governors, particularly the chairman, was increased. The FDIC restored confidence, and reduced the incentive to "run", by providing deposit insurance, initially up to USD 2,500 per deposit. All banks paid a flat rate fee to cover the insurance premiums. Over time, the government increased the deposit insurance to USD 100,000 (before the Great Financial Crisis) and USD 250,000 afterwards. Fees are now differentiated based on the riskiness of the bank, to prevent moral hazard. Bank branching across state-lines remained, however, prohibited – even for national banks.

The National Banking Act of 1933 called for the separation of commercial banking from investment banking. This act is better known as the Glass-Steagall Act, after the two congressmen who framed the legislation. The lines between banking and securities services had blurred in the wake of lax rulings by the OCC, that had allowed national banks to engage in investment banking. The Securities and Exchange Commission (SEC) was created as the new body to oversee the investment banking activities of the broker dealers.

The last major restriction imposed in the 1930s was an interest rate ceiling. Regulation Q of 1937, gave the Fed the authority to impose interest rate ceilings to protect banks from excessive competition. In 1966, these ceilings were also extended to S&Ls, savings banks and credit unions. The banking literature argues that interest ceilings paved the way for more disintermediation of banks and thrifts. When market rates rose far above the ceiling, (even after the ceiling had been adjusted upward) in the high inflation period of the 1970s and 1980s, depositors migrated to higher yielding money market funds, and banks began to obtain funds through commercial paper, Eurodollar deposits and on the Repo markets. To counter the outflow of funds, regulators were forced to create the 6-month "certificate of deposit" with an interest rate pegged to the Treasury bill. Interest rate ceilings were eventually removed except for demand deposits.

Until the 1930s, the government had limited the thrift institutions' geographic expansion. In 1933 and 1934, the government allowed S&Ls and credit unions to obtain federal charters as well. This only became possible for savings banks in 1978.

An important regulatory gap had occurred with the creation of one-bank holding companies, which were exempt from Fed supervision. These holding companies were used to expand into non-banking activities or to buy banks in other states, which was otherwise not allowed. The Bank Holding Act of 1970 closed this gap, and gave the Fed responsibility for defining appropriate non-bank activities for bank holding companies. All non-permissible activities had to be divested by 1980.

The International Banking Act of 1978, made sure that international banks active in the US were treated on a par with national banks. The Depository Institutions Deregulation and Monetary Control Act (DIDMCA) of 1980 finally phased out the interest rate ceiling, and eliminated state usury ceilings on mortgages. The act subjected all transaction accounts to the Fed's reserve requirements. It also gave thrift institutions greater leeway on the asset side; the lines between the different types of depository institutions were blurring.

The crisis of the 1980s and early 1990s, including the banking crisis in Texas, resulted in two important changes. Firstly, with banks and S&Ls confined to single states, regulators could not find enough banks to take over failed institutions and reduce resolution costs. For this reason, in the early 1980s, the government began to permit interstate acquisition of distressed institutions. This permission was the only way for large institutions to expand their activities until further deregulation took place in the 1990s. Secondly, and more importantly, the Federal Deposit Insurance Corporation Improvement Act (FDICIA), which Congress passed in 1991, encouraged banks to measure and manage risk more precisely and allowed the FDIC to take prompt corrective action in the fight against bank forbearance.

The 1990s were characterized by the deregulation of banking. The Riegle-Neal Interstate Banking Act of 1994, effectively repealed the McFadden Act of 1927, and allowed interstate banking – initially for bank holding companies, and later for banks. The 1999 Graham-Leach-Bliley Act, repealed the Glass-Steagall Act and parts of the Bank Holding Act, allowing for investment banking, commercial banking, and insurance activities to be combined in one financial holding structure. Both pieces of legislation triggered a wave of significant consolidation in the US, and accelerated the movement towards a financial market-based economy. They also led to an increase in the complexity of large financial conglomerates and banking groups.

The Great Financial Crisis of 2007–2009 exposed significant gaps in US financial architecture. As the importance of financial markets had increased, it became obvious that the Fed lacked the necessary tools to effectively deal with bank-like runs in the financial markets. Parts of the financial institutions were not supervised, as the case of AIG had clearly demonstrated. Systemic risk across markets and institutions had not been monitored properly in the run up to crisis. This insight led to the establishment of the Financial Stability Oversight Council (FSOC). Large, systemically-important financial institutions would henceforth be subject to a more stringent regulatory regime, and a dedicated restructuring regime.

When we reflect on optimal financial policies for the Eurozone, what are the relevant conclusions from our journey through the history of banking regulation in the US?

(1) Centralized deposit insurance, plus the ability to resolve and shut down banks, helped the US to deal with the regional and state banking crises of the 1980s, and early 1990s. In fact, interstate transfers are less politicized if done centrally as opposed to bilaterally.
(2) Most crises led to a strengthening of the role of the federal (that is to say, central) level.
(3) Financial integration in the US was only made possible with the deregulation of banking in the 1990s. Although financial policies were centralized at that time, the next financial crisis could not be avoided. In fact, given the level of financial integration and global financialization, it spread across the entire country and beyond.
(4) With Dodd-Frank, the regulatory response to the crisis has been comprehensive, adding systemic oversight, and a special regulatory regime for large and complex financial institutions, making the US financial system safer – for now, at least.[243]

243 See Acharya et al. (2011) for a complete review of the Dodd-Frank Act. The Trump administration is currently considering the repeal of significant parts of the Dodd-Frank Act.

In summary

The Great Financial Crisis exposed significant weaknesses in Europe's financial architecture. National financial policies proved incompatible with financial stability and financial integration in the Eurozone. In the case of a serious banking crisis, as Ireland shows, lack of a centralized rescue mechanism pushes the sovereign into a debt crisis. The Greek crisis demonstrates how an over-indebted sovereign and a collapsing economy can affect the banking system, and how the negative feedback loop is reinforced if the banks hold significant amounts of sovereign debt. If we do not want to give up the benefits of financial integration in Europe, we must centralize financial policies. Looking at the US and the Texas banking crisis of the 1980s, we can learn important lessons for the design of optimal financial policies both for the Eurozone, and the framework of a Banking Union.

Chapter 12: Blueprints, optimal policies to choose from

"In all that people can individually do well for themselves government ought not to interfere"[244]

Abraham Lincoln, President of the United States of America, (1854)

"Since the onset of the global financial crisis, we have developed and begun implementing sweeping reforms to tackle the root causes of the crisis and transform the system for global financial regulation"[245]

G-20 Leaders Statement: The Pittsburgh Summit, 25th September, 2009

Banking regulation and supervision in Europe obviously shielded neither European banks, nor Europe itself from the effect of the global financial crisis, and the subsequent European debt crisis. The protracted weakness of European banks has held back economic recovery in the EU. As we go back to the drawing board, we need to ask ourselves how we can avoid the mistakes of the past. What should the regulation of financial institutions look like going forward? Given the massive interventions of central banks and governments, how can we contain moral hazard going forward, and firmly re-establish the link between liability and responsibility? How can we change the framework of financial markets for both wholesale bank debt and government debt from ex ante implicit guarantees and ex post bail-outs, to credible bail-in threats? And what role should policies on state aid and competition play in European banking going forward? In this regard, specifically, what is the trade-off between the efficiency of the financial system and its stability? And last, but not least, have we done enough, or do we need structural reforms in the style of the US Glass-Steagall Banking Act?

244 See Lincoln (1854).
245 See G20 (2009), p 5.

What should the regulation of financial institutions look like? Going back to the drawing board

The Great Financial Crisis exposed many significant weaknesses in the financial system, such as the regulation of banks. The regulation of banks in Europe had slavishly followed the Basel II accord, which had been developed by the BCBS between 1999 and 2004, and introduced in the EU in 2008.[246] The shortcomings of the regulatory framework were well known beforehand. As Danielsson et al. (2001) summarize in their 2001 "Academic Response to Basel II": "Perhaps our most serious concern is that these proposals, taken altogether, will enhance both the pro-cyclicality of regulation and the susceptibility of the financial system to systemic crises, thus negating the central purpose of the whole exercise." And they forcefully add: "Reconsider before it is too late",[247] as if they already knew that they would not be listened to, but re-read after a financial crisis. Danielsson and his colleagues expressly refer to the following shortcomings of the Basel II framework:

(1) *Endogenous risk:* the Basel II framework treats risk as exogenous, whereas at the level of the financial system it is endogenous, that is, not only emanating from external shocks, but strongly influenced by the actual trading, lending, and herding behaviors of financial institutions themselves. In this regard, Danielsson et al., (2001), note that "Value-at-Risk", or VaR, measure that uses a loss history to forecast future losses can destabilize an economy and induce crashes when they would not otherwise occur.[248] "The market outcome changes if everybody moves in the same direction – euphoria and risk-taking on the way up and depression and risk-aversion on the way down – and this is amplifying the financial cycle."

(2) *Limitations of risk models:* the statistical models used in the Basel framework are not reliable. In particular, they are "under-estimating the joint downside risk of different assets," that is, the contagion and correlation experienced in the recent financial crisis across most markets. Such critical correlations are even more difficult to forecast.

(3) *Reliance on rating agencies:* governments need to reconsider their reliance on rating agencies in the Basel II framework, because the agencies are providing conflicting and inconsistent forecasts of individual clients' creditworthiness. One flaw that Danielsson et al. note is the fact that unrated firms receive a lower risk-weight (100 percent in the standardized approach) than firms below BB- (at 150 percent), which creates incentives for risky

246 See BCBS (2004).
247 Compare Danielsson, Embrechts, Godhart, Keating, Mueenich, Renault, Shin (2001), p 5.
248 See Danielsson et al. (2001), p 3.

firms to forego ratings altogether. In addition, ratings are, for the most part, inconsistent across agencies, types of issuer and time; most importantly, they lag market developments.

(4) *Capital charge for operational risk:* the BCBS has not made a convincing argument for capital requirements for operational risk. Thus, banks perceive the requirements as a way "merely to provide a cumulative add-on factor to the capital charge, that may have fallen as a result of the increased use of internal rating based-calculated market- and credit risk weightings." The charge has done nothing to improve operational risk management within banks, which should have been the desired outcome.

(5) *Supervisory discretion:* the Pillar II Supervisory Review Process leaves room for supervisory discretion, thereby opening the door for bank and supervisory forbearance and posing risks to a level playing field.

In summary, Danielsson et al. (2001) maintained that Basel II is inherently pro-cyclical and, as such, will not reduce the likelihood of systemic crises: the Great Financial Crisis of 2007–2009 proved them right. In the run-up to the financial crisis the regulatory framework proved to be very pro-cyclical, in that it allowed the build-up of significant leverage coupled with large funding maturity mismatches. The long intermediation chains, involving complex originations and off balance sheet investment vehicles, led to a decline in transparency and trust. This decline made European banks vulnerable to a bank run. When the music stopped, and the storm hit, there were significant shortages in liquidity, funding and, ultimately, loss-absorbing capital.

In the subsequent Euro sovereign-debt crisis, the large exposures to Eurozone sovereign debt made banks vulnerable to a deterioration in sovereign credit. In addition, the idea of "too-big-to-fail", that was reinforced by massive government interventions in 2008 and 2009, made sovereign credit vulnerable to weaknesses in banks' balance sheets – thereby creating the infamous "doom-loop."[249]

The new Basel III framework has addressed several key weaknesses in Basel II that the financial crisis and the Euro crisis exposed: specifically, Basel III has introduced more stringent regulation on capital, and new regulations on liquidity and funding:[250]

(1) *Increasing capital requirements:* During the Great Financial Crisis, bank supervisors realized that subordinated capital securities, that counted as regulatory capital, were not able to absorb losses on a going-concern basis: only in the case of a bankruptcy of the bank did holders of subordinated debt

249 See Haldane and Alessandri (2009).
250 See BCBS (2011, 2013, 2014).

face losses. However, this scenario was exactly the type of moral hazard that governments and supervisors were seeking to avoid.[251] Basel III, therefore, attempts to increase the loss-absorbing capacity of capital securities. This change has a much larger emphasis on common equity, with less emphasis on Tier 2 and upper Tier 1 securities.[252] Moreover, supervisors – once they have established that a bank has reached the point of non-viability – can now convert these new additional Tier 1 and Tier 2 securities into equity or reduce their value (a so-called haircut). The calculation of risk-weighted assets for the banking book follows the Basel II approach. The risk-weighting of assets in the trading book (dubbed Basel II.5) had already been changed in 2009, and had led to a significant increase in the capital requirements for trading book assets. These requirements reduced the incentives for moving assets from the banking book to the trading book. Basel III's capital rules also involve a triple hurdle:

a. the minimum requirement remains at 8 percent, but now has a built-in minimum of 4.5 percentage points of Tier 1 common equity;
b. there is a capital conservation buffer of 2.5 percentage points, which means that the bank will remain under close watch by the supervisor between the 8 percent and 10.5 percent capital ratios;
c. a second additional buffer of 2.5 percentage points of Tier 1 capital corrects for the pro-cyclicality of Basel II by giving the supervisor the discretion to demand higher capital buffers in upswings of the business cycle;
d. the introduction of IFRS 9, a new accounting standard for loans, should also help to reduce the pro-cyclicality of regulatory accounting by forcing banks to recognize expected losses over the lifetime of a loan once the credit quality deteriorates;[253]
e. additionally, Basel III imposes a capital surcharge on global, systemically-important banks (G-SIBs), that ranges from 1 to 3.5 percent based on the degree of systemic relevance of the institution.[254]

251 The EU Commission tried to correct this shortcoming in the state aid proceedings.

252 Basel III hardens the definition of capital by deducting goodwill and capping the reliance on deferred tax assets, mortgage servicing rights, and investments in other financial institutions at 15 percent of tier 1 capital.

253 Only in "stage 2" are "expected losses over the lifetime of the loan" required to be recognized according to IFRS 9.

254 See BCBS (2013a), p 6, table 1 for an overview of the indicator-based measurement approach that comprises five equally weighted categories; namely, cross-jurisdictional activity, size, interconnectedness, substitutability, financial institution infrastructure, and complexity.

Taken together, these measures mean that banks must potentially hold 16.5 percent of capital. Basel III allows the new capital requirements to be phased in by 2019 (see Figure 37).

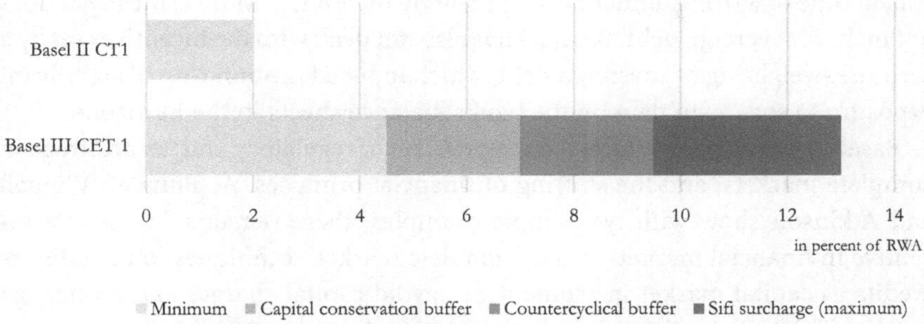

(Figure 37: Basel III capital regulations, see Huertas (2014), p 22)

(2) *Introducing an un-weighted leverage ratio as a backstop:* before the crisis, banks had been able to arbitrage the Basel system by holding assets with a reported low probability of default. This arbitrage led to a significant build-up of leverage in the system and made the banks more vulnerable to smaller losses and bank runs. For this reason, and to put a lid on gaming behavior, Basel III has also introduced an un-weighted leverage ratio requirement of at least 3 percent.[255] The leverage ratio also includes certain off balance sheet exposures.

(3) *Introducing new regulation on liquidity and funding:* Basel III is also introducing the liquidity coverage ratio (LCR) and the net stable funding ratio (NSFR) requirements. The LCR requirement, which is being introduced between 2015 (60 percent threshold) and 2019 (100 percent threshold), requires banks to cover their 30-day stress cash outflows with high-quality liquid assets. This coverage demonstrates their ability to survive a temporary shut-down in short-term funding markets. The NSFR requirement, which is scheduled to become a minimum standard in 2018, ensures that banks can withstand a protracted crisis scenario of 12 months without access to external funding.

Whilst Basel III is dealing with some of the criticism of its framework, significant gaps and shortcomings remain. Basel III continues to suffer from the assumption of portfolio invariance, or linear weighting, that facilitates the additivity in the model. It does not penalize concentration risks in Pillar I and a single global

255 The leverage ratio will be imposed in 2018. Requirements outside the Eurozone are higher, in particular, in Switzerland, the United States and the UK.

risk factor still underpins the core Credit Risk model. The BCBS could deal with concentration risk, for example, by introducing a quadratic risk weighting applied to deviations from a diversified benchmark portfolio.[256]

Basel III has introduced a framework for large exposures framework but is still, at time of writing, under development by the EBA.[257] More critically, it does not include sovereign debt. Basel III has also not dealt with the incentives set by a zero risk-weighting of sovereign debt, which induced the build-up of significant exposure to sovereign debt on the banks' balance sheets in the Eurozone.

Basel III has also not addressed the problem of regulatory and tax arbitrage in complete markets, and the shifting of financial promises. As Blundell-Wignall and Atkinson show with two simple examples, there remains "a massive incentive in financial markets to use 'complete market' techniques to reconfigure credits as capital market instruments, to avoid capital charges and reduce tax burden. This will continue despite the proposed reforms."[258]

The EBA has not yet finalized the calibration of NSFR. The ratio's quality will ultimately depend on the ability of banks and supervisors to be able to model the behavior of investors as "stable" or "unstable" in a crisis situation.

The BCBS has only lately begun to deal with Interest Rate Risk (IRR) in Pillar I, although, given where the interest curve is right now, this is arguably one of the biggest risks to bank solvency going forward.[259]

In addition to quantitative standards for capital ratios, leverage, liquidity, and funding, regulators have also made recommendations, and defined minimum requirements, for risk governance and risk data. The objective is to implement best practices and make risk data systems as reliable and responsive as accounting systems. Last, but not least, regulators have also begun to devise rules for compensation incentives that banks can provide to their management and staff.

Not only have the reforms in the Basel framework itself increased the complexity of the regulatory landscape, but the pursuit of a more political agenda outside the framework, sometimes with the outright populist view to penalize banks and bankers, has created additional complexities. This is especially the case for the hitherto unsuccessful efforts to introduce a financial transaction tax. As Dewatripont et al. (2010) clearly recognize, the first challenge on the road to efficient regulation is "the need to avoid overreaction: regulation should mimic for banks the corporate governance of non-financial firms, not 'punish' banks just in order to place blame for the crisis." [260]

256 Compare Blundell-Wignall and Atkinson (2010), pp 12–14.
257 Compare BCBS (2014a).
258 See Blundell-Wignall and Atkinson (2010), pp 12–14.
259 The BCBS has finally issued a proposal on how to deal with interest-rate risk.
260 Compare Dewatripont et al. (2010), p 8.

Tighter regulation is not the only reform to make banks more resilient. Central banks need to implement tighter supervision, both at the micro- as well as macro-prudential level.[261] At the level of individual organizations, authorities are becoming more forward looking, by ensuring good governance and robust capital, liquidity, and recovery planning and – if need be – preparing for supervisory interventions.

The implementation of regulatory reforms in the EU took time. In 2009, the BCBS agreed on the key elements of the Basel III framework, enabling the EU to implement the necessary legislation; namely, the Capital Requirements Directive IV (CRD IV), which each respective member country had to transpose into national laws, and the Capital Requirements Regulation (CRR). The timing was difficult, as the European banks' regulatory capital positions were under pressure from the Great Financial Crisis and the subsequent severe recession. In addition, smaller banks continued to struggle with the fixed costs of regulatory compliance, which arguably put them at a disadvantage to larger banks. The tightening of capital rules for trading books forced banks to reduce inventories and undermined their ability to act as market-makers, which contributed to increased volatility in thin market trading.

Taking a step back, and putting the regulatory reforms into a larger context, Basel III has not dealt with at least four serious shortfalls:

(1) *The "boundary problem" of financial regulation:* the current regulation focuses on banks as institutions and not on the functions of financial intermediation that they and other players perform. Increasing thresholds and oversight in the system provides incentives for activities to migrate outside the regulated entities. This problem is also referred to as the "boundary problem of financial regulation."[262] The last crisis was – to a large extent – nurtured and spread through the non-banking sector: broker, dealers, ABCP-vehicles, and money market funds. As Brunnermeier et al. (2009) conclude: "These problems of setting, and policing, the regulatory boundary are real and severe. There are no easy answers. But perhaps the first step towards resolving such problems effectively is to be aware of them."[263] Whether the BCBS can design an "interface between the regulated and the unregulated" in which the resulting incentive to shift business into unregulated channels is so low that it never becomes systemic remains to be seen.

261 See Huertas (2014), chapter 3, pp 50–81 for a comprehensive summary of post crisis changes in bank supervision.
262 See Brunnermeier et al. (2009), pp 63–69.
263 See Brunnermeier et al. (2009), pp 69.

(2) *Risk modeling:* Basel III still relies on a model of risk which has significant shortcomings. In particular, because the market data it uses to estimate risk models is endogenous, that is, depends on the behavior of market participants, the statistical analysis made in terms of stability cannot provide much guidance in times of instability, such as a crisis.[264] In fact, many supervisors, when they want to test the resilience of the largest banks, do not rely on the Basel risk-weightings and ratios alone, but are devise their own risk scenarios and stress tests to correct for these shortcomings. The former president of the Fed, Alan Greenspan (2008), is not the only one to question, "whether we will ever have a perfect model of risk?"[265] In that sense, the Basel framework arguably creates a false sense of security: most certainly for those that do not understand its inherent limitations.

(3) *Increasing complexity:* regulation and supervision have become very complex. In fact, the history of the BCBS's rulemaking over the last 50 years or so can be interpreted as a history of increasing complexity, adding rules to existing rules to deal with shortcomings exposed in the previous crisis ie mostly reactive, rather than proactive. From a European perspective, this build-up in complexity needs to be multiplied by the number of different supervisory traditions and differences in fundamental law. Haldane (2012), Chief Economist at the Bank of England, argues convincingly that, as regards regulation and supervision, less might be more: "Because complexity generates uncertainty, not risk, it requires a regulatory response grounded in simplicity, not complexity."[266] But he also concludes, somewhat skeptically, that simplification of the regulatory system "would require an about-turn from the regulatory community from the path followed for the better part of the past 50 years. If a once-in-a-lifetime crisis is not able to deliver that change, it is not clear what will."[267]

(4) *Undermining market discipline:* the increasingly complex regulatory and supervisory framework means more reliance on regulators and supervisors – who are subject to regulatory capture by market participants and political forces at the expense of market discipline. Barth et al., building on the analysis of a new database on bank regulation and supervision in 107 countries, "raise a flag regarding policies that rely excessively on direct government supervision and regulatory restrictions on banks."[268]

264 Compare Danielsson (2002).
265 See Greenspan (2008).
266 See Haldane (2012), p 19.
267 See Haldane (2012), p 19.
268 Compare Barth et al. (2002), p 1.

If there are so many objections to the current regulatory and supervisory framework, are there more radical solutions that should be considered? Indeed, there are:

(1) *More equity capital:* Admati and Hellwig (2013) propose raising the equity capital requirements for banks significantly.[269] The standard objection to this is that equity capital is more expensive than debt. In a world of tax-deductible coupon payments, deposit insurance, lender of last resort facilities, and implicit too-big-to-fail guarantees, banks have an incentive to issue more debt and thus increase leverage. Even if governments remove these distortions, the cost of debt and equity still depends on the risk associated with the assets of the bank and the mix of debt and equity. The less risky assets are, the less debt the bank carries and the lower the cost of equity. Therefore, whether banks can be funded with more equity is not the question. Instead, the question is whether governments would be prepared to change the tax system on bank debt, whether they would credibly withdraw implicit guarantees for bank debt, and whether investors would provide enough equity capital to fund the current asset portfolios of banks.

(2) *Taxing run-prone, short-term debt:* Cochrane (2012) builds on this line of thinking in his outline of a "run-free financial system." He argues that if "a demand for separate bank debt really exists, the equity of 100 percent equity-financed banks can be held by a downstream institution or pass-through vehicle that issues equity and debt tranches."[270] Starting from the premise that the Great Financial Crisis was essentially a systemic bank run, he maintains that the central focus of the regulatory response should be to eliminate such runs. Therefore, he proposes taxing run-prone, short-term debt contracts, especially deposits and overnight debt. He argues that these contracts are information sensitive in terms of crisis, and induce runs due to their sequential service constraint. He proposes that for "each dollar of run-prone, short-term debt issued, the bank or other intermediary must pay…Pigouvian taxes…"[271] Specifically, he suggests that banks and other intermediaries pay a tax for every dollar of short-term debt, that they issue. "That tax could, in principle, decline smoothly with maturity, be larger depending on capital ratios and other measures of how run-prone the institution is."[272]

(3) *Towards an altogether new monetary system:* Mayer (2016) proposes an entirely new monetary system that decouples money creation and bank

269 See Admati, Hellwig (2013), chapter 13, pp 100–114.
270 Compare Cochrane (2012), p 198.
271 See Cochrane (2012), p 199.
272 Compare Cochrane (2012), p 217.

lending. Block-chain, that is, distributed ledger technology that is subject to the availability of the required decentralized computing power, could become the back-bone of new money. Building on the idea of currency competition introduced by von Hayek, he suggests that "competition among different issuers of reputation money would be the best, if not only, way to arrive at sound money" and that "with today's payment technology competition of several monies does no longer appear as an insurmountable problem."[273]

In conclusion, the optimal regulatory policies should:
(1) aim for a functional approach that deals as much as possible with the boundary problem of financial regulation;
(2) focus on clearly identified market failures and externalities, particularly the cost of bank-runs on other financial institutions and the financial system at large;
(3) rely on a set of simple rules and regulations to minimize both direct (salaries of regulators and supervisors and administrative compliance costs for banks) and indirect costs (ie, the distortions created);
(4) be enforced by independent supervisors; and
(5) should be subject to regular independent cost-benefit analyses themselves.[274]

In the search for blue prints and optimal policies to choose from, considering a general framework of regulatory analysis makes sense (see Figure 38). This analysis can prevent us from falling "prey to a naïve view of the world," as Freixas and Santomero (2002) state, "where powerful regulators act in the best interest of society, and the regulated banks will submissively abide by the regulation."[275] Instead, regulators could deviate from their ideal objective function, and banks could react strategically. In other words, the recent instability of the financial system can also be interpreted as banks reacting to the wrong incentives, set by regulators with mostly good intentions.

Optimizing the current regulatory and supervisory framework, however, is challenging. Changing rules and regulations always means proving the superiority of the counter-argument, dealing with path dependencies and the vested interests in the status quo. And it invariably takes place in the political realm.

273 Compare Mayer (2016), p 6.
274 Cochrane (2014) notes on p 29: "Although "Systemic stability" is one of the main goals of financial regulation, yet neither systemic nor stability has a well agreed-on, quantifiable definition or measurement procedure."
275 See Freixas and Santomero (2002) and compare Freixas and Rochet (2008), p 312.

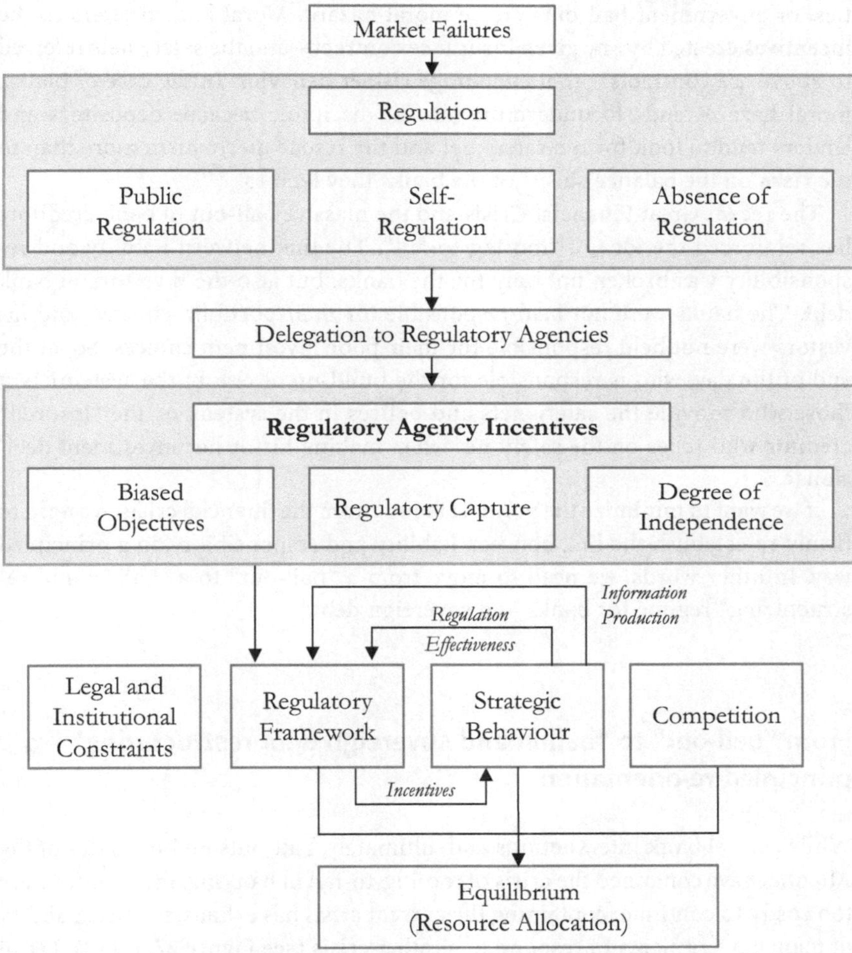

(Figure 38: Banking regulation in perspective, Freixas, Rochet (2008), Fig. 9.1, p 311)

Lessons from the Great Financial Crisis – moral hazard and the link between liability and responsibility

Until we find the optimal policies to regulate our financial system, we will face the prospect of bank runs, failures, and systemic crises. Whether these crises are because of ill-designed regulations, bad bank behavior, insufficient supervision, or external shocks, there will be a need for safety nets.

Safety nets, whether they are deposit insurance, lender-of-last resort facilities, or government bail-outs create moral hazard. Moral hazard refers to the incentives created by any given insurance contract – and the safety nets referred to above are contracts – that encourage riskier behavior. In the case of banks, moral hazard tends to undermine market discipline because depositors and lenders tend to look for the safety net and the rescue mechanism more than to the risks on the balance sheets of the banks they lend to.

The recent Great Financial Crisis and the massive bail-out of bank creditors has reinforced the idea of "too-big-to-fail". The link between liability and responsibility was broken not only for the banks, but also the investors in bank debt. The banks were not held responsible for their portfolio choices, and investors were not held responsible for their poor investment choices. So, at the end of the day, who is responsible for the build-up of risk in the system? Is it those who provide the safety nets and polices in the system, or the "insured" creditor who relies on the safety net when making his or her investment decisions?

If we want to minimize the political fallout from the financial crisis, we need to firmly re-establish the link between liability and responsibility, in a principled way. In other words, we need to move from a "bail-out" to a "bail-in and restructuring" regime for banks and sovereign debt.

From "bail-out" to "bail-in and sovereign debt restructuring" – a principled re-orientation

While central bank interventions and, ultimately, bail-outs on both sides of the Atlantic, have contained the crisis of too-big-to-fail in banking, these actions are too costly to continue: containing the current crisis has exhausted the capability of many governments to respond to another crisis (see Figure 27, p 118). Fiscal flexibility has evaporated, and monetary policy is running out of options. "Too-big-to-fail" not only destroys public finances, it also distorts competition, removes market discipline, and encourages risk-taking.[276]

Therefore, the end of "too-big-to-fail" in banking, unsurprisingly, has been a top priority. The Basel reforms have focused on reducing the likelihood of failure through tighter regulation and supervision. Similarly, the introduction of bank resolution regimes has focused on making banks "safe to fail." As the FSB (2014) puts it, "the objective of an effective resolution regime is to make feasible the resolution of financial institutions without severe systemic disruption and without exposing taxpayers to loss, while protecting vital economic functions

276 Compare Huertas (2014), chapter 1, pp 4–20.

through mechanisms which make it possible for shareholders, unsecured and uninsured creditors to absorb losses in a manner that respects the hierarchy of claims in liquidation."[277]

The FSB (2014) defines nine key attributes of effective resolution regimes for financial institutions. Per the FSB, *"an effective resolution regime should:*

(1) ensure continuity of systemically important financial services, and payment, clearing, and settlement functions;

(2) protect…such depositors, insurance policy holders, and investors as are covered by such schemes and arrangements, and ensure the rapid return of segregated client assets;

(3) allocate losses to shareholders and unsecured and uninsured creditors in a manner that respects the hierarchy of claims;

(4) not rely on public solvency support and not create an expectation that such support will be available;

(5) avoid unnecessary destruction of value, and therefore seek to minimize the overall cost of resolution in home and host jurisdictions;

(6) provide for speed and transparency and as much predictability as possible through legal and procedural clarity and advanced planning for orderly resolution;

(7) provide a mandate in law for cooperation, information exchange, and coordination domestically and with relevant foreign resolution authorities;

(8) ensure that non-viable firms can exit the market in an orderly way; and

(9) be credible and thereby enhance market discipline and provide incentives for market-based solutions."[278]

Once the supervisors have determined that a bank fails to meet the threshold conditions for a going concern, it will then be put into resolution. Once in resolution, the most important task is to recapitalize the failed bank, primarily through a bail-in by creditors. The bail-in ensures the provision of adequate liquidity and funding, ensures both continued authorization and access to financial markets' infrastructures, primarily exchanges and payment and settlement systems. A main challenge is to implement an automatic stay on qualified financial contracts.[279] Subsequently, the bank needs to be restructured expeditiously, either by selling it to a third party, re-launching it on the market, or winding it (or parts of it) down. Creditors, in any case, should be no worse off than they would have been under liquidation.

---

277 See FSB (2014).

278 See FSB (2014).

279 Compare Huertas (2014), pp 82–109 for a comprehensive discussion of the critical steps in resolution and bail-in.

There are several additional barriers to resolution that need to be overcome. Firstly, adequate amounts of bail-in funds need to exist, that is, debt that investors can bail in without causing a systemic run (elsewhere) in the system, and that they can afford. From a systemic risk perspective, leveraged institutions that are short-term funded are not the best place for banks to look for bail-in debt. Secondly, the resolution regime needs to ensure a clear separation between the obligations of investors and the more sensitive obligations of customers. This is best achieved in a holding company structure, which limits the investors' obligations to the holding company level, and the customers' obligations to the operating level of the bank subsidiary. Thirdly, cross-border issues need to be dealt with in advance, with both home- and host-country agreeing on a single-point-of-entry approach. In summary, a constructive certainty – for all market participants involved – is key for financial stability. Investors need to know in advance that they can be bailed-in in a resolution scenario, and customers need to know that there is enough bail-in debt to protect them in case of a bank failure. This constructive certainty might, in fact, create incentives for banks and investors to reach bail-in type solutions in times of stress without going through a formal resolution procedure.

Dewatripont and Freixas (2011) identify two critical limitations in the design of a bank resolution regime: multiple regulators and the ability to make credible commitments.[280] Cross-border banks always pose a challenge for effective bank resolution, given the number of authorities with conflicting goals that are involved: one major German bank, for example, has close to 80 different regulators globally. More importantly, the credibility of the bail-in threat rests on constructive certainty for investors with regards to its possibility. Dewatripont (2014), with respect to the specific European context, identifies the need for a pre-funded resolution fund – ideally with some government backstop to ensure access to enough liquidity in a systemic crisis – and the enforcement of a minimum level of bail-in debt.[281]

The Eurozone also needs to enforce the bail-ins of creditors to sovereigns. The serial bail-out and "cash for reforms" policy in the Eurozone has failed.[282] The political fallout across Europe is considerable. The ECB is trying to buy time, and keep the cost of debt financing at a sustainable level, with its bond buying programs, but the stock of debt is what is holding back growth.

A restructuring regime for sovereign debt would help break the "doom loop" between the banks' balance sheets and sovereign debt. Mandatory collective action clauses for sovereign debt are clearly a first important step in this di-

280 See Dewatripont and Freixas (2011), pp 431–432.
281 Compare Dewatripont (2014).
282 See Sandbu (2015).

rection.[283] Banks could not treat sovereign debt in the Eurozone as a zero risk-weight, risk-free asset anymore and would give up their home bias as far as the sovereign debt is concerned.

In this context, it makes sense to revisit the 2001 proposal by IMF First Deputy Managing Director, Anne O Krueger (2001), to create a new legal and institutional framework – the "Sovereign Debt Restructuring Mechanism" (SDRM) – for resolving sovereign debt crises.[284] Not unlike bank restructuring mechanisms, the "objective of an SDRM is to facilitate the orderly, predictable, and rapid restructuring in of unsustainable sovereign debt, while protecting asset values and creditor rights."[285]

Krueger (2002) identifies two key challenges to the successful design of an SDRM:

(1) the mechanism should provide incentives for debtors with unstainable debt burdens to restructure their debt early and promptly, without creating incentives for the misuse of the mechanism;
(2) once activated, the SDRM should incentivize all parties to reach a quick agreement that allows the debtor to reach a sustainable debt level and regain its growth path. [286]

Building on key attributes of a successful corporate reorganization model, Krueger identifies the following core features of a SDRM:[287]

(1) *majority restructuring* should be possible with the affirmative vote of the majority of creditors and should bind the dissenting minority to the terms of the agreement;
(2) *a stay on creditor enforcement:* before such an agreement is reached, there should be a temporary stay on creditor litigation;
(3) *protection of creditor interests:* an SDRM would need to include safeguards that protect creditors against payments by the debtor to non-priority creditors or value-destroying policies.
(4) *priority financing:* all new money from private creditors should get priority over existing debt.

---

283 The Sub-Committee on EU Sovereign Debt Markets has developed a Eurozone model collective action clause that is now mandatory for timely introduction in all Eurozone government securities issued from January 1st, 2013, onwards.

284 See Krueger (2002). For more recent discussion of "The Economics and Law of Sovereign Debt and Default". See Panizza et al. (2009).

285 Compare Krueger (2002), p 4.

286 See Krueger (2002), p 5.

287 See Krueger (2002), pp 14–17.

Debt from official creditors such as the World Bank or the IMF, and possibly bilateral official debt from other sovereigns, would be excluded from the SDRM.

A principled reorientation from the bail-out of creditors to a bail-in would create constructive certainty and enhance market discipline for banks and sovereigns. There is evidence that, not unlike banks, sovereigns that undergo prompt restructuring return to the sustainable growth path much sooner.[288] Market discipline can only work if there are transparent rules and no place for discretionary interventions that would prevent a time-consistent application of the rules.

What is the right role for competition policy in European banking? State aid, competition, and bank resolution

The implementation of bail-ins would also help with the competitive distortions caused by implicit "too-big-to-fail" guarantees because governments would reduce these guarantees. Instead of dealing with the question of state aid distortions in bail-out situations, the new role for competition policy in European banking would be to measure the size of the implicit government guarantees. In this way, competition policy in European banking would effectively become the supervisor of the resolution regime and their national implementations.

State aid proceedings, and the negotiation of compensation measures, would only be necessary if states chose not to implement a bail-in and still proceed with a bail-out. For this scenario, states could follow the principles behind the evaluation of the competition policy for the rescue plans of banks as proposed by Beck et al. (2010).[289] The starting point is the recognition that a bank bail-out is different. A bail-out not only has the potential to distort competition but generally helps competitors who would otherwise suffer from a failure of the bank due to interconnections and contagion. Specifically, the following questions should guide any assessment of bail-out plans:[290]

(1) does the bail-out process in one member state affect banks in other member states either positively or negatively (positive or negative externalities)?
(2) does the recapitalization of a bank significantly increase the incentives for future marginal lending (excessive moral hazard)?
(3) do the terms of the bail-out unduly incentivize the bank to dispose of assets in a specific market (national discrimination)?

288 Compare Sandbu (2015).
289 Compare Beck et al. (2010), pp 57–58.
290 Compare Beck et al. (2010), ibid.

(4) are the recapitalization plans connected to the distortions that have led to the failure of the bank in the first place (elimination of existing distortions)?
(5) is the bank viable after the bail-out (viability)?
(6) is there an exit strategy for the state aid?

When determining the appropriate corrective actions that banks need to take in exchange for receiving state aid, Dewatripont et al. (2010) highlight the risk of excessive penalties on bailed out banks that would unduly put them at a competitive disadvantage to their competitors, which also indirectly benefit from the bail-out. In addition, a risk exists that the compensation measures favor domestic lending over international activities; in other words, state aid proceedings might undermine financial integration in Europe in times when it is most needed to achieve more growth.[291]

Competition policy in banking, going forward, must play an important role in terms of regulating "dynamic competition." Digitalization and the FinTech revolution are an important development to make our financial system more efficient. In particular, governments will have to design policies for the banking sector in such a way that they do not discriminate against new technologies that ultimately make the provision of financial services cheaper.

Do we need more structural reforms? Completing the regulatory and supervisory framework

Last, but not least, will these policies sufficiently reduce the likelihood and potential damage done by the failure of a large institution? Or do we need further structural reforms that would separate riskier banking activities from retail deposit activities?

In the US, the legislature introduced the "Volcker rule" with Section 619 of the Dodd-Frank Act of 2010. This section prohibits licensed US banks or bank holding companies with US subsidiaries from engaging in proprietary trading, and both investing in or sponsoring hedge funds and private equity funds. The section does not affect the underwriting of securities by banks and still allows a subsidiary within the bank holding company to also do so. The rule was enabled in 2011, and become law in July, 2012. Banks have had to comply since 2014. In the UK, the proposals of the UK Independent Commission on Banking (Vickers (2011)) mandates a ring-fencing of retail banking activities with higher equity capital requirements.[292] Banks have until 2019, to implement the reforms. In

291 See Dewatripont et al. (2010), p 9.
292 See Vickers (2011).

October 2012, the EU's High-Level Expert Group under the leadership of Errki Liikanen (2012), governor of the Bank of Finland, proposed that the investment banking activities of universal banks be placed in an entity separate from the remainder of the banks.[293] There is no legislation on this recommendation yet. Some EU members, France and Germany, in particular, have passed legislation along the lines of the recommendation of the Liikanen report.

The common denominator in all of these structural reform proposals is the separation of investment banking from retail and commercial banking. This separation, undoubtedly, can help to limit the risk of cross-contamination in a crisis. Whether it will crowd out investment banking activities remains to be seen. And there are undoubtedly loopholes in these proposals that will be exploited over time. The biggest risk from a financial stability point of view is clearly the risk that more activities will migrate outside the regulated financial system as a consequence of these structural reform proposals being passed into law. These reform proposals will also reduce the economies of scale and scope of the diversification available in larger banking groups. However, whether these structural reforms are binding, or whether these economies of scale and scope are disappearing because of the introduction of bank resolution regimes and bail-ins, remains to be seen. In any case, the markets and the resolution authorities might be better off – via their review and approval of the "Living Will" – implementing structural reforms in a "tailor-made" fashion and with a view to making banks resolvable instead of prescribing one size fits all banking structures.

In Summary

Since the outbreak of the Great Financial Crisis, governments have initiated and implemented many reforms. The BCBS has reformed the Basel framework and has strengthened supervision. Bail-in for bank debt has been introduced with a view to strengthen market discipline, and make banks safe to fail without recourse to the taxpayers' money. More needs to be done in terms of sovereign debt restructuring.

On the one hand, the hope would now be that the system can deal with a failure of a systemically relevant bank. But – given the shortcomings in risk modeling and specific incentives of bank resolutions – the system cannot deal with another crisis. Given the elevated sovereign debt levels, we will need to watch – and maybe limit – the size of the largest institutions relative to the GDP of their home country. On the other hand, we cannot afford to focus only on policies on

293 See Liikanen (2012).

financial stability, but must also be mindful of the overall economic growth objectives and the efficiency of the financial system. Strong economies need their banks to function properly. But strong banks also need the economy to grow.

Ultimately, the question is how we implement these blueprints and optimal policies going forward in the context of the newly-established European Banking Union.

Chapter 13: Banking union – realm of the possible

"...financial integration is essential for a well-functioning single currency, but it is not something we can take for granted. ... With the banking union, I am confident we are laying the foundations for a more complete financial integration in the future."[294]

Mario Draghi, President of the European Central Bank, 12th February, 2014

"The crisis painfully demonstrated the clear need to remove the asymmetry between integrated financial markets and a financial stability architecture that was primarily organized along national lines."[295]

Daniele Nouy, Chair of the Supervisory Board at the European Central Bank, 27th April, 2015

The introduction of the Euro on 1st January, 1999, marked a milestone in the history of European integration. The introduction of a banking union – beginning with the onset of banking supervision by the ECB on 4th November 2014 – is another important milestone. If we want to maintain financial stability and financial integration across Europe, financial policies need to be centralized as well, particularly the rulebook, banking supervision and resolution, as well as deposit insurance. Coordination among the national entities, alone, is not sufficient. Thus, a banking union needs to translate the global Basel consensus on minimum standards into European law, and complement this process with a common supervisory manual, or "Single Handbook". Currently, the banking union consists of three pillars: the Single Supervisory Mechanism (SSM); the Single Resolution Mechanism (SRM); and, a yet to be agreed on, but critically important European Deposit Insurance Scheme (EDIS).

As the banking union develops, it is important to take a step back and look at whether the centralization of financial policies in Europe is, in fact, working toward financial stability and financial integration. Is the implementation of the banking union helping to put European banks and Europe back on track? What

294 See Draghi (2014).
295 See Nouy (2015).

is working and what needs fixing? Is the SSM working properly? Does the introduction of the SRM mark the beginning of the end of "too-big-to-fail" in European banking? Why do we need the EDIS to complete the banking union and what are the roadblocks to implementation?

Single Supervisory Mechanism – Is European supervision working properly?

The SSM is the first of the three pillars of the European banking union. Under the SSM, which became operational on 4th November, 2014, the ECB became the banking supervisor for all banks in the Eurozone, and is responsible for the direct supervision of the largest 128 "significant" banking groups. All other banks (more than 6,000 in the Eurozone alone), are supervised by national authorities. However, the ECB has ultimate supervisory authority over these banks, and also has the authority to take over direct supervision if necessary.[296]

A bank is deemed significant when it meets one the following five criteria:
(1) The value of the assets exceeds EUR 30 billion.
(2) The value of its assets exceeds both EUR 5 billion and 20 percent of the GDP of the member state in which it is located.
(3) The bank is among the three most significant banks of the country in which it is located.
(4) The bank has sizeable cross-border activities.
(5) The bank has applied for or already receives assistance from ESM.

The SSM builds on the existing legal framework of the EU, specifically on Article 127 (6) of the TEUF. To ensure the separation of monetary policy from banking supervision, whilst at the same time respecting the ECB's Governing Council as the sole decision-making body, the ECB created an SSM Supervisory Board. The Supervisory Board consists of the national supervisors who participate in the SSM, in addition to a chair, vice-chair, and four ECB representatives. The Supervisory Board makes draft decisions, which are then passed to the Governing Council for a final decision. The banking union foresees a strict administrative "Chinese wall" separation between the ECB's monetary and supervisory tasks: however, in both areas, final decisions are made by the same body, the Governing Council.[297]

296 See Houben et al. (2008) on the optimal set-up for supervising cross-border banks in Europe.

297 For a general discussion of the pros and cons of combining monetary and supervisory policy making in one institution compare Goodhart (1988) and Hellwig (2014).

To prepare for assuming its new responsibilities in banking supervision, the ECB conducted a Comprehensive Assessment (CA) of 130 banks.[298] The CA was broad in scope.[299] The banks under assessment had total assets of EUR 22 trillion as of 31st December, 2013, which accounts for over 80 percent of the total banking assets in the SSM. The CA had two components: an Asset Quality Review (AQR) and a stress test. The AQR was an assessment of the accuracy of the carrying value of the banks' assets as of December 2013, which provided the starting point for the stress test. The stress test provided a forward-looking examination of the resilience of the solvency of individual banks under two hypothetical scenarios. In the baseline, banks were required to maintain a minimum CET1 ratio of 8 percent and, under an adverse scenario, of 5.5 percent. The European Banking Authority (EBA) had developed the scenarios, in collaboration with the European Systemic Risk Board. The AQR resulted in the aggregate adjustment of EUR 47.5 billion to the carrying value of participating banks' assets, as of 31st December, 2013. Additionally, non-performing exposures increased by EUR 135.9 billion across all banks, as the ECB harmonized the definitions of non-performing exposures (including the examination of forbearance as a trigger). All in all, the CA identified a capital shortfall of EUR 24.6 billion across 25 participating banks.[300]

The objectives of the CA were to:

(1) strengthen a "bank's balance sheets by repairing the problems identified, through the necessary remedial actions,"
(2) enhance "transparency by improving the quality of information available on the condition of banks," and
(3) ultimately of building "confidence by assuring that, on completion of the identified remedial actions, banks will be soundly capitalized."[301]

No specific backstop for remedial actions was available at the European level. The CA therefore had to strike a delicate balance between jeopardizing the credibility of the stress test with too much leniency, and destabilizing the banking sector with too much severity. The task was further complicated by the fact that market participants did not consider the results of the two previous stress tests in 2010 and 2011, also under the auspices of the EBA, to be credible.

Several significant shortcomings in the methodology, implementation, and

298 Compare ECB (2014), in particular, subsection 3.1 for an explanation of the differences in scope between SSM direct supervision and the Comprehensive Assessment.
299 See ECB (2014).
300 Compare ECB (2014) p 10, table 1 for a list of the participating banks with a shortfall.
301 ECB (2014), p 2.

documentation of the CA have been identified.[302] These clear shortcomings undermine the credibility of the stress test results.[303] In particular, the stress test:
(1) does not include the scenario of a sovereign default, contrary to the recent sovereign debt crisis in the periphery of the Eurozone,
(2) does not include the adverse scenario of deflation, an issue that was already a concern in earlier stress tests,
(3) is exclusively calibrated on a risk-weighted capital ratio and not on the leverage ratio, and
(4) does not include further litigation charges or costs of misconduct in the adverse scenario.

An independent set of benchmark analyses, published ahead of the CA in December 2013, uses only publicly available data as at 31st December, 2012 or 30th June, 2013, and four stressed capital shortfall measures. It discloses significantly higher capital shortfalls than those "produced" by the EBA stress test:[304]
(1) *Book capital shortfall:* using thresholds of 4 percent and 7 percent for the book value of equity and the assets leverage ratio respectively, corresponding capital shortfalls of between EUR 82 and EUR 176 billion, and between EUR 509 and 767 billion were predicted. A recent update of this analysis, based on the final set of banks subject to the CA on 31st December 2013, continued to show capital shortfalls of between EUR 53 and EUR 88 billion or between EUR 451 and 571 billion respectively.[305]
(2) *Market capital shortfall:* similarly, using thresholds of 4 percent and 7 percent for the market value of equity and the book value of assets respectively, a calculation of the leverage ratio results in capital shortfalls of between EUR 230 and EUR 620 billion for the 41 publicly-listed banks. An update of this analysis using financials as of 31st December, 2013, for the, by then, 40 publicly-listed banks still showed capital shortfalls between EUR 118 and EUR 411 billion.
(3) *The SRISK or the capital shortfall in a systemic crisis:* estimates of SRISK (40 percent market decline over a six-month period, assuming a capital ratio of 5.5 percent) was EUR 579 billion for the 41 publicly-listed banks. The updated analysis still indicated a capital shortfall of EUR 454 billion for the 40 publicly-listed financial institutions.[306]

302 Compare Steffen and Steinruecke (2015).
303 Compare Beck (2014).
304 Compare Acharya and Steffens (2013).
305 For the updated results using financials as at December 31, 2013, see Steffens and Steinruecke (2015).
306 For SRISK compare Acharya et al. (2012).

(4) *Capital shortfall after the write-down of net nonperforming loans:* these estimates range from EUR 232 billion (using Core Tier 1 threshold of 8 percent) to EUR 435 billion (using a tangible equity/tangible assets ratio and a 4 percent threshold). This measurement is motivated by the tendency of banks to extend loans to unhealthy borrowers to prevent a write-down of their loans, a behavior that is sometimes also referred to as "zombie lending."

Compared to these independent benchmark analyses, the results of the CA, specifically the relatively minor capital shortfall of EUR 25.6 billion across 25 banks, do not seem credible at all. On the contrary, they clearly suggest that member states may have forced the ECB to err on the side of leniency, since there is no credible European backstop facility that could have underwritten these large capital shortfalls. Only time will tell to what extent the CA has either strengthened or undermined financial stability and economic growth in Europe.

In addition to institutional challenges, the SSM faces legal challenges with regards to substantive and procedural law, as well as accountability.[307] Contrary to EU regulations, its directives are not directly applicable, but require transposition into national law. This incomplete harmonization of substantive law poses a challenge for the ECB: because the ECB is responsible for the consistent application of the SSM, the ECB has to apply 19 or more different national laws which, in turn, raises the issue of consistency across member states.

Procedural law aspects with regards to the interplay between the ECB and the national authorities also pose a challenge. A particular challenge for the ECB is to ensure consistent supervision of the less significant banks, which are still supervised by the national authorities. Again, the jury is still out on whether this indirect influence of the ECB in the form of common procedures, and its right to assume supervision and/or instruct the national authorities will work in practice, or become a new fault line in the European banking system.

Last, but not least, there are questions around accountability, not only to the EU and national institutions, or to the public, but also with regard to a judicial review of supervision by the SSM. Internally, all supervisory decisions can be subject to review by an Administrative Board of Review on request by affected parties. Such a review, however:

(1) does not put supervisory decisions on hold;
(2) is not binding upon the SSM governance bodies;
(3) or a precondition for a court review.

307 Compare Schmies (2015).

All of the ECB's decisions which affect a bank, including instructions to national authorities, plus the national authorities' decisions which directly affect a bank, are subject to a court review. However, there is a question as to whether the responsible court will be that of the Court of Justice of the European Union (CJEU), or the national courts. In this context, it also relevant to note that the different national courts have different traditions in the judicial review of administrative decisions.[308] As Hellwig (2014) notes:

> *"In the context of the SSM, the difference in judicial attitudes to the exercise of judgment by an administrative authority is important, because much supervisory activity does involve such an exercise of judgment; judgment about the quality of assets that a bank holds; about the riskiness of a bank's strategy; and even the professional quality of its management."*

In that context, it should come as no surprise that the ECB has recently announced its focus on the harmonization of supervisory practices with regards to the licensing of bank management and institutional support schemes.[309]

Ultimately, it is the exercise of supervisory judgment where the centralization of supervision and the movement to an SSM should have the biggest impact. That is why a further harmonization of supervisory legislation and jurisdiction is critical if both a level playing field and a reduction in related complexities and uncertainties is to be achieved.

Is European supervision working properly? It is probably too early to tell. The CA seems to have cost credibility rather than build it, at least with the capital markets, which are discounting bank equity more heavily than the supervisors have done in the recent stress test. The SSM has certainly been costly for the banks which have to comply with both ongoing and ad hoc reporting requirements. In that context, the ECB might ultimately have to recalibrate the regulatory and supervisory burdens on smaller banks. Otherwise, the SSM could have the unintended consequence of distorting competition among banks. In any case, for it to function properly, the SSM needs to be complemented by a working SRM and EDIS. In the longer run, the success of the SRM should lead to more "safe" banking failures in Europe, and an increase in cross-border banking.

308 See Hellwig (2014), pp 14–15.

309 Compare Lautenschläger (2016).

The Single Resolution Mechanism – The beginning of the end of "too-big-to-fail" in European banking?

The Single Resolution Mechanism (SRM) is the second pillar of the European banking union. It complements the centralized supervision of the SSM, with centralized decision-making on a common resolution fund. The objective of the SRM is to ensure that if a bank that is subject to the SSM faces serious difficulties, its resolution can be managed in an orderly and efficient way, with minimal costs to taxpayers and the real economy.

The SRM regulation has been applicable since 1st January, 2016, together with the bail-in provisions of the Bank Recovery and Resolution Directive (BRRD).[310] The SRM is governed both by its regulation, and an inter-governmental agreement relating to some specific aspects of the Single Resolution Fund (SRF). The main institutional components of the SRM are the Single Resolution Board (SRB), and the SRF, to which all banks in the banking union contribute, regardless of size (see Figure 39).

The SRM is responsible for resolution planning and actual resolution of banks directly supervised by the ECB, as well as cross-border groups. According to the BRRD, the national resolution authorities retain responsibility for all other banks in the respective member states.

The SRB operates in two sessions: an executive session and a plenary session. The executive session comprises the chairman, the vice-chair, four permanent members, and the relevant national authorities of the countries in which the troubled bank is established. In this session, the SRB takes the key preparatory and operational decisions for resolving individual banks, including use of the SRF, and the decisions addressed to national authorities. Representatives from the ECB and the European Commission participate in the process as permanent observers. The plenary session comprises the participants in the executive session, and representatives of all national resolution authorities. In this session, the SRB makes all decisions of a general and budgetary nature.

The SRF consists of contributions from all banks established in the member states. It has an estimated target level of EUR 55 billion which is to be reached by 2024, and can borrow from the market and third parties if the SRB agrees. During the transition time, the SRF is composed of individual national compartments that incrementally mutualize lending between compartments, and bridge financing is possible.

The BRRD contains the new crisis management framework for banks in

310 Compare European Commission (2014).

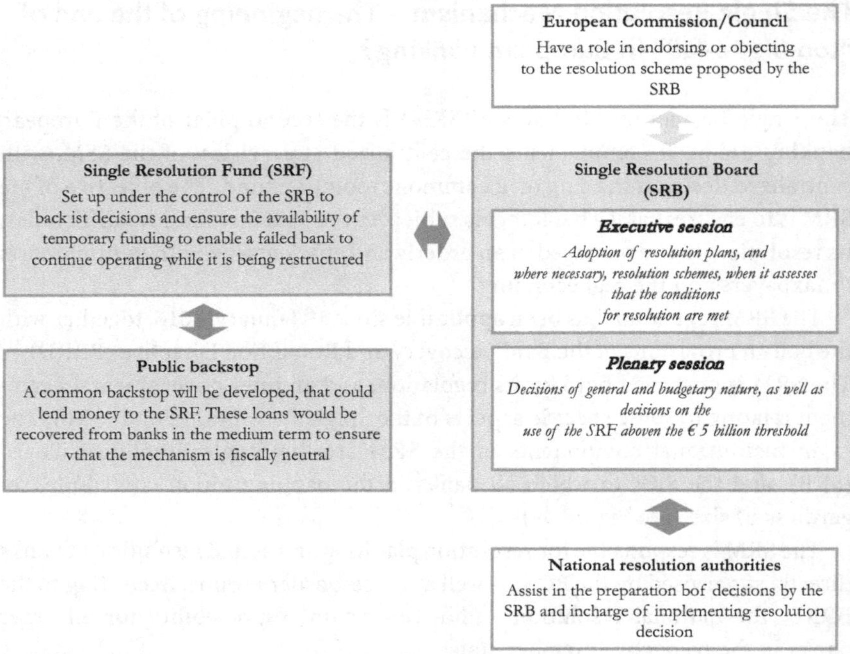

(Figure 39: SRM structure, compare de Haan et al., (2016), Figure 13.7, p 478)

Europe. It provides authorities with more comprehensive and effective arrangements to deal with failing banks.

(1) *Preparation and prevention:* banks and resolution authorities are required to draw up recovery-and-resolution plans ("living wills") on how to deal with situations of financial stress or even failure. If authorities identify obstacles to the resolvability as part of the resolution planning, they can require a bank to take appropriate measures, such as changes to corporate and legal structures, to ensure that resolution is possible without threatening financial stability or imposing a cost on taxpayers. Typical obstacles to resolvability are qualified financial contracts such as derivatives, the separation between investor and customer obligations, and dealing with cross-border issues. Recovery and resolution plans are not made public. Avgouleas et al., (2012), find that resolution plans can be used not only to reduce legal entity complexities of banking groups but also, in particular, for non-EU cross-border banking situations, to agree on specific burden-sharing agreements between countries, and ultimately to trigger a harmonization of the legal framework for bank resolution across all G-20 countries.[311]

311 Compare Avgouleas et al. (2012).

(2) *Early interventions:* supervisory authorities are granted new powers enabling them to intervene if a bank faces financial distress, but before the situation deteriorates beyond repair. These powers include the ability to dismiss the management and appoint a temporary administrator as well as convening a shareholder meeting to adopt necessary reforms and draw up a plan for debt restructuring.

(3) *Resolution:* resolution ultimately occurs when the relevant authorities determine that a bank has reached the "point of non-viability," respectively the status of failing or likely to fail, ie there is no other private-sector intervention that can restore the institution back to viability within a certain time frame, and that normal insolvency proceedings would lead to financial instability. Resolution means the restructuring of a bank to ensure the continuity of critical functions. Resolution tools include the power to sell or merge the business with another bank; to set up a temporary bridge bank to operate critical functions; to separate good assets from bad ones; and to convert shares or write down the debt of failing banks (bail-in).

(4) *Bail-in:* bail-in effectively enables the authorities to recapitalize a failing bank, so that it can continue as a going concern. To ensure that banks always have sufficient loss-absorbing capacity, the BRRD provides for the SRM to set Minimum Requirements for Eligible Liabilities (MREL) for each institution. Bail-in applies to all liabilities that are not backed by assets or other collateral. To effectively minimize contagion, bail-in does not apply to deposits:
   a. protected by deposit guarantee schemes;
   b. client assets;
   c. short term interbank lending;
   d. claims of clearing houses and payment and settlement systems (that have a remaining maturity of seven days);
   e. liabilities such as salaries, pensions, or taxes.

   Authorities can exclude certain other liabilities on a discretionary basis to prevent contagion. The write-down follows the ordinary allocation of losses and ranking in insolvency (see Figure 40). Deposits from small and medium sized enterprises (SMEs) and natural persons are preferred over other senior creditors. In order to protect the interest of creditors, the bail-in is subject to the principle of "no creditor worse-off than in normal insolvency proceedings".

(5) *Resolution funding:* the SRF should primarily be used for the resolution costs that cannot be funded through bail-in, for example, the financing of a bridge bank. The BRRD provides that only after stakeholders have born losses equal to 8 percent of liabilities, through write-downs or conversions, can the SRF bear the remaining losses, but only up to 5 percent of the bank's liabilities.

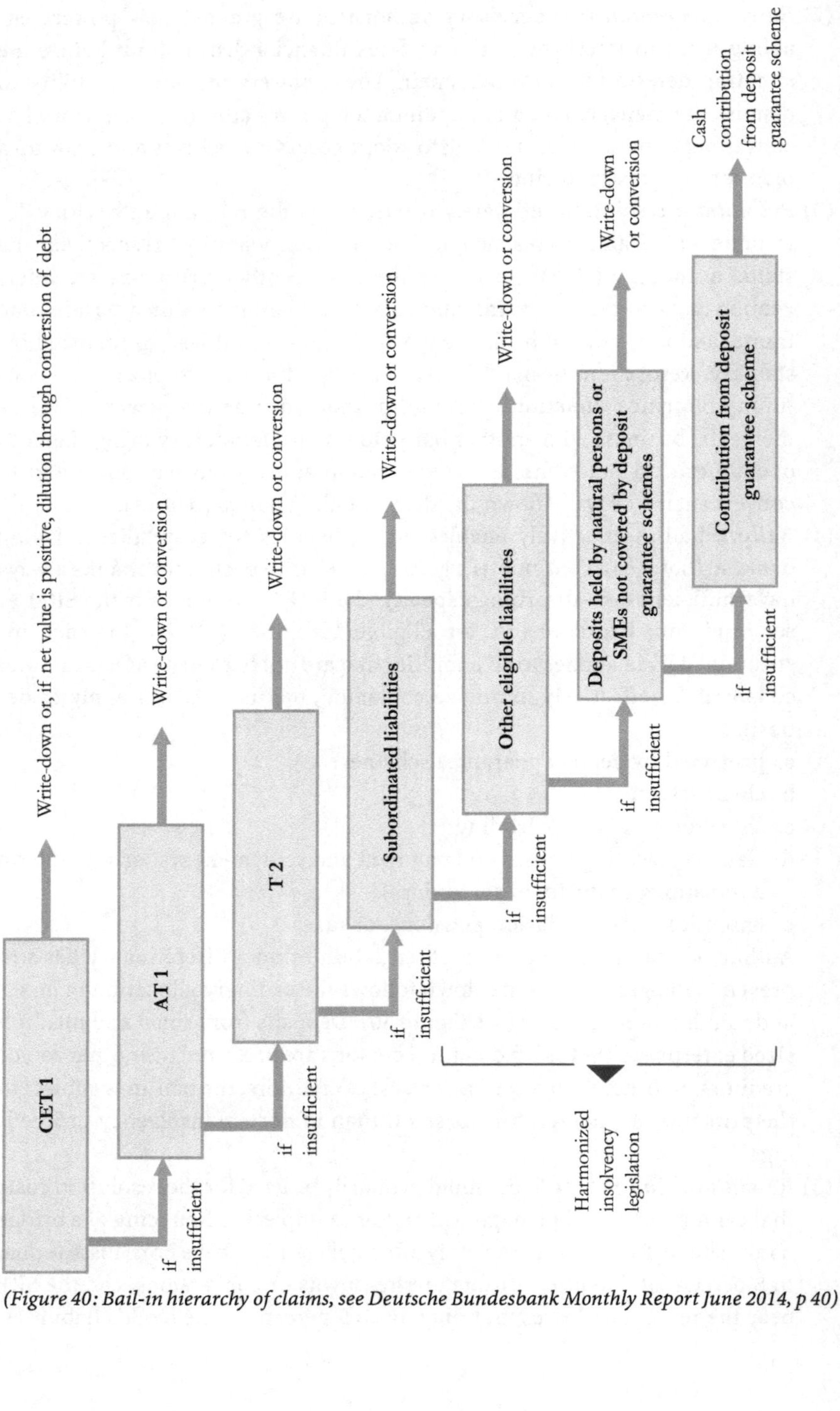

(Figure 40: Bail-in hierarchy of claims, see Deutsche Bundesbank Monthly Report June 2014, p 40)

The introduction of the bail-in tool links liability and responsibility. It is clearly an important step towards restoring the principles of the market economy. Compared to the bail-out policies in the aftermath of the Great Financial Crisis a bail-in has significant advantages. In particular, it:[312]

(1) reduces moral hazard by raising the funding costs for banks and improving the ex ante behavior of bank management,
(2) provides bank creditors with stronger incentives to monitor the bank and its management,
(3) places the burden of bank failures more fairly, and
(4) ultimately protects taxpayers and mitigates the sovereign to bank-debt "doom-loop."

However, it fails to completely eradicate the need for bail-outs in situations when there is the threat of a systemic collapse, or in the event of a large complex cross-border bank. In these situations, the essential conditions for a successful bail-in process, namely, a rapid restoration of market confidence, an accurate evaluation of losses, and a swift restructuring to avoid successive rounds of bail-in rescues, is very difficult for the authorities to achieve. More importantly, the bail-in process itself might trigger contagion, that is, a flight of creditors from other banks which are not yet affected, that might require greater subsequent liquidity injections to restore confidence.

Hellwig (2014) echoes some of the same concerns and has identified four critical issues in his evaluation of the BRRD and the SRM:

(1) *Cross-border banks with systemically important subsidiaries in countries outside the banking union:* in these cases, the SRM has not settled the issue of loss-sharing in resolution. In particular, the US authorities seem to insist on the ring-fencing of US subsidiaries in the case of the resolution of the European mother-group. In addition, because the UK does not participate in the banking union or the SRM, the SRM does not address a major part of the multiple-entry problem.
(2) *The need for interim funding:* the BRRD underestimates both the timeline for restructuring and the need for interim funding to keep systemically important operations going. The SRF, when compared to the balance sheets of the largest European banks, is clearly too small. The banking union needs to provide the necessary "wall of money" to ensure the funding of critical operations in resolution.
(3) *Asset valuations and bail-ins:* asset valuations take time to perform properly; this creates uncertainty in the restructuring process and adds to funding difficulties.

312 Compare Avgouleas and Goodhart (2014).

(4) *Fiscal backstops:* the BRRD includes important exceptions from bail-ins; it allows for "pre-emptive" government recapitalizations even before the bank enters resolution.

In addition to these more fundamental concerns that would call for a significant retooling of the SRM, the uneven and occasionally arbitrary implementation of bail-ins has increased the uncertainty for investors and calls into question the "singleness" of the SRM:

(1) While some member countries of the banking union, such as Germany, insist that the resolution authorities "should continue to have full discretion to request the amount of bank-specific add-ons deemed necessary for smooth resolution," the EU commission has proposed the capping of MREL (at least for the systemically important institutions) at the level of Total Loss Absorbing Capacity (TLAC), as defined by the FSB.[313] In any case, there needs to be a sufficient layer of loss absorbing capacity to absorb a bail-in, to reassure other more senior claimholders, and to prevent them from taking to the hills if resolution is imminent.[314]
(2) The BRRD and TLAC requirements have also led to significant differences in bail-in debt definitions across the different member states. The result is a "bail-in hotchpotch" with three discernible versions of senior subordination: contractual, statutory, and structural. Spain has opted for contractual subordination, creating a new de facto class of "Tier 3" bonds. In Germany, legislators have passed a law that retroactively leads to a statutory subordination of senior bank bondholders to other unsecured depositors. Structural subordination prevails in the UK where holding company debt is considered a loss-absorbing capacity. This is likely to lead to an uneven repricing of senior bank bonds across Europe.
(3) Two recent bail-ins in Europe have created additional uncertainty for bondholders, namely the selective bail-in of the senior unsecured bonds of Novo Banco in Portugal, and the attempt by the Republic of Austria to apply the implementation of the BRRD retroactively to the outstanding bonds of the Heta Asset Resolution AG. The latter is the "bad bank" formed from the ashes of the Hypo Alpe-Adria-Bank. Whilst the Novo Banco bondholders are still fighting their bail-in in court, the Republic of Austria has, in the meantime, reached a settlement with the (mostly) German and Italian Heta bondholders.

313 See Jennen, Groendahl (2016); for the definition and calibration of TLAC see FSB (2015); and see BBVA Research (2014), for a comparison of the European MREL with the global TLAC requirements for systemically important banks.
314 Compare Dewatripont (2015).

(4) In two situations, contrary to the stated intentions of the SRM, there have been (partial) bail-outs of bondholders. In Greece, the banking sector has received a EUR 25 billion capital injection as part of the most recent bail-out package; this exception was largely motivated by the Greek sovereign debt crisis, and the fact that "the sovereign has held the banks hostage." In Italy, the creation – with government support – of the Atlante fund as a back-stop for the capital measures required for the troubled regional lenders Banco Popolare di Vicenza and Banco Veneto, has called into question the resolve of Italian authorities to fully implement BRRD. The situation in Italy is complicated by the fact that bonds subject to a bail-in are owned by the retail customers of these same banks. This situation, of course, raises the broader issue of who should ultimately (be allowed to) hold bail-in bank bonds.

All in all, these implementation issues show significant tensions between the incentives for politicians (local and national) and European supervisors. Local and national politicians clearly have an incentive to bail in foreign bondholders and protect domestic bondholders, as this protects taxpayers and voters. Centralization of financial policies might not be enough to achieve financial stability, financial integration, and economic growth in Europe. True harmonization of the fundamental laws and the steps toward a political union are probably necessary if bail-ins are to work as they should, and further reduce the implicit government guarantees for large, interconnected banks.[315] Until then it is both premature, and wishful thinking, to say good-bye to government bailouts and "too-big-to-fail."

Single Deposit Insurance Scheme – Why we need it and how it could be working?

The EU has introduced a single deposit insurance scheme, EDIS, as the third pillar of a European banking union. As a first step, the Union agreed on a Deposit Guarantee Scheme Directive (DGSD).[316] The DGSD ensures that deposits in all member states will continue to be guaranteed up to EUR 100,000 per depositor and bank. The DGSD also ensures faster payouts with specific repayment deadlines, which will be gradually reduced from 20 working days to 7 working days. The banking union requires national deposit insurance schemes to reach a level of ex ante funding of 8 percent of insured deposits by 2014.

315 Schich and Kim (2012) provide some early evidence for a reduction in implicit government guarantees due to the introduction of bank resolution regimes.
316 Compare EC (2015a).

However, a truly common pan-European deposit insurance scheme, that requires all deposit insurance premiums to be paid into a common fund, does not exist. Such a scheme requires breaking the doom loop in times of crisis, because national budgets would still be exposed to banking crises if they needed to back stop their national deposit insurance schemes. It would also allow the risks and costs of financial shocks to be diversified.[317]

Not unlike the SRF, a common EDIS would be privately funded through ex ante, risk-based fees that all of the participating banks would pay. The use of risk-based variable fees, set and collected by an independent European agency, would be designed in such a way as to limit moral hazard. In that sense, the scope of the EDIS would coincide with that of the SSM, that is, it would be mandatory for all Eurozone member states and optional for other EU banking systems. Instead of creating a new authority, the EDIS could be housed by the SRB. The joint institution would become the European Deposit Insurance and Resolution Authority (EDIRA). The role model for this new agency is of course the US FDIC. Similar to the FDIC, the EDIRA would need to be well-funded ex ante and would need access to a fiscal backstop, which could be provided by the ESM.[318] The ESM could also house the new European SDRM (see Figure 41).

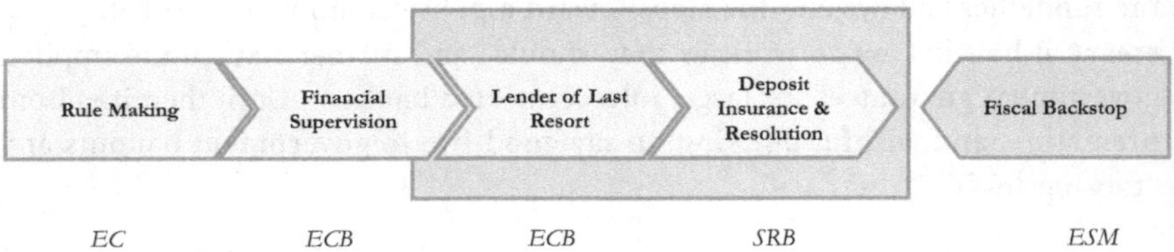

(Figure 41: European bodies in the Banking Union, see de Haan et al. (2015), Figure 3.3, p 104)

Such a proposal, however, has been met with strong opposition from the German government, which points to the need to properly account for sovereign risk on member banks' balance sheets before implementing a European deposit insurance scheme. The Dutch government, which currently holds the EU presidency, has set out five options for the treatment of sovereign risk on banks' balance sheets. The two main options involve either limiting the sovereign exposure of a bank in relation to its capital, or the introduction of a risk weighting for sovereign bonds. These proposals have been met with resistance from the French and Italian governments, with no immediate compromise in sight. Referring the issue back to the BCBS might help to maintain banking harmony, but will certainly hinder a full banking union in Europe.

317 See EC (2015b).
318 See Gros, Schoenmaker (2013).

In summary

A full European banking union is clearly in the realm of the possible. However, to fully reap its benefits in terms of increased financial stability, deeper financial integration and more economic growth, the union needs to be fully implemented. Completing the institutional framework by establishing an EDIRA, modeled after the US FDIC, and implementing the ESM as a common fiscal backstop, would allow the banking union to function properly. But centralization of financial policies might not be enough to get European banking (and Europe) back on track. More harmonization is required to break the gridlock of national banking deals in Europe. A true European banking deal still seems far away. In a true banking union, it should not matter whether an individual member country has a functioning banking system, and where the banks that are providing services in that country are ultimately headquartered.

Chapter 14: The larger context – how much (political) union does the EMU need?

"J'ai toujours pensé que l'Europe se ferait dans les crises, et qu'elle serait la somme des solutions qu'on apporterait à ces crises" [319]

Jean Monnet, French political economist, regarded as a founding father of the European Union. (1976)

"…, we think the euro is irreversible."[320]

Mario Draghi, current President of the European Central Bank, (2012)

"We are convinced that the majority of people believe in the fundamental idea of the European Union and its reformability and development and does not want to sacrifice it to nationalist tendencies. Nothing less than the protection of an alliance, which secures peace and guarantees individual freedom, justice and legal security are at stake." [321]

#PULSEOFEUROPE, a pro-EU citizens' initiative, (2016)

As the protracted banking crisis and sovereign debt crisis have demonstrated, the European Economic and Monetary Union (EMU) has been inherently fragile. That fragility resulted partly from a flawed regulatory regime which allowed the build-up of outsized leverage in the banking system. It also resulted from a lack of banking union, ie the lack of a comprehensive framework of common supervision, crisis management and deposit insurance. Plus, it resulted from a lack of budgetary union.

To increase the stability of the EMU, more political union is required. Member states must relinquish their sovereignty, not only in terms of monetary policy, but also in terms of banking policies and, more importantly, in terms of budget and sovereign debt policies. This becomes even more crucial as the EU continues to expand in size and in heterogeneity. Let us examine the broader picture: Why is the EMU in its current form inherently unstable? And what steps could, should

319 See Monnet (1976), p 488.
320 See Draghi (2012).
321 See #PULSEOFEUROPE (2017).

and are being taken to complete it? And what challenges are being encountered on the way?

More (political) union in Europe, however, will not come about without a renewed sense of common purpose. Perhaps the rise of populism will spark a strong reaction among Europeans; perhaps a reaction to overcome the centrifugal forces generated by the Great Financial Crisis, and enable more progress on the thorny path to European union.

Europe's incomplete union

European Monetary Union, in its current form, is incomplete. It is inherently unstable, as the recent banking, sovereign debt and economic crises, which occurred in the wake of the Great Financial Crisis, have shown. The incompleteness of the EMU arises because it is a monetary union without a risk sharing mechanism, in other words, a monetary union without budgetary union. The main disadvantage of the EMU is that there is one clear monetary authority, the ECB, but many independent national governments with their own government budgets. These national governments issue their own debt, all denominated in a common currency. In this set up, the sovereign bonds of weaker member states are vulnerable to self-fulfilling market speculation in the wake of asymmetric external shocks, ie shocks which affect the economies of individual member states differently.

De Grauwe, (2014), analyzes the instability of monetary union without budgetary union:[322]

(1) *No liquidity provider of last resort:* without a central bank acting as a liquidity provider of last resort for the government, sovereign debt is vulnerable to speculative attacks following external shocks such as a recession or a sudden loss in competitiveness. Put another way, "a speculative selling of governments bonds out of fear that the government may have insufficient cash would not be possible", if a central bank could act as the liquidity provider of last resort. The vulnerability to speculative attacks increases with the level of sovereign debt, the size of the externally held debt, and the inefficiency of the tax system.

(2) *Negative spill-overs into the banking sector:* countries in an incomplete monetary union are not only vulnerable to speculative attacks on their sovereign bonds, they will also see their banking system affected negatively. As investors try to avoid being caught in a default scenario, they pull out of sovereign bonds and move their funds into a safer currency. Banks therefore

322 See de Grauwe (2014), pp 101–118.

suffer valuation losses on their bond holdings and experience a funding crisis. The sovereign debt crisis spills over into the banking sector, even if the banking sector was safe and sound to begin with. Rescuing the banking system on its own will further weaken – if not overstretch – the sovereign and make sovereign debt even more vulnerable to market speculation.

(3) *Inability to use automatic stabilizers:* Moreover, higher sovereign spreads make funding of counter-cyclical economic programs more difficult, and can force a country into austerity and deflation. For example, as spreads widen under speculative attacks, the sovereign can no longer raise the required levels of debt needed to pursue counter-cyclical economic policies. In fact, it is pushed into austerity.

The situation analyzed by de Grauwe was exactly the situation in the EU periphery after the Great Financial Crisis. Whilst the shock in Greece was probably so great that default within the EMU was a rational choice for the Greek government (but apparently not for the other members of the EMU due to fears of contagion risk), Ireland, Portugal, Spain and, still later, Greece, Cyprus and Italy saw significant spread widening of their sovereign bonds as investors anticipated their default and began to sell their bond holdings. In Ireland, Portugal and Spain it was a rapidly deteriorating economy and a real-estate-related banking crisis that forced the hand of the sovereign. In Greece, at a later stage, and in Cyprus, it was the spilling over of the Greek sovereign-debt restructuring into the banking systems that led to a banking crisis. The inherent fragility of the EMU became manifestly evident in the "Euro crisis".

Ultimately, it was the ECB, as a provider of liquidity of last resort, which helped to calm markets and stop contagion in Europe. In fact, following Mario Draghi's (2012) famous "the ECB is ready to do whatever it takes to preserve the Euro. And, believe me, it will be enough"[323] speech in London on 26th July, 2012, sovereign spreads in the periphery started to recover. Draghi's statement was further backed up by the ECB announcement of 2nd August, 2012, in which the ECB articulated its intention to perform Outright Monetary Transactions (OMTs) in secondary Euro bond markets. A necessary condition for OMT is strict conditionality attached to an appropriate European Stability Mechanism (ESM) program. In other words, Eurozone countries needed to come to the support of a fellow member state before the ECB would start buying in the secondary bond market. Although never enacted to date, OMT has been quite effective in addressing the distortions in the bond markets which originated from unfounded fears of investors about the reversibility of the Euro.

In January 2015, following other central banks such as the Fed, the Bank of

323 See Draghi (2012).

England, and the Bank of Japan, the ECB decided to embark on an expanded program of asset purchases, a policy also referred to as Quantitative Easing (QE).[324] The objective of this policy has been to address the risks of a prolonged period of too-low inflation. However, as inflation is once again beginning to rise but minimal or zero interest rates become negative real rates, political pressure in the core countries is mounting to exit from QE policy, and start raising interest rates. In fact, the QE policy of the ECB can only buy time and simultaneously increases the risk of moral hazard. If the periphery does not use the opportunity of low interest rates to increase its competitiveness, reduce its debt levels and improves the efficiency of their tax systems, they will be without air cover if, and when, the ECB raises interest rates again.

The question going forward, therefore, will be whether the battered economies on the periphery have recovered enough by then to be able to fund their deficits at higher rates. But what would happen, if the world fell into a currency and trade war, or the populist movement gained pace in certain European member states? Could all European member states withstand the next shocks and defend their sovereign bond markets? It is clear, that the ECB cannot remain the only game in town. Put differently, we need to assess and evaluate options to complete the EMU today if we want to have a more stable EMU tomorrow.

...and options to make Europe more resilient, more prosperous

What are the options to make Europe more resilient and more prosperous? Creating a United States of Europe would certainly solve the problem of an incomplete monetary union: but it is Utopia. Even if populist voters are not in the majority, it is both unlikely and risky to think that the majority of the population in Europe would support the creation of a United States of Europe.

More steps towards political unification, however, are necessary. Let us look at two important steps in that regard: the consolidation of government budgets and debts as well, as the coordination of budgetary and economic policies.

In terms of government budgets and debts, full consolidation remains unrealistic as long as there is no one European sovereign. Therefore, the pertinent question is, what small steps can be taken in the same direction? One step, clearly would be the joint issuance of common bonds. Other, perhaps politically more achievable, steps would be the implementation of a "blue" and "red" bond structure[325] or the creation of European Safe Bonds (ESBies)[326]:

324 See de Haan et al. (2015), pp 138–139, for a discussion of QE.

325 See Delpla and von Weizsäcker (2010).

326 See Brunnermeier et al. (2011).

(1) *Joint issuance of common bonds:* by jointly issuing common bonds, the participating member states become jointly liable for the debt they have issued together. This would send a visible and strong signal to the market. By pooling their sovereign debts, the members of the EMU would protect themselves against the destabilizing speculative attacks which arise from their inability to control the currency in which their debt has been issued, ie by devaluation. Two issues arise, however, with common Eurobonds. Firstly, the issue of moral hazard: common bonds represent an implicit insurance for participating members. The joint liability creates an incentive for participating member states to cheat and issue too much debt. Obviously, this risk creates strong push back from the stronger members participating in the common bonds. Strengthening mechanisms to improve fiscal and budgetary discipline are key. The second problem results from the fact that a common bond would make debt finance more expensive for those countries like Finland, Germany and the Netherlands which have a AAA country rating and therefore very low stand-alone funding costs.

(2) *Tiered "blue" and "red" bond structure:* one proposal to deal with the second issue is that of a tiered "blue" and "red" bond structure. Countries would only be able to participate by up to 60 percent of their GDP in joint Eurobond issuance, so called "blue" bonds. Anything above 60 percent of GDP would have to be issued on the national debt markets as so called "red" bonds. The red bonds would carry a higher risk premium than the blue bonds. In other words, beyond 60 percent debt-to-GDP ratio the marginal cost of debt would jump, creating a strong incentive for keeping the debt at or below the 60 percent of GDP level. The blue bond/red bond proposal would also shield a significant portion of sovereign debt from speculative attacks. Banking regulation could be revised in such a way that it maintained a zero-percent risk weighting for blue bonds and put increased risk weightings on red bonds. Blue bonds would create joint incentives for enhancing the competitiveness of the union altogether.

(3) *Creation of European Safe Bonds (ESBies):* Another proposal would be the creation of ESBies, via a simple securitization structure with two different tranches of debt. These bonds do not involve any joint liability of debt. Although they would not fully shield members of the monetary union from speculative attacks following adverse shocks, this structure would, nevertheless, limit negative banking spill overs and cross-border flight to quality distortions, thereby breaking the "devilish nexus" between bank and sovereign risk. The proposal involves the pooling of national bonds and the subsequent tranching of the pool into a senior and junior bond. The senior tranches could be favored by banking regulation in terms of lower risk weighting.

Another important step toward consolidation of government budget and debts would be the completion of European banking union, more especially, the introduction of a common deposit insurance and crisis resolution mechanism. In order to fully break the devilish and divisive bank-sovereign debt nexus, a common European back-stop would be required, a role that could be assumed by the ESM.

The key issue of all proposals to consolidate government budgets and debts in the Eurozone is the risk of moral hazard. Weaker sovereigns have an incentive to increase their budget deficits, effectively piggy-backing on the implicit insurance provided by common bonds and banking union. Centralized banking supervision is one protection against moral hazard. The other protection would be a more stringent regulation of government-debt risk weighting and exposure sizes. Even more important would be the tighter coordination of budgetary and economic policies, and an increased accountability vis-à-vis the European Community for budgetary discipline.

Clearly, there is a need to protect the EMU from two pivotal risks, the internal moral hazard risk – members becoming more reckless in their spending and financing patterns – and the external risk of investors speculating on sovereign debt default. More solidarity is the right answer to the second risk but it also opens the door for moral hazard: finding the right balance remains a challenge. The irony of the current situation is that, while the population might feel we need less "Europe" because crisis management has been so flawed, in actuality we need more European unification and integration.[327] Muddling through is less and less of an option. The bigger the EU, the higher the necessity – and the greater the benefits – of making progress towards more unification.

Let us look how the moral hazard risk is being addressed in the EMU. In order to tighten fiscal and economic policies, European policy makers have taken several important steps, especially the introduction of the Six-Pack and the Two-Pack, the Treaty on Stability Coordination and Governance (TSCG), and the Macroeconomic Imbalance Procedure (MIP):[328]

(1) *The Six-Pack:* the Six-Pack, consisting of five Regulations and one Directive, entered into force on 13th December, 2011. Most importantly, it reinforces the preventive and corrective arm of the Stability and Growth Pact (SGP). Financial sanctions for a country may eventually reach 0.5 percent of GDP.
(2) *The Two-Pack:* the Two-Pack added two more Regulations, entering into force on 30th May, 2013. It requires member states to submit their draft budget plan to the European Commission, which is authorized to check it beforehand, and can request revisions.

327 See Economist (2017).
328 See de Haan et al. (2015), pp 96–97, for a good summary of these measures.

(3) *The TSCG:* on 1st January, 2013, the TSCG came into force. The articles in Title III of the Treaty referring to fiscal policy are also known as the Fiscal Compact. The most important elements are a balanced budget rule and a strengthening of the sanctioning mechanism of excessive deficits. A balanced budget rule must be introduced in the national law of the member states concerned. Going forward, at each stage of the Excessive Deficit Process (EDP), member states will support the Commission's proposals for corrective action, unless a qualified majority is against them.

(4) *The MIP:* to prevent large financial and macro-economic imbalances within the Eurozone, policy-makers have also introduced the continuous monitoring of a "score-board", consisting of a set of 11 indicators covering the major sources of macro-economic imbalances. For each indicator, thresholds have been defined to identify sources of imbalances. By analogy to the SGP, the MIP has a preventive and a corrective arm. Non-compliance with the Council's recommendations may lead to sanctions that could eventually reach 0.2 percent of GDP.

While these are important steps in the right direction, doubts remain as to whether mere contractual provisions can really achieve tighter policy coordination. It remains to be seen, how determined the EC will be in sanctioning violations by individual member states. It will be all about accountability and adherence to rules.

European politicians have clearly recognized this and are pushing in the direction of more European integration. In 2016, Jean-Claude Juncker, President of the EC, Donald Tusk, President of the European Summit, Jeroen Dijsselbloem, President of the Euro Group, Mario Draghi, President of the ECB, and Martin Schulz, President of the EP, published their report on "Completing Europe's Economic and Monetary Union", the so-called "five Presidents'" Report.[329] Amongst others, the report builds on the van Rompuy report, (2012). It stresses the need for more "risk-sharing" within the EMU. In particular, it argues for the achievement of four unions: economic; financial; fiscal; and political. This would take place in two stages. In stage one, by June 2017, ("deepening by doing"), the EU institutions and member states would build on existing Treaties. In stage two, more far-reaching measures would be agreed to complete the EMU's economic and institutional architecture.

(1) *Economic Union:* the notion of convergence is at the heart of the economic union proposal. Stronger focus will be put on employment and social performance. Significant and sustained convergence towards similarly resilient economies should become more binding. The report also proposes a

329 See EC (2015).

strengthened implementation of the MIP as well as stronger coordination of economic policies.

(2) *Financial Union:* in stage one, a major step would be to complete European banking union, by (amongst others):
   a. setting up a bridging finance mechanism for the Single Resolution Fund (SRF),
   b. implementing concrete steps towards the common backstop to the SRF,
   c. agreeing on a common deposit insurance scheme, and
   d. improving the effectiveness of the ESM for bank recapitalization.
   e. the launch of capital markets union, and
   f. a reinforcement of the ESRB.

(3) *Fiscal Union:* stage one involves the creation of a new, and advisory, European fiscal board to provide an independent, public assessment of how budgets and their execution would perform against the European fiscal framework. Stage two would involve the setting up of a macro-economic stabilization function for the Eurozone.

(4) *Political Union:* political union should provide the foundations for economic, financial and fiscal union through more European democratic accountability, legitimacy and institutional strengthening.

Key immediate steps proposed in stage one are:

(1) a revamp of the annual cycle of macro-economic policy coordination (also referred to as the "European semester")
(2) strengthening of parliamentary control as part of the European semester
(3) increasing the level of cooperation between the European parliament and national parliaments
(4) reinforcing the steer of the Euro Group
(5) taking steps towards a consolidated external representation of the Eurozone, and
(6) integrating into European law a few of the inter-governmental, bilateral mechanisms such as the TSCG.

Ultimately, in stage two, the goal would be to integrate ESM into the EU legislative framework and set up a Eurozone treasury accountable at the European level.

Whilst the proposals clearly point in the direction of more European union, they remain fairly unspecific, and the timeline lacks a sense of urgency, with stage two only due to be completed in 2025. The report also refers to another white paper to be presented in the spring of 2017, which will detail the next steps needed to make the transition from stage one to stage two, including a comprehensive legislative roadmap. The report does not discuss improvements in the ESM's governance structure nor does it propose specific measures to deal with a sovereign default in the Eurozone.

The report clearly demonstrates how difficult it is to strike a balance between the economic necessity to strengthen the EMU and achieve more European union, whilst at the same time facing the lack of political support from member states. For European banks, the most important measure would clearly be the completion of banking union.

In summary

European Economic and Monetary Union remains incomplete without full implementation of banking union, and tangible steps towards more fiscal and budgetary union. This ultimately requires more political unification in Europe. More (political) union in Europe, however, will not come about without a renewed sense of common purpose. Perhaps the rise of populism will spark strong a reaction among Europeans to overcome centrifugal forces at work and make more progress on the thorny path to more European union.

Politicians had hoped that a monetary union would ultimately bring about more political union. In hindsight, this is proving to be a risky bet. The incompleteness of monetary union has been undermining the credibility of our common project. In the long run, an incomplete EMU will do more harm than good. Therefore, the EMU needs to be completed as soon as possible. Banking union is a key component. Completion of the EMU and implementation of banking union requires more political union. And more political union means more accountability from member states, not less.

Epilogue

It is time for a short recap:

Where did we start from?

Europe, and its economy, is very dependent on the well-being of the banks. The European banking landscape pre-crisis was characterized by the emergence of large, highly-leveraged, and complex international banking groups. Banks are special institutions; their leverage makes them vulnerable to bank runs. Since bank runs are contagious, and can bring the financial system to a grinding halt – with negative consequences for the real economy – there is a need for regulation, supervision, and additional safety nets such as deposit insurance and central bank lending of last resort. But regulation, supervision and safety nets can also increase moral hazard, ie the risk of increased negligent – even reckless – behavior, and create a false sense of security, whilst also undermining market discipline.

What did European banking and finance look like in less troublesome times?

The re-engineering of European banking moved higher up the European political agenda in the 1980s, and was seen as an important condition for the completion of the Internal Market. As barriers to entry were gradually eroded by EU legislation, banks began to branch out and make cross-border acquisitions. Wholesale banking markets, including money markets, began to integrate more quickly than the market for retail banking services. On the eve of the Great Financial Crisis of 2007–2009, the Eurozone was operating with one money, but (too) many different banking systems; monetary union was incomplete – with a weak contractual budgetary union, no political union – and a decentralized bank supervision architecture.

What happened as the crisis was hitting – and multiplying?

The global Great Financial Crisis started in the US subprime mortgage market. Through securitizations and off-balance-sheet vehicles, with significant mismatches between leverage and funding maturities, the crisis spread to Europe. It exposed significant weaknesses in the regulatory and supervisory framework and the banks' own risk management practices. Amid mounting losses, and increasing uncertainty, the inter-bank market broke down, and forced significant liquidity injections by the ECB. The shortage of liquidity forced the banks to sell assets at discount prices, which set off a deadly loss-spiral that, in turn, led to further devaluations and write-downs, thereby turning the liquidity crisis into a full-blown solvency crisis. Ad hoc support coordinated by central banks was not enough to prevent a total meltdown. Governments were forced to bail out the banks, both in the US and in Europe.

How did the crisis become existential in Europe?

Early lessons drawn from the Great Financial Crisis were incomplete in a Europe shackled by outdated principles. Micro-prudential supervision was only coordinated at the level of the ESAs, as national governments were unwilling to transfer supervisory authority to a central institution. Giving the ECB a bigger role in macro-prudential supervision, and entrusting it with micro-prudential supervision of banks, was prevented by the principle of a central bank focused solely on monetary stability. Bank bail-outs and restructurings, necessary to preserve financial stability, were held back by the state aid framework. As a consequence, bank rescues and restructurings were only undertaken half-heartedly. Nevertheless, the salvaging of the banks both burdened government budgets and created the expectations of more rescues across the EU. The "Euro crisis" was caused by a lack of fiscal discipline, diverging financial boom-bust cycles, diverging competitiveness, and the devilish sovereign debt-bank nexus. Initially, politicians were reluctant to let a Eurozone sovereign default, and undergo debt restructuring. Crisis management at the European level was uncoordinated, relying initially on inter-governmental bail-out agreements, instead of building the necessary institutions and introducing market discipline right away. The bail-outs created the perception of violating the spirit (if not the substance) of the Maastricht Treaty. The IMF lost its credibility in agreeing to the first Greek bail-out. The introduction of PSI came too late.

How can we finish the business of repairing European banking – in a principled way?

The Great Financial Crisis exposed significant weaknesses in Europe's financial architecture. National financial policies proved incompatible with financial stability and financial integration in the Eurozone. In a serious banking crisis, as Ireland showed, lack of a centralized rescue mechanism pushes the sovereign into a debt crisis. The Greek crisis demonstrated how an over-indebted sovereign and a collapsing economy affect the banks, and how the negative feedback loop is reinforced if the banks hold significant amounts of sovereign debt. Since the outbreak of the Great Financial Crisis, governments have initiated and implemented many reforms: the BCBS has reformed the Basel framework and has strengthened supervision; bail-in for bank debt has been introduced with a view to strengthen market discipline and making banks safe to fail without recourse to taxpayers' money. More still needs to be done in terms of sovereign debt restructuring. Banking union needs to be fully implemented, so as to fully reap the benefits of increased financial stability, deeper financial integration and more economic growth. EMU remains incomplete without full implementation of banking union and tangible steps towards more fiscal and budgetary union. This ultimately requires more political unification in Europe. More (political) union in Europe, however, will not come about without a renewed sense of common purpose.

Where does this leave us in terms of – tentative – recommendations for European regulators, supervisors, bankers, academics and politicians?

In terms of bank regulation, we need to push for more simplicity, less complexity and more accountability. And we need to increase awareness of the limitations of the current regulatory framework. Clearly, exposure limits and proper risk weightings for sovereign debt are crucial, not only with regards to Eurozone sovereign debt, but also for other sovereign debt, given the mounting geopolitical tensions globally.

In terms of supervision, we need more centralization, more rights for early interventions and more independence from the influence of national financial policies. There should be less tolerance for protracted forebearance, for instance with regards to overexposure and under-provisioning of NPLs, or insufficient cyber-risk prevention and risk concentrations individually or in aggregate. Brexit creates additional challenges as more banking activities are set to migrate from the UK to the Continent.

Bank management also needs to focus on reducing complexity and leverage, building capital buffers and reducing costs. The restructuring of bank balance sheets and business models needs to be accelerated. The FinTech revolution is an opportunity to accelerate this restructuring, not a threat. Banking in the digital age, however, poses new challenges for risk management and financial stability.

At the national level, the political focus should be on improving the financial situation and competitiveness – in a coordinated way. At the European level, politicians should pursue a two-pronged strategy of a) strengthening the common cause and b) taking steps to complete economic and monetary union: the ultimate goal must be political union. We need more political leadership for Europe as a whole; not less for (the false) fear of appearing undemocratic. Completing banking union and creating a common fiscal back-stop for bank resolution is a must, as is creating a true capital markets union while implementing Brexit and therefore London exit, harmonizing fundamental law on the way.

Academic research, last, but not least, needs to focus on finding fault-lines in the overall European financial architecture and introduce their insights into public and political debate.

We need to recognize that the rehabilitation of European banking is very much unfinished business; we must recognize that we need to put European banking back on track if want prosperity.

In the end, it is about accountability: the accountability of bankers, regulators, supervisors, politicians and academic researchers. All of us are accountable for putting European banking back on track.

List of Abbreviations

ABCP	Asset-Backed Commercial Paper
AIG	American International Group
AQR	Asset Quality Review
ASC	Advisory Scientific Committee
AT	Austria
AT1	Additional Tier 1
ATC	Advisory Technical Committee
BCBS	Basel Committee on Banking Supervision
BE	Belgium
BRRD	Bank Recovery and Resolution Directive
CA	Comprehensive Assessment
CAPM	Capital Asset Pricing Model
CDO	Collateralized Debt Obligation
CDS	Credit Default Swap
CEBS	Committee of European Banking Supervisors
CEE	Central and Eastern Europe
CEO	Chief Executive Officer
CEPS	Centre for European Policy Studies
CET1	Common Equity Tier 1
CJEU	Court of Justice of the European Union
CoE	Cost of Equity
CRA	Community Reinvestment Act
CRD	Capital Requirements Directive
CRR	Capital Requirements Regulation
CT1	Core Tier 1
DG	Directorate General
DGSD	Deposit Guarantee Scheme Directive
DIDMCA	Depository Institutions Deregulation and Monetary Control Act
EBA	European Banking Authority
EBC	European Banking Committee
EBT	Earnings before Taxes
ECB	European Central Bank
ECSC	European Coal and Steel Community

ECU	European Currency Unit
EDIRA	European Deposit Insurance and Resolution Authority
EDIS	European Deposit Insurance Scheme
EDP	Excessive Deficit Procedure
EEA	European Economic Area
EEC	European Economic Community
EFC	Economic and Financial Committee
EFSF	European Financial Stability Facility
EFSM	European Financial Stability Mechanism
EIOPA	European Insurance and Occupational Pension Authority
ELA	Emergency Liquidity Assistance
EMI	European Monetary Institute
EMS	European Monetary System
EMU	Economic and Monetary Union
EONIA	Euro OverNight Index Average
ERM	European Exchange Rate Mechanism
ES	Spain
ESA	European Supervisory Authority
ESB	European Safe Bonds
ESCB	European System of Central Banks
ESFS	European System of Financial Supervision
ESM	European Stability Mechanism
ESMA	European Securities and Market Authority
ESRB	European Systemic Risk Board
ESRC	European Systemic Risk Council
EU	European Union
EUR	Euro
FDIC	Federal Deposit Insurance Corporation
FDICIA	Federal Deposit Insurance Corporation Improvement Act
Fed	Federal Reserve Bank
FHA	Federal Housing Agency
FI	Finland
FICO	Fair Isaac Company
FR	France
FSAP	Financial Services Action Plan
FSB	Financial Stability Board
FSOC	Financial Stability Oversight Council
GDP	Gross Domestic Product
GR	Greece
G-SIB	Global, systemically-important bank
HR	Human Resources
HRE	Hypo Real Estate Group
ICAAP	Internal Capital Adequacy Assessment Process
IE	Republic of Ireland
IEO	Independent Evaluation Office
IFRS	International Financial Reporting Standards

IMF	International Monetary Fund
IRBA	Internal Ratings-Based Approach
IRR	Interest rate risk
IT	Italy
KDB	Korea Development Bank
KGSM	Kellogg Graduate School of Management
LCR	Liquidity coverage ratio
LLP	Loan Loss Provision
M&A	Mergers and Acquisitions
MiFID	Markets in Financial Instruments Directive
MIP	Macro-economic Imbalance Procedure
MoU	Memorandum of Understanding
MREL	Minimum Requirements for Eligible Liabilities
MRO	Main Refinancing Operations
NAMA	National Asset Management Agency (Ireland)
NCB	National Central Bank
NL	The Netherlands
NPL	Non-performing loans
NSFR	Net stable funding ratio
OCC	Office of the Comptroller of the Currency
OECD	Organisation for Economic Co-operation & Development
OFS	Office of Financial Stability
OMT	Outright Monetary Transaction
OTS	Office of Thrift Supervision
P&L	Profit and loss
PSI	Private Sector Involvement
PT	Portugal
PV	Present Value
QE	Quantitative Easing
Repo	Repurchase Agreement
RMBS	Residential Mortgage-Backed Securities
RoA	Return on Assets
RoE	Return on Equity
RoW	Rest of World
RWA	Risk-weighted Assets
S&L	Savings and loans
SDRM	Sovereign Debt Restructuring Mechanism
SEA	Single European Act
SEC	Securities and Exchange Commission
SGP	Stability and Growth Pact
SIFI	Systemically Important Financial Institution
SIV	Structured Investment Vehicle
SME	Small-and medium-sized enterprises
S&P	Standard & Poor's Rating Agency
SPV	Special Purpose Vehicle
SRB	Single Resolution Board

SRF	Single Resolution Fund
SRM	Single Resolution Mechanism
SSM	Single Supervisory Mechanism
TARGET	Trans-European Automated Real-Time Gross Settlement Express Transfer System
TARP	Troubled Asset Relief Program
TFEU	Treaty on the Functioning of the European Union
TLAC	Total Loss Absorbing Capacity
TSCG	Treaty on Stability Coordination and Governance
UK	United Kingdom
US	United States
USA	United States of America
USD	United States Dollar
VaR	Value at Risk
WestLB	Westdeutsche Landesbank

List of Figures

List of References

#PULSEOFEUROPE (2017): Website, found at http://pulseofeurope.eu/?lang=en, last accessed on 14th March, 2017.

Acharya, Viral, Cooley, Thomas, Richardson, Matthew, Walter, Ingo (eds.) (2010): Regulating Wall Street: the Dodd-Frank Act and the New Architecture of Global Finance, Wiley, 2010.

Acharya, Viral, Drechsler, Itamar, Schnabel, Philipp (2014): A Pyrrhic Victory? Bank Bailouts and Sovereign Credit Risk, in: The Journal of Finance, Vol. LXIX, No. 6, December, 2014.

Acharya, Viral, Engle, Robert, Richardson, Matthew (2012): Capital Shortfall: A New Approach to Ranking and Regulating Systemic Risks, in: American Economic Review Papers & Proceedings, Vol. 102, pp 59–64.

Acharya, Viral, Philippon, Thomas, Richardson, Matthew, Roubini, Nouriel (2009): Prologue: A Bird's Eye View – The Financial Crisis of 2007–2009: Causes and Remedies, in: Acharya, Richardson (eds.): Restoring Financial Stability – How to Repair a Failed System, Wiley, pp 1–56.

Acharya, Viral, Richardson, Matthew (eds.) (2009): Restoring Financial Stability – How to Repair a Failed System, Wiley.

Acharya, Viral, Schnabl, Philipp (2010): Do Global Banks Spread Global Imbalances? Asset-Backed Commercial Paper during the Financial Crisis of 2007–2009, in: IMF Economic Review, Vol. 58, No. 1, pp 37–73.

Acharya, Viral, Steffen, Sascha (2013): Falling Short of Expectations? Stress-Testing the European Banking System, Policy Paper, 20th December, 2013, later appeared as CEPS Policy Brief, No. 315, 15th January, 2014.

Acharya, Viral, Sundram, Rangarajan (2009): The Financial Sector Bail-out. Sowing the Seeds for the next Crisis, in: Acharya, Richardson (eds.): Restoring Financial Stability – How to Repair a Failed System, Wiley, pp 327–351.

Admati, Anat, DeMarzo, Peter, Hellwig, Martin, Pfleiderer, Paul (2010): Fallacies, Irrelevant Facts, and Myths in the Discussion of Capital Regulation: Why Bank Equity is Not Expensive, Stanford GSB Working Paper No. 2063.

Admati, Anat, Hellwig, Martin (2013): The Bankers' New Clothes: What's wrong with Banking and What to do about it, Princeton University Press.

Adrian, Thomas, Shin, Hyun Song (2010): The Changing Nature of Financial Intermediation and the Financial Crisis of 2007–09, Federal Reserve Bank of New York Staff Reports 439.

–. (2010a): Liquidity and Leverage, Federal Reserve Bank of New York Staff Report No. 328, May 2008, revised December, 2010.

Allard, Julien, Blavy, Rodolphe (2011): Market Phoenixes and Banking Ducks – Are Recoveries Faster in Market-Based Economies?, IMF Working Paper WP/11/213 found at https://www.imf.org/external/pubs/ft/wp/2011/wp11213.pdf, last accessed on 22nd March, 2017.

Allen, Franklin, Beck, Thorsten, Carletti, Elena, Lane, Philip, Schoenmaker, Dirk, Wagner, Wolf (2011): Cross-Border Banking in Europe: Implications for Financial Stability and Macroeconomic Policies, Center for Economic Policy Research (CEPR).

Allen, Franklin, Carletti, Elena, Gu, Xian (2012): The Role of Banks in Financial Systems, in: Allen N Berger, Philip Molyneux, John O S Wilson (eds.): The Oxford Handbook of Banking, 2nd edition, Oxford University Press.

Allen, Franklin, Gale, Douglas (2008): Comparing Financial Systems, MIT Press.

Angeloni, Ignazio (2012): Toward a European Banking Union, in CESifo Forum 4/2012, pp 10–14.

Angeloni, Ignazio, Ehrmann, Michael (2003): Monetary Policy transmission in the Eurozone: Any Changes after EMU?, ECB Working Paper No. 240, July, 2003.

Antoniades, Adonis (2015): Commercial Bank Failures During the Great Recession: The Real (Estate) Story, BIS Working Papers No. 530, November, 2015.

Avgouleas, Emilios, Goodhart, Charles (2014): A critical evaluation of bail-in as a bank recapitalisation mechanism, CEPR Discussion Paper Series, No. 10065, July, 2014.

Avgouleas, Emilios, Goodhart, Charles, Schoenmaker, Dirk (2012): Bank Resolution Plans as a catalyst for global financial reform, in: Journal of Financial Stability, Vol.9, No. 2, 2012, pp 210–218.

Bagehot, Walter (1962): Lombard Street – The classic book on the money market and the Bank of England, Harriman House.

Bande, Armand (2012): Banking Integration in the EU: a process marked by a battle between systems, Financial Stability Research Group University of Twente, found at https://www.utwente.nl/en/bms/pa/staff/donnelly/Thesis%20-%20A%20%20Bande%2020%2008%2012.pdf, last accessed on 5th February, 2017.

Bank of England (2009): Financial Stability Report, Issue No. 25, June, 2009, found at http://www.bankofengland.co.uk/publications/Documents/fsr/2009/fsrfull0906.pdf, last accessed on 23rd March, 2017.

–. (2009a): Financial Stability Report, Issue No. 26, December, 2009, found at http://www.bankofengland.co.uk/publications/Documents/fsr/2009/fsrfull0912.pdf, last accessed on 23rd March, 2017.

Barnier, Michel (2014): quoted in Euractive, Europe's bank stress test were unreliable, EU auditors say, by James Crisp, 3rd July, 2014, found at http://www.euractiv.com/section/euro-finance/news/europe-s-bank-stress-tests-were-unreliable-eu-auditors-say/, last accessed on 3rd March, 2017.

Barth, James, Caprio, Jr, Gerard, Levine, Ross (2002): Bank Regulation and Supervision: What Works Best?, NBER Working Paper No. 9323.

Barth, James, Li, Tong, Lu, Wengling (2009): Bank Regulation in the US, in: CESifo Economic Studies, 2009, pp 1–29.

Basel Committee on Banking Supervision (BCBS) (2004): Basel II: International Convergence of Capital Measurement and Capital Standards: A Revised Framework, June, 2004.

–. (2011): Basel III: A global regulatory framework for more resilient banks and banking systems, revised version June, 2011.

–. (2013): Basel III: The liquidity coverage rate and liquidity monitoring tools, January, 2013.

–. (2013a): Global systemically important banks: updated assessment methodology and the higher loss absorbency requirement, July, 2013.

–. (2014): Consultative Document – Basel III leverage ratio framework and disclosure requirements, final version January, 2014.

–. (2014a): Standards – Supervisory framework for measuring and controlling large exposures, April, 2014.

–. (2016): Consultative Document – Interest rate risk in the banking book, final version April, 2016.

BBVA Research (2014): Europe Regulation Watch: The European MREL: main characteristics and TLAC similarities and differences, 3rd December, 2014.

Beck, Thorsten, Coyle, Diane, Dewatripont, Mathias, Freixas, Xavier, Seabright, Paul (2010): Bailing out the Banks: Reconciling Stability and Competition – An analysis of state-supported schemes for financial institutions, CEPR, 2010.

Beck, Volker (2014): After AQR and stress test – where next for banking in the Eurozone, Vox Policy portal, 10th November, 2014.

Bernanke, Benjamin S (2005): The Global Saving Glut and the US Current Account Deficit, Remarks at the Sandridge Lecture, Virginia Association of Economists, Richmond, Virginia, 10th March, 2005.

–. (2010): Lessons from the Failure of Lehman Brothers, Testimony before the Committee on Financial Services, US House of Representatives, Washington, DC, 20th April, 2010.

Bijlsma, Michiel, Zwart, Gijsbert (2013): The Changing Landscape of Financial Markets in Europe, The United States and Japan, Bruegel Working Paper 2013/02.

Bikker, Jakob, Spierdijk, Laura, Finnie, Paul (2006): The Impact of Bank Size on Market Power, DNB Working Paper 120.

Bini Smaghi, Lorenzo (2009): Regulation and supervisory architecture: Is the EU on the right path?, speech, Brussels, 12th February, 2009, found at https://www.ecb.europa.eu/press/key/date/2009/html/sp090212.en.html, last accessed on 25th March, 2017.

Black, Susan, Fisher, Chay (2008): The Asset-Backed Commercial Paper Market, in: Bulletin Reserve Bank of Australia, January, 2008, pp 1–10.

Blundell-Wignall, Adrian (2012): Solving the Financial and Sovereign Crisis in Europe, in: OECD Journal: Financial Market Trends, Volume 2011, Issue 2, pp 1–23.

Blundell-Wignall, Adrian, Atkinson, Paul (2010): Thinking beyond Basel II: Necessary Solutions for Capital and Liquidity, in: OECD Journal: Financial Market Trends, Volume 2010, Issue 1, pp 1–23.

Blundell-Wignall, Adrian, Slovik, Patrick (2011): A Market Perspective on the European Sovereign Debt and Banking Crisis, in: OECD Journal, Financial Market Trends, Volume 2010, Issue 2, pp 1–28.

Bolkestein, Frits (2004): Progress on Financial Services Action Plan and Taxation, Address to European Parliament Committee on Economic and Monetary Affairs, Brussels, 16th March 2004, found at http://europa.eu/rapid/press-release_SPEECH-04-136_en.htm, last accessed on 9th February, 2017.

–. (2004a): Learning the lessons of the Financial Services Action Plan, Address at Edinburgh Finance and Investment Seminar, Edinburgh, 29th January, 2004, found at http://europa.eu/rapid/press-release_SPEECH-04-50_en.htm?locale=en, last accessed on 11th February, 2017.

Borio, Claudio (2003): Towards a Macroprudential Framework for Financial Supervision and Regulation?, CESifo Economic Studies, Vol. 49 (2), pp 181–216.

–. (2003): Towards a Macro-Prudential Framework for Financial Supervision and Regulation?, BIS Working Papers No. 128, February, 2003.

Brunnermeier, Markus (2008): Deciphering the Liquidity and Credit Crunch 2007–08, NBER Working Paper No. 14612, December, 2008.

–. (2011) ESBies: A Realistic Reform of Europe's Financial Architecture, VOX, October 2011, found at http://voxeu.org/article/esbies-realistic-reform-europes-financial-architecture, last accessed on 15th March, 2017.

Brunnermeier, Markus, Crocket, Andrew, Goodhart, Charles, Persaud, Avinash, Shin, Hyun Song (2009): The Fundamental Principles of Financial Regulation, Geneva Reports on the World Economy – Preliminary Conference Draft, 2009.

Brunnermeier, Markus, James, Harold, Landau, Jean-Pierre (2016): The Euro and the Battle of Ideas, Princeton University Press, 2016.

Bundesministerium der Finanzen (BMF) (2002): Anstaltslast und Gewährträgerhaftung; Entscheidung der Europäischen Kommission vom 27. März 2002, Geschäftszeichen E C 3 – F2505–104/02, 12th April, 2002.

Calello, Paul, Wilson, Ervin (2010): From bail-out to bail-in, in: The Economist, 28th January, 2010.

Calomiris, Charles, Haber, Stephen (2014): Fragile by Design, The Political Origins of Banking Crises & Scarce Credit, Princeton University Press.

Cecchini, Paolo (1988): The European Challenge, 1992: The Benefits of a Single Market, Gover, Aldershot.

Center for European Policy Studies (CEPS) Task Force Report (2010): Bank State Aid in the Financial Crisis, Fragmentation or Level Playing Field?, Brussels, October, 2010.

Cochrane, John (2012): Towards a Run-free Financial System, in: Marin Neil Baily, John B Taylor (eds.): Across the Great Divide, New Perspectives on the Financial Crisis, Hoover Institution Press, 2012, pp 197–249.

–. (2014): Challenges for Cost-Benefit Analysis of Financial Regulation, Working Paper, August, 2014.

Commission of the European Communities (1983): Financial Integration, Communication from the Commission to the Council, COM (83) 207, Brussels, 20th April 1983, found at http://aei.pitt.edu/5070/1/5070.pdf, last accessed on 5th February, 2017.

–. (1985): Completing the Internal Market, White Paper from the Commission to the European Council, COM (85) 310 final, Brussels, 14th June, 1985, available at http://europa.eu/documents/comm/white_papers/pdf/com1985_0310_f_en.pdf, last accessed on 8th February, 2017.

–. (1988): Europe 1992, The Overall Challenge, SEC (88) 524 final, Brussels, 13th April 1988, found at http://aei.pitt.edu/3813/1/3813.pdf, last accessed on 6th February, 2017.

Committee for the Study of Economic and Monetary Union (Jacques Delors, Chairman) (1989): Report on economic and monetary union in the European Community, presented 17th April, 1989, found at http://aei.pitt.edu/1007/1/monetary_delors.pdf, last accessed on 8th February, 2017.

Committee of Wise Men (2001): Final Report of the Committee of Wise Men on the Regulation of European Securities Markets, Brussels, found at http://ec.europa.eu/internal_market/securities/docs/lamfalussy/wisemen/final-report-wise-men_en.pdf, last accessed on 29th January, 2017.

Constancio, Vitor, (2016): Challenges for the European banking industry, Lecture at the Conference on "European Banking industry: what's next?", organized by the University of Navarra, Madrid, 7th July, 2016, speech last retrieved on 26th January, 2017, from https://www.ecb.europa.eu/press/key/date/2016/html/sp160707_1.en.html.

Copeland, Tom, Koller, Tim, Murrin, Jack (1994): Valuation – Measuring and Managing the Value of Companies, J. Wiley & Sons, Second Edition, chapter 16, pp 476–512.

Dallara, Charles (2012): Interview in ekathimerini.com, found at http://www.ekathimerini.com/141602/article/ekathimerini/business/iifs-dallara-says-greek-euro-exit-not-foregone-conclusion, last accessed on 12th March, 2017.

Danielsson, Jon (2002): The emperor has no clothes: Limits to risk modeling, in: Journal of Banking & Finance, 26 (2002), pp 1273–1296.

Danielsson, Jon, Embrechts, Paul, Goodhart, Charles, Keating, Con, Muennich, Felix, Renault, Olivier, Shin, Hyun Song (2001): An Academic Response to Basel II, Special Paper No. 130, LSE Financial Markets Group, May 2001.

de Grauwe, Paul (2014): Economics of Monetary Union, Tenth Edition, Oxford University Press.

de Haan, Jakob, Oosterloo, Sander, Schoenmaker, Dirk (2015): Financial Markets and Institutions: A European Perspective: Third Edition, Cambridge University Press.

de Spinoza, Benedict (2016): The chief works of Benedict de Spinoza, Two Volumes in one, translated from Latin by RHM Elwes, first edition 1884, reprinted with new formatting 2016, Kshetra Books.

Delpla, Jacques, von Weizsäcker, Jakob (2010): The Blue Bond Proposal, bruegelpolicybrief, issue 2010/03, May 2010, found at http://bruegel.org/wp-content/uploads/imported/publications/1005-PB-Blue_Bonds.pdf, last accessed on 15th March, 2017.

Dermine, Jean (1996): European Banking with a Single Currency, Working Paper 96–54, The Wharton Financial Institutions Center.

–. (2002): European Banking, Past, Present and Future, INSEAD, Fontainebleau, October 2002.

–. (2005): European Banking Integration: Don't Put the Cart before the Horse, INSEAD Research Paper, 17th September, 2005.

–. (2015): Bank Valuation and Value-Based Management, McGraw Hill, Second Edition.

Deutsche Bank (2015): Annual Report 2015, found at https://www.db.com/ir/en/download/Deutsche_Bank_Annual_Report_2015.pdf, last accessed on 23rd March, 2017.

Deutsche Bank (DB) Research (2013): Bank performance in the US and Europe – An ocean apart, Jan Schildbach, 26th September, 2013, found at https://www.dbresearch.com/

PROD/DBR_INTERNET_ENPROD/PROD0000000000320825.pdf, last accessed on 23rd March, 2017.

Deutsche Bundesbank (2014): Monthly Report June 2014: Europe's new recovery and resolution regime for credit institutions, p 40, found at https://www.bundesbank.de/Redaktion/EN/Downloads/Publications/Monthly_Report/2014/2014_06_monthly_report.pdf?__blob=publicationFile, last accessed on 22nd March, 2017.

Dewatripont, Mathias (2014): European Banking: Bail-out, bail-in and state aid control, in: International Journal of Industrial Organization, Vol. 34, 2014, pp 37–43.

–. (2015): The Banking Crisis and Its Responses, 4th EBA Policy Research Workshop, London, 18th November, 2015.

Dewatripont, Mathias, Freixas, Xavier (2011): Bank resolution: a framework for the assessment of regulatory intervention, in: Oxford Review of Economic Policy, Vol. 27, Number 3, 2011, pp 411–436.

Dewatripont, Mathias, Rochet, Jean-Charles, Tirole, Jean (2010): Balancing the Banks – Global Lessons from the Financial Crisis, Princeton University Press, 2010.

Diamond, Douglas, Dybvig, Philip (1983): Bank Runs, Deposit Insurance, and Liquidity, in: Journal of Political Economy, Vol. 91, No. 3, pp 401–419.

Donnelly, Shawn (2011): The regimes of financial market regulation in Europe, in: The European Financial Review, 23rd October, 2011.

Draghi, Mario (2012): Speech at the Global Investment Conference in London, 26th July, 2012, found at https://www.ecb.europa.eu/press/key/date/2012/html/sp120726.en.html, last accessed on 14th March, 2017.

–. (2014): Financial integration and banking union, speech at the conference for the 20th anniversary of the establishment of the European Monetary Institute, Brussels, 12th February, 2014, found at https://www.ecb.europa.eu/press/key/date/2014/html/sp140212.en.html, last accessed on 11th March, 2017.

Duisenberg, Wim (2001): EMU: Experiences to Date and Challenges for the Future, in: INTERECONOMICS, March/April 2001, p 59–61.

Emerson, Michal, Gros, Daniel, Italianer, Alexander, Pisani-Ferry, Jean, Reichenbach, Horst (1992): One Market, One Money: An Evaluation of the Potential Benefits and Costs of Forming an Economic and Monetary Union, Oxford University Press.

Eurozone Summit (2008): Declaration on a concerted European Action Plan of the Euro Area Countries, 12th October, 2008, found at http://ec.europa.eu/economy_finance/publications/pages/publication13260_en.pdf, last accessed on 31st March, 2017.

Eurozone Summit (2012): Joint Statement, June 28–29, 2012, found at https://www.bankingsupervision.europa.eu/about/milestones/shared/pdf/2012-06-29_euro_area_summit_statement_en.pdf, last accessed on 31st March, 2017.

European Banking Authority (EBA) (2011): 2011 EU-wide Stress Test, Methodological Note, 18th March, 2011, found at https://www.eba.europa.eu/documents/10180/15932/EBA-ST-2011-004-Detailed-Methodological-Note_1.pdf, last accessed on 3rd March, 2017.

–. (2017): EBA Homepage, found at http://www.eba.europa.eu/, last accessed on 25th February, 2017.

European Central Bank (1999): Possible Effects of EMU on the EU Banking System in the Medium to Long Term, found at https://www.ecb.europa.eu/pub/pdf/other/emubnken.pdf?adb30f1e82baef005598a4e72895d9c9, last accessed on 8th February, 2017.

–. (2007): Financial Stability Review, December, 2007, found at https://www.ecb.europa.eu/pub/pdf/other/financialstabilityreview200712en.pdf?4ea457b0f9ce90962ec70beb3e961230, last accessed on 26th February, 2017.
–. (2008): Financial Integration in Europe, April 2008, found at https://www.ecb.Europa.eu/pub/pdf/other/financialintegrationinEurope200804en.pdf, last accessed on 21st February, 2017.
–. (2011): The Monetary Policy of the ECB, 2011, found at https://www.ecb.Europa.eu/mopo/implement/html/index.en.html, last accessed on 21st February, 2017.
–. (2014): Aggregate Report on the Comprehensive Assessment, Summary, October, 2014.
–. (2015): Financial Integration in Europe, April, 2015.
–. (2015a): Presentation at BVI Asset Management, Peter Praet, 1st October, 2015.
–. (2016): Report on Financial Structures, October 2016.
–. (2017): Economic and Monetary Union (EMU), 2017, found at https://www.ecb.Europa.eu/ecb/history/emu/html/index.en.html, last accessed on 13th February, 2017.
European Commission (EC) (2008): EMU@10, Successes and challenges after ten years of Economic and Monetary Union, European Economy 2, 2008.
–. (2008a): Press release, High-Level Expert Group on EU financial supervision to hold first meeting on 12th November, 11th November, 2008, found at http://europa.eu/rapid/press-release_IP-08-1679_en.htm, last accessed on 24th February, 2017.
–. (2009): Communication from the Commission, European financial supervision, COM (2009) 252 final, Brussels, 27th May, 2009, found at http://ec.europa.eu/internal_market/finances/docs/committees/supervision/communication_may2009/C-2009_715_en.pdf, last accessed on 26th February, 2017.
–. (2009a): Report of The High-Level Group on Financial Supervision in the EU, chaired by Jacques de Larosière, Brussels, 25th February 2009, can be accessed at http://ec.europa.eu/finance/general-policy/docs/de_larosiere_report_en.pdf, last retrieved on 21st January, 2017.
–. (2009b): Communication from the Commission – The recapitalization of financial institutions in the current financial crisis: limitation of state aid to the minimum necessary and safeguards against undue distortions of competition (2009/C 10/03), Brussels, January, 2009, found at http://eur-lex.europa.eu/legal-content/EN/ALL/?uri=CELEX:52009XC0115(01), last accessed on 27th February, 2017.
–. (2011): European System of Financial Supervision, 2011, found at https://ec.europa.eu/info/business-economy-euro/banking-and-finance/financial-supervision-and-risk-management/european-system-financial-supervision_en#theeuropeansystemoffinancialsupervision, last accessed on 25th February, 2017.
–. (2014): EU Bank Recovery and Resolution Directive (BRRD): Frequently Asked Questions, Memo/14/297, EC, Brussels, 2014.
–. (2015): Completing Europe's Economic and Monetary Union, report by Jean-Claude Juncker, 2015, in close collaboration with Donald Tusk, Jeroen Dijsselbloem, Mario Draghi and Martin Schulz, found at http://www.todiktio.eu/images/pdf/presidents.pdf, last accessed on 13th March, 2017.
–. (2015a): Five President's Report Series, 01/2015, Towards a European Deposit Insurance Scheme, November, 2015.
–. (2015b): Deposit Guarantee Scheme – Frequently Asked Questions, Brussels, November, 2015.

European Court of Auditors (ECA) (2014): European banking supervision taking shape – EBA and its changing context, Special Report 05, 2014, found at http://www.eca.europa.eu/Lists/ECADocuments/SR14_05/SR14_05_EN.pdf, last accessed on 3rd March, 2017.

European Insurance and Occupational Pension Authority (EIOPA) (2017): Homepage, found at https://eiopa.europa.eu, last accessed on 25th February, 2017.

European Markets and Securities Authority (ESMA) (2017): Homepage, found at https://www.esma.europa.eu/, last accessed on 25th February, 2017.

European Systemic Risk Board (2015): ESRB report on the regulatory treatment of sovereign exposures, found at http://www.esrb.europa.eu/pub/pdf/other/esrbreportregulatorytreatmentsovereignexposures032015.en.pdf?c0cad80cf39a74e20d9d5947c7390df1, last accessed on 3rd March, 2017.

–. (2017): ESRB Homepage, found at http://www.esrb.europa.eu/home/html/index.en.html, last accessed on 25th February, 2017.

Eurostat (2017): National accounts (including GDP) database, found at http://ec.europa.eu/eurostat/web/national-accounts/data/database, last accessed on 23rd March, 2017.

–. (2017a): Unemployment statistics, found at http://ec.europa.eu/eurostat/statistics-explained/index.php/Unemployment_statistics, last accessed on 23rd March, 2017.

Federal Deposit Insurance Corporation (FDIC) (2015): US Banks Total Assets Data, found at https://ycharts.com/indbicators/us_banks_total_assets, data retrieved on 13th January, 2017.

Ferguson, Niall (2008): The Ascent of Money, A Financial History of the World, Penguin Press.

–. (2014): The Great Degeneration: How Institutions Decay and Economies Die, 2014, Penguin Press.

Fichtner, Ferdinand, Koenig, Philipp (2015): A Stronger Union through Crisis? 25 Years of Monetary Integration in Europe, in: DIW Economic Bulletin, No 27/2015 of July, 2015, pp 376–384.

Financial Stability Board (2011): Key Attributes of Effective Resolution Regimes for Financial Institutions.

–. (2014): Key Attributes of Effective Resolution Regimes for Financial Institutions, update October, 2014.

–. (2015): Principles on Loss-absorbing and Recapitalisation Capacity of G-SIBs in Resolution – Total Loss-absorbing Capacity (TLAC) Term Sheet, 9th November, 2015.

Financial Times (2009): Hypo Real bailed out by German peers, 29th September, 2008, by James Wilson in Frankfurt and Bertrand Benoit in Berlin, can also be found at https://www.ft.com/content/60cec9cc-8df0-11dd-8089-0000779fd18c, last accessed on 18th March, 2017.

Fisher, Irving (1935): 100 % Money, Yale University, Chapter 1: Introduction.

Fonseca Marinheiro, Carlos (2003): Output Smoothing in EMU and OECD: Can We Forgo Government Contribution? A risk sharing approach, Estudos do GEMF, Faculdade de Economia da Universidade de Coimbra, No. 2, 2003, found at http://gemf.fe.uc.pt/workingpapers/pdf/2003/gemf03_02.pdf, last accessed on 18th February, 2017.

Fonteyne, Wim (2007): Toward a Single Financial Market, in: Decressin et al. (eds.) (2007): Integrating Europe's financial markets, IMF, Washington, 2007.

Freixas, Xavier, Giannini, Curzio, Hoggarth, Glenn, Soussa, Farouk (2000): Lender of Last Resort: What have we learned since Bagehot?, in: Journal of Financial Services Research, Vol. 18:63.

Freixas, Xavier, Rochet, Jean-Charles (2008): Microeconomics of Banking, Second Edition, MIT Press, 2008.

Freixas, Xavier, Santomero, Anthony (2002): Working Paper No. 02-1, An Overall Perspective on Banking Regulation, Federal Reserve Bank of Philadelphia, February 2002.

Funke, Manuel, Schularick, Moritz, Trebesch, Christoph (2015): Politics in the Slump: Polarization and Extremism after Financial Crises, 1870–2014, CESIFO Working Paper No. 5553, October 2015, found at http://www.statewatch.org/news/2015/oct/financial-crises-cesifo-wp-5553.pdf, last accessed on 2nd March, 2017.

G20 (2009): Leaders' Statement: The Pittsburgh Summit, September 24–26, 2009, found at http://www.bmjv.de/SharedDocs/Downloads/EN/G20/G20%20Leaders%27s%20Statement%20(Pittsburgh%20Summit).pdf?__blob=publicationFile&v=2, last accessed on 12th March, 2017.

Gambacorta, Leonardo, van Rixtel, Adrian (2013): Structural bank regulation initiatives: approaches and implications, BIS Working Papers No. 412, April 2013.

Goddard, John, Molyneux, Philip, Wilson, John (2010): Banking in the European Union, in: Allen N Berger, Philip Molyneux, John Wilson (eds.): The Oxford Handbook of Banking, Oxford University Press, pp 806–843.

Goodhart, Charles (1988): The evolution of Central Banks, MIT Press.

Gorton, Gary (2009): Slapped in the Face by the Invisible Hand: Banking and the Panic of 2007, Prepared for the Federal Reserve Bank of Atlanta's 2009 Financial Markets Conference: Financial Innovation and Crisis, 11th-13th May, 2009.

–. (2013): Misunderstanding Financial Crises: Why we do not see them coming, Oxford University Press.

Greenspan, Alan (2008): We will never have a perfect model of risk, in: Financial Times, 16th May, 2008.

Gros, Daniel, Schoenmaker, Dirk (2013): European Deposit Insurance and Resolution in Banking Union, Working Paper, December, 2013.

Group of Ten (2001): Consolidation in the Financial Sector, Basle, January 2001, found at http://www.bis.org/publ/gten05.pdf, last accessed on 9th February, 2017.

Group of Thirty (2009): Financial Reform, A Framework for Financial Stability, Washington, January, 2009.

Haldane, Andrew (2012): The Dog and the Frisbee, Speech at the Federal Reserve Bank of Kansas City's 366th Economic Policy Symposium, Jackson Hole, WY, 31 August, 2012.

–. (2012a): On being the right size, Speech, Bank of England, 25th October, 2012.

Haldane, Andrew G, Alessandri, Piergiorgio (2009): Banking on the state, paper based on a presentation delivered at the Federal Bank of Chicago twelfth annual International Banking Conference on "The International Financial Crisi: Have the Rules of Finance Changed?", Chicago, September 25th 2009, found at http://www.bis.org/review/r091111e.pdf, last accessed on 31st March, 2017.

Hale, Galina, Obstfeld, Maurice (2014): How the Euro changed the pattern of international debt flows, in: VOX, CEPR's policy portal, at voxeu.org/article/how-Euro-changed-international-debt-flows, last accessed on 14th February, 2017.

Hellwig, Martin (2014): Yes Virginia, There is a European Banking Union! But It May Not Make Your Wishes Come True, Research Paper, Max Planck Institute for Research on Collective Goods.

High-Level Group on Financial Supervision in the EU, chaired by Jacques de Larosière (2009): Report, Brussels, February, 2009, found at https://www.esrb.europa.eu/shared/pdf/de_larosiere_report_fr.pdf?4712c00718855033ea74f6d4cbbf82ee, last accessed on 25th February, 2017.

Houben, Aerdt, Schrijvers, Iskander, Willems, Tim (2008): Supervising cross-border banks in Europe, in: Journal of Banking Regulation, Vol. 9, 4, pp 227–246.

Huertas, Thomas (2014): Safe to Fail – How Resolution Will Revolutionise Banking, Palgrave Macmillan.

Huettl, Pia, Schoenmaker, Dirk (2016): Should the 'outs' join the European Banking Union?, Bruegel Policy Contribution, Issue 2016/03, February 2016.

Independent Evaluation Office of the IMF (IEO) (2016): The IMF's Role in Greece in the Context of the 2010 Stand-By Arrangement, Background Paper 16-02/by: Charles Wyplosz and Sylvia Sgherri, found at http://www.ieo-imf.org/ieo/files/completedevaluations/EAC__BP_16-02_11__The_IMFs_Role_in_Greece_in_the_Context_of_the_2010_SBA.PDF, last accessed on 11th March, 2017.

International Monetary Fund (2009): Global Financial Stability Review, Chapter 3: Market Interventions During the Financial Crisis: How Effective and How to Disengage, October, 2009, pp 117–152.

–. (2010): Staff Position Note No. 2010/12, 2010, found at https://www.imf.org/external/pubs/cat/longres.aspx?sk=24134.0, last accessed on 4th March, 2017.

–. (2011): Working Paper 11/269, Mody, Ashoka, Sandri, Damiano: The Eurozone Crisis: How Banks and Sovereigns Came to be Joined at the Hip.

–. (2011a): Staff Country Report 11/175.

Issing, Otmar (2009): Some Lessons from the Financial Market Crisis, in: International Finance, Vol. 12(3), 2009, pp 431–444.

J.P. Morgan Chase & Co (2015): Annual Report 2015.

Jakab, Zoltan, Krumhof, Michael (2015): Banks are not intermediaries of loanable funds – and why this matters, Bank of England Working Paper No. 529, May 2015.

Jennen, Birgit, Groendahl, Boris (2016): Germany on Track for New EU Clash over Bank-Failure Rules, Bloomberg, 6th April, 2016.

Johnson, Mark Anthony, Mamun, Abdullah (2012): The failure of Lehman Brothers and its impact on other financial institutions, Applied Financial Economics, 22:5, pp 375–385.

Kashyap, Anil, Stein, Jeremy (1997): The role of banks in monetary policy: A survey with implications for the European monetary union, in: Economic Perspectives, Federal Reserve Bank of Chicago, pp 2–12.

Kotz, Hans-Helmut (2010): EMU's Response to the North Atlantic Financial Crisis: Policymaking from Incompatible Views, in: Robert M. Solow, Daniel S Hamilton: Europe's Economic Crisis: Transatlantic Perspectives, 2010, pp 29–44.

Krueger, Anne (2002): A New Approach to Sovereign Debt Restructuring, IMF, April 2002.

Laano, Karel (2009): A bit more clarity, please, M. de Larosière, in: CEPS Commentaries, 3rd March, 2009.

Lane, Philipp (2010): The Irish Crisis, IIIS Discussion Paper no. 356, 2010, found at https://pdfs.semanticscholar.org/36c7/4679bb1df06cc581684593ee74dccc8b1415.pdf, last accessed on 4th March, 2017.

–. (2012): The European Sovereign Debt Crisis, in: Journal of Economic Perspectives – Volume 26, Number 3, 2012, pp 49–68.

Lastra, Roda Maria (2006): Legal Foundations of International Monetary Stability, Oxford University Press.

Lautenschläger, Sabine (2016): Banking Supervision needs further harmonization, speech, Frankfurt, 1st June, 2016.

Liikanen, Errki (2012): High-level Expert Group on reforming the structure of the EU banking sector, Final Report, Brussels, 2nd October, 2015, found at http://ec.europa.eu/internal_market/bank/docs/high-level_expert_group/report_en.pdf, last accessed on 31st March, 2017.

Lincoln, Abraham (1854): Fragment on government (July 1, 1854?) – The Collected Works of Abraham Lincoln, ed. Roy P. Basler, vol. 2, pp 220–21 (1953).

Lintner, John (1965): The Valuation of Risk Assets and the Selection of Risky Investments in Stock Portfolios and Capital Budgets, in: Review of Economics and Statistics, Vol. 47, pp 13–37.

Mayer, Thomas (2016): From Zirp, Nirp, QE and helicopter money to a better monetary system, FvS Research Institute, Economic Policy Note 16/3/2016.

McDonald, Robert, Paulson, Anna (2014): AIG in Hindsight, Federal Reserve Bank of Chicago, WP 2014–07, October, 2014.

McKittrik, David (2012): Sir George Blunden – banker who helped avert financial crises, The Independent (online edition), News, Obituaries, 20th April, 2012, from http://www.independent.co.uk/news/obituaries/sir-george-blunden-banker-who-helped-avert-financial-crises-7578020.html, last accessed 14th January, 2017.

McLeay, Michael, Radia, Amar, Thomas, Ryland (2014): Money creation in the modern economy, in: Quarterly Bulletin Bank of England, 2014 Q1, pp 1–14.

Merkel, Angela (2011): Regierungserklärung, Deutscher Bundestag, Berlin, 26th October 2016, found at https://www.cdu.de/system/tdf/media/dokumente/26_10_2011_Regierungserklaerung.pdf?file=1, last accessed on 12th March, 2017.

Merton, Robert (1977): An Analytic Derivation of the Cost of Deposit Insurance and Loan Guarantees, in: Journal of Banking and Finance (1), pp 3–11.

Merton, Robert, Bodie, Zvi (1995): A conceptual framework for analyzing the financial system, HBS Paper based on chapters 1 and 8 of The Global Financial System: A Functional Perspective, Harvard Business School Press.

Mody, Ashoka, Sandri, Damiano (2011): The Eurozone Crisis: How Banks and Sovereigns Came to be Joined at the Hip, IMF Working Paper 11/269.

Moenninghoff, Sebastian, Wieandt, Axel (2011): The Financial Crisis: Observations and Implications, the Case of Hypo Real Estate (HRE), Zeitschrift für betriebswirtschaftliche Forschung (zfbf), 2011, Vol. 63, pp 508–530.

Monnet, Jean (1976): Mémoires, Librairie Arthème Fayard, 1976.

Mundell, Robert (1961): A Theory of Optimal Currency Areas, in: American Economic Review, volume 51 (4), pp 657–665.

–. (1962): Capital mobility and stabilization policy under fixed and flexible exchange rates, in: Canadian Journal of Economic and Political Science, vol. 29, pp 475–485.

Noeth, Bryan, Sengupta, Rajdeep (2010): Global European Banks and the Financial Crisis, in: Federal Reserve Bank of St. Louis Review, November / December, 2012, pp 457–479.

Nouy, Daniele (2015): The banking union and financial integration, Speech at the joint EC / ECB conference, Brussels, 27th April, 2015.

O'Keefe, John (1990): The Texas Banking Crisis, Causes and Consequences, 1980–1989, Division of Research and Statistics, Federal Deposit Insurance Corporation (FDIC), July, 1990.

Onado, Marco (2010): Is the Larosière Proposal on European Financial Regulation on the Right Path?, in: The International Spectator, Vol. 45 (1), pp 59–73.

Orphanides, Athanasios (2015): The Eurozone Crisis Five Years After the Original Sin, 19th October, 2015. MIT Sloan Research Paper No. 5147-15.

Padoa-Schioppa, Tomas (1999): EMU and banking supervision, Lecture at the London School of Economics, Financial Markets Group, on 24th February, 1999, found at https://www.ecb.europa.eu/press/key/date/1999/html/sp990224.en.html, last accessed on 13th February, 2017.

Pagano, Marco (2015): Lessons from the European Financial Crisis, in: Ester Faia, Andreas Hackethal, Michael Haliassos and Katja Langenbucher (eds.): Financial Regulation, A Transatlantic Perspective, pp 23–48.

Panetta, Fabio, Faeh, Thomas, Grande, Guiseppe, Ho, Corinne, King, Michael, Levy, Aviram, Signoretti, Federico, Taboga, Marco, Zaghini, Andrea (2009): An assessment of financial sector rescue programs, BIS Papers No 48, July, 2009.

Panizza, Ugo, Sturzenegger, Federico, Zettelmeyer, Jeromin (2009): The Economics and Law of Sovereign Debt and Default, in Journal of Economic Literature, Vol. 47, 2009, pp: 651–698.

Peltzman, Samuel (1976): Toward a More General Theory of Regulation, in: Journal of Law and Economics, Vol. 19, No. 2, pp 211–240.

Rajan, Raghuram (2010): Fault Lines, How Hidden Fractures Still Threaten The World Economy, Princeton University Press.

Rajan, Raghuram, Zingales, Luigi (1996): Financial Dependence and Growth, NBER Working Paper 5758, September 1996.

Reinhart, Carmen, Rogoff, Kenneth (2010): Growth in a Time of Debt, in: American Economic Review: Papers & Proceedings, Vol. 100, pp 573–578.

Sandbu, Martin (2015): Europe's Orphan, The Future of the Euro and the Politics of Debt, Princeton University Press, 2015.

Schich, Sebastian, Kim, Byoung-Hwan (2012): Developments in the Value of Implicit Guarantees for Bank Debt: The Role of Resolution Regimes and Practices, in: OECD Journal: Financial Market Trends, Volume 2012 – Issue 2, pp 1–31.

Schmidt, Reinhard, Hackethal, Andreas, Tyrell, Marcel (1999): Disintermediation and the Role of Banks in Europe: An international comparison, in: Journal of Financial Intermediation, Vol. 8, No. 1–2, pp 36–67.

Schmies, Christian (2015): Legal Challenges of the SSM, Hengeler Mueller presentation, 2nd November 2015.

Schoenmaker, Dirk (2011): The financial trilemma, in: Economic Letters, Vol. 111 (2011), pp 57–59.

Shambaugh, Jay (2012): The Euro's Three Crises, Brookings Papers on Economic Activity, 2012, pp 157–207.

Shambaugh, Jay (2012): The Euro's Three Crises (with comments), Brookings Papers on Economic Activity, 2012, pp 157–231.

Sharpe, William (1964): Capital Asset Prices: A Theory of Market Equilibrium under Conditions of Risk, in: Journal of Finance, Vol. 19, pp 425–442.

Shin, Hyun Song (2011): Global Banking Glut and Loan Risk Premium, Mundell-Fleming Lecture, Conference Draft for the 12th Jacques Polak Annual Research Conference, 2011, found at https://www.imf.org/external/np/res/seminars/2011/arc/pdf/hss.pdf, last accessed on 23rd March, 2017.

Solbes, Pedro (2001): New European Union, EMU and Enlargement, in: INTERECONOMICS, March/April 2001, pp 68–71.

Steffen, Sascha, Steinruecke, Lea (2015): Funktionsweise und Einschätzung des Comprehensive Assessment, in: zfbf, Vol. 67, December 2015, pp 418–443.

Stigler, George (1971): The Theory of Economic Regulations, in: The Bell Journal of Economics and Management Science, Vol. 2, No. 1, pp 3–21.

Story, Jonathan, Walter, Ingo (1997): Political Economy of Financial Integration in Europe – the battle of the systems, MIT Press, Cambridge.

The Economist (2017): Not enough Europe, Free exchange, Finance and Economics, p 64, 18th February, 2017.

The New York Times (2011): Adding up the Government's Total Bailout Tab, 24th July, 2011.

The World Bank (2015): GDP & Population Data for European Union, United States, United Kingdom, Eurozone, from http://data.worldbank.org/?locations=EU-GB-US-XC, data retrieved on 14th January, 2017.

Tobin, James (1963): Commercial Banks as Creators of "Money", Cowles Foundation Discussion Paper No. 159, Yale University, 24th July, 1963.

Trichet, Jean-Claude (2009): The financial crisis and the response of the ECB, Speech by Jean-Claude Trichet, President of the ECB at the Ceremony conferring the honorary title of Doctor Honoris Causa at the University of National and World Economy, Bulgari in Sofia on 12th June, 2009, found at https://www.ecb.europa.eu/press/key/date/2009/html/sp090612.en.html, last accessed on 2nd March, 2017.

UK Office for National Statistics (2017): GDP database, found at https://www.ons.gov.uk/economy/grossdomesticproductgdp/timeseries/ihyq/pn2, last accessed on 22nd March, 2017.

Valukas, Anton (2010): United State Bankruptcy Court Southern District of New York, Chapter 11 Case No. 08–13555 (JMP), Report of Anton Valukas, Examiner, 11th March, 2010.

Van Rompuy, Hermann (2012): Towards a genuine economic and monetary union, in close collaboration with José Manuel Barroso, Jean-Claude Juncker, and Mario Draghi, 5 December 2012, found at http://www.consilium.europa.eu/uedocs/cms_Data/docs/pressdata/en/ec/134069.pdf, last accessed on 13th March, 2017.

Vickers, John (2011): Independent Commission on Banking, Final Report, September 2011, found at http://webarchive.nationalarchives.gov.uk/20131003105424/https:/hmt-sanctions.s3.amazonaws.com/ICB%20final%20report/ICB%2520Final%2520Report[1].pdf, last accessed on 31st March, 2017.

Vives, Xavier (2009): Europe's Regulatory Chaos, The Wall Street Journal, 18th March, 2009.

Walkner, Christoph, Raes, Jean-Pierre (2005): Integration and Consolidation in EU Banking – an Unfinished Business, in: European Economy, European Commission, Economic Papers, No 226, April 2005, pp 1–48.

Werner, Pierre (1970): Report to the Council of the Commission on the Realisation by Stages of Economic and Monetary Union in the Community, Bulletin of the European Communities, Supplement 11, pp 1–65.

Williamson, Oliver (1973): Markets and Hierarchies: Some Elementary Considerations, American Economic Review: Papers & Proceedings Vol. 63, pp 316–325.

Zavvos, George (1989): Banking integration in the European Community, Northwestern Journal of International Law & Business, Volume 9, Issue 3 Winter 1989, pp 572–587.

Zettelmayer, Jeromin, Trebesch, Christoph, Gulati, Mitu (2013): The Greek Debt Restructuring, An Autopsy, Working Paper, The Peterson Institute for International Economics, August 2013.

Index of Names

Subject Index

Bei Fragen zur Produktsicherheit wenden Sie sich bitte an:
If you have any questions regarding product safety, please contact:

Brill Deutschland GmbH
Robert-Bosch-Breite 10
37079 Göttingen
info@v-r.de